CRP

I AM
MY BROTHER

I AM
MY BROTHER

JOHN LEHMANN

REYNAL & COMPANY

NEW YORK

LIBRARY OF CONGRESS CATALOG CARD NUMBER 59-34181

Printed in Great Britain

INTRODUCTION

IN this book I have tried to tell the story of the war years in Britain from the point of view of an author who was at the same time deeply involved in the literary scene from many other sides. The war kept me, a civilian, from many of the activities and adventures that varied my life both before and after. The adventures I had were chiefly of the mind; and I beg the reader's pardon that it contains no descriptions of hair-raising exploits in exotic theatres of war.

And yet, humdrum as that may sound, life in London was extraordinarily enthralling during those years, not merely because we were under siege in the essential stronghold the enemy had to take if his plans for world conquest were to succeed, but also because of the revolution that was taking place in men's minds while this struggle went on. Under the extreme pressure of total war, one saw English life, as conservative and traditional as any way of life in the world, changing and yet resisting change in a ferment that released unsuspected energies in every layer of the population. I believe this ferment showed itself in the records of the thoughts and experiences men tried to give shape to in the more permanent and imaginative form of poetry, stories and novels than in the speeches and newspaper reports and articles of the time; and as editor of *New Writing*—as this book will, I believe, show—I was especially fortunately placed to see and to evoke these records, often for young people who had never thought of using words in this way before.

I am my Brother is, then, not merely the continuation of the autobiography that I began in *The Whispering Gallery*; I would like to think that it also contributes to the understanding of a crucial moment in the spiritual history of my countrymen.

My grateful thanks are due to my sister Rosamond, Mr. William Plomer, and Miss Barbara Cooper for both criticism and encouragement as this book was being prepared; to Mr. Walter Allen, Mr. John Betjeman, Mr. William Chappell,

v

Mr. E. M. Forster, Mr. Roy Fuller, Mr. Denis Glover, Mr.
Robert Graves, Mrs. Violet Hammersley, Mr. John Hillier,
Mr. John Irwin, Mr. Christopher Isherwood, Mr. Julian
Maclaren-Ross, Mr. V. S. Pritchett, Mr. Henry Reed, Mr.
Alan Ross, Mr. Frank Sargeson, Dame Edith Sitwell, Mr. John
Sommerfield, Mr. Terence Tiller, Mr. Keith Vaughan, Mr.
Leonard Woolf, Mr. Henry Yorke, and to the executors and
heirs of Norman Cameron, André Gide, Lord Inverchapel (Sir
Archibald Clark-Kerr), John Lepper, Alun Lewis, Gully Mason,
Dylan Thomas, Sir Hugh Walpole, Denton Welsh and Virginia
Woolf, for permission to quote from letters I received from them
during the years covered by this narrative. I also wish to
thank Mr. Roy Fuller and The Hogarth Press for allowing me
to use one poem entire from *The Middle of a War*.

JOHN LEHMANN

CONTENTS

PLATES

My brother Cain, the wounded, liked to sit
Brushing my shoulder, by the staring water
Of life, or death, in cinemas half-lit
By scenes of peace that always turned to slaughter.

He liked to talk to me.   His eager voice
Whispered the puzzle of his bleeding thirst,
Or prayed me not to make my final choice,
Unless we had a chat about it first.

And then he chose the final pain for me.
I do not blame his nature: he's my brother;
Nor what you call the times: our love was free,
Would be the same at any time; but rather

The ageless ambiguity of things
Which makes our life mean death, our love be hate.
My blood that streams across the bedroom sings:
' I am my brother opening the gate.'

DEMETRIOS CAPETANAKIS
(*Abel*)

I

TO THE END OF THE RIVER

O<small>N</small> September 1st, 1939, when the news came through that Hitler had opened his attack on Poland, I had the feeling that I was slipping down into a pit, clutching at grass on the ledges but failing to stay the accelerating descent into darkness. This feeling must have been shared by many others. It was more than the knowledge that we should obviously be at war ourselves within a few days: listening to the broadcasts of Hitler's speeches, it seemed to me that the frightening irrational note in his voice, the lunatic evil that I had become more and more acutely conscious of since the invasion of Austria, had drowned everything else. It had led me deeply to distrust both the school of thought that held that he could be handled on traditional foreign policy lines, and the other, that everything the Nazis did could be explained on orthodox Marxist lines as part of a shrewdly ruthless plan for capitalist expansion. Now it afflicted me like nausea; and I am certain that I knew from that moment, in spite of the hopes of last-minute withdrawal we all talked about during the tense forty-eight hours between the two decisions, that war to the ruinous end, until either Hitler was destroyed or we ourselves were finished for ever, had become inevitable.

And yet the upper part of our minds clung to straws: I remember during that morning Stephen Spender came in to see me, and like prisoners tapping every corner of a cellar into which they have been flung in the hope of finding a loose stone, we went through every tiniest possibility of escape we could imagine in the situation. He was oppressed with the same weight of foreboding as I was, and though we made our usual jokes to one another, melancholy kept falling on us like a fog. That night—the first night of black-out—I struggled out in the slithery rainy darkness to dine up in Highgate with my sister Beatrix, who had just returned from a holiday abroad and the adventure of getting across France in the middle of the confusion of mobilization. Her experience had made her feel, as I felt, that it was only a matter of days or hours; and yet we fell to arguing whether the Chamberlain Government might not still try to put across a gigantic sell-out to the Nazis.

When the actual declaration of war came on the 3rd, the immediate uppermost sensation was, curiously enough, relief. The whole point, after all, of the movement I and my friends had belonged to and believed in, was that Hitler must be thwarted and stopped by every means possible. War we dreaded, but war was better than giving in to Hitler if it came to that. It had not been prevented; but at least England was going to show that her—perhaps too tardy—threats were no bluff, and the whole nation was in it at last. We were not alone; and yet, ironically enough, the country we had so lightly thought to be the great champion and leader of our cause, was not one of our allies. Even in those early days, before the partition of Poland, the attempt of the comrades to prove that what had broken out was just one more imperialist war, was an eye-opener for those who were not too irremediably blinded to read the signs.

All the same, the blow was grim enough. Everyone, except possibly those who scented in the war the chance to infuse meaning into lives that had hitherto been meaningless, had his own hardships and disappointments to bear. For those who were younger than I was, there was the prospect of an early call-up, the unassessable danger of the front line and a sponge wiped right over the immediate hopes of their careers. During those September days I saw many of them, and was struck by the quiet, undemonstrative way they were taking it, haunted by the slightly dazed look that would come over their faces. For me, there seemed to be an end to many things: a new life had come, and almost everything that mattered in the old life had to be tied up like letters in bundles, and locked away in a drawer for the duration—or for ever. Irrevocably, I was cut off from all my friends and all that I had loved so much in Austria: my flat in Vienna would probably be taken over by the Reichswehr, and young people I had talked and laughed and drunk with as intimate friends up to only a few weeks ago would soon be marching—or flying—against my English friends. My career as a publisher seemed to be broken again, for in those days it was difficult to see how ordinary book-publishing could survive the transformation of civilian life that had already begun and the onslaught we expected any moment, even if I was not drafted into war-work or put into uniform at once. *New Writing*, too, seemed utterly doomed. I felt I had lost everything.

About eighteen months before, when it had become clear to me that my centre of activities must once more be London, I had taken a flat on the north side of Mecklenburgh Square, only a few doors away from the new abode of The Hogarth Press which had just emigrated from Tavistock Square. I had two big rooms on the second floor. From the window of the back room, which I made into a bed-workroom, pasting up maps just as I had in my Vienna flat, I looked over Heathcote Street where I had started my London life nine years before; from the front room the view was over the tall, shadily spread-ing, pom-pom-hung plane-trees of the Square garden; to the right, across the Foundling Estate playground, I could just glimpse Lansdowne Terrace where Stephen Spender had taken a ground-floor flat. On the long wall opposite the fire-place in this room I decided to have a large mural, and called in my old friend John Banting. After inspecting the wall, John decided that the only feasible scheme was to paint it on canvas pasted to the plaster. This plan had one advantage that seemed considerable in the anxious days of 1938: if I had to leave the flat suddenly, the canvas could be detached, rolled up and carried off to my next home.

The painting that John executed on this canvas, after making numerous coloured sketches and blue-prints, each one a treasure to me in itself, was as ingeniously imaginative as anything he had done. It was also prophetic in its symbolism. A huge classical façade appeared on one side, not giving on to any temple or palace as one might expect but merely a front that was propped up from behind by a dead tree-trunk, round the base of which fire had broken out. On the other side of the picture was an equally huge, ancient brick wall, also propped up from behind by a tree-trunk with flames licking its base.

In the foreground stood the proud figure—minute by comparison with the two structures—of an athletic young man,
casting an enormous elongated shadow on the classical façade;
in this shadow, however, he appeared with head bowed, a
noose or halter round his neck. The end of the rope-shadow
led across the pillars of the façade to the point where it was
met by the brick wall: a strange figure formed by the leafage
of the tree that was growing against the wall, and vaguely suggesting the Italian dictator, seemed to hold the end in its hand
like a marionette master manipulating a dejected captive doll.
All around stretched a desert landscape, but in a corner just
behind the wall was assembled a group of tiny, chess-like,
surrealist figures who might, from a hint here and there in
their posture or garb, be taken to represent an effete aristocracy
or bourgeoisie: the wall was clearly going to overwhelm them
in its fall when the fire had consumed the dead tree.

How much further up the tree the flames seemed to have
risen, as I sat, during those early days of the war, on the
window seat watching the searchlight unit practising their drill
in the Foundling playground. I had scarcely had time to make
the flat feel like home when the war had come; but the flat in
the Invalidenstrasse, occupied since the year before by my
Viennese secretary Toni and his wife Gretl, was already slipping
away from me. I had made two visits, one at the end of
March, and a longer one in the summer—returning only a few
weeks before war broke out. I remembered how I had stood
at the window and seen in the railway station below the troop
trains filled with Reichswehr soldiers travelling eastwards, a
sight that began to drain out of my heart the hopes I still entertained that war could be avoided. It was some comfort to me
that I had at least left the flat in the hands of friends, with my
furniture and a few of my books and pictures around them.
It seemed to me then to make the break that was surely coming
a little less total; and now I could envisage the life that was
going on there, in a kind of secret code that passed over the
angry frontiers of war. There had been a last reunion that
Toni had organized, a dinner party for the circle of friends he
had introduced me to. One of them, a young carpenter who
had never interested himself in politics before, disgusted by

what he had already seen of Hitler in action since the Anschluss, had joined the illegal Communist party at the most dangerous hour to do so. It was heart-rending to hear him speak of the blow to the hopes of himself and his friends that the German occupation of Czechoslovakia had been, to hear him saying: ' I listen in to Moscow every night, and still the Russians say nothing. How much longer is this going to go on, when will a halt be called? When will England move? We are powerless unless England and the rest move at last—you can at least still try to organize opposition to this monster, you can still say what you think, write the truth, denounce the crimes and point out the dangers, but all we can do here is to wait in silence and secrecy, and have our hopes broken down by the waiting.' But Marabu had not long to wait before Russia spoke—before the Nazi–Soviet pact cleared the road for the invasion of Poland and the war for which the troops were already rolling eastwards, only a few hundred yards away from the inn where we were drinking our wine.

In my work-bedroom at the back of the flat, where I put the finishing touches to this last volume—so I imagined—of *New Writing*, the maps on the wall reminded me of another part of my life that was gone for good: the explorations I had made so happily through all the countries of the old Austro-Hungarian Monarchy, down the course of the Danube to the sea. Nostalgically I thought of week-ends spent in Bratislava, only a couple of hours' run from Vienna, and expeditions from there up into the Slovakian hills, the wild forests and the high pastures where the shepherds in their white-woollen leggings and coloured jackets slung over one shoulder guarded their flocks; of long trips in the river-steamers of the pompously named Donau Dampfahrtschiff Gesellschaft, through the Hungarian plain where the river spread into an ever huger lake with the shimmering silver-green of the willows always accompanying it; of a drive with my sister Helen on a hot Summer's day along the straight road to Budapest, when we stopped at an inn hung with golden ripe cobs of *kukuruz* and drank a carafe of the cold, sharp wine of the place; of an exciting week-end in Belgrade during which I had been introduced by journalist friends to

some of the political leaders who were working in secret against
the royal dictatorship; of the night journey by steamer from
there down to the Kazan Pass, getting up at dawn to find the
willows and the plains had vanished, as we thumped and
churned our way through the narrowing twists of a rocky de-
file that led to the Iron Gate, skilfully navigating past a train
of barges coming up from the Sip Canal, drawn by a tug
flying—to my surprise—an English flag and carrying unmis-
takably the name *Princess Elizabeth*. As I lovingly studied the
map, I could see again some children on the first barge waving
back to me as I shouted good morning to them.

On the last trip I had made, only a few months before, to
collect the final details for my book *Down River*, I had realized
the ambition that had for so long tantalized me: one afternoon
I had found myself within sight of the Danube's ultimate
lighthouse. From the deck of the steamer, as it slid along the
straight, rush-bordered canal that forms the middle arm of the
Delta, the little port of Sulina appeared like a mirage, the
wharves and buildings balanced on air and quivering. This
unreal vision was the first sign of a bewitched quality that had
haunted me all through the country of the Danube mouths:
I had found myself continually thinking of *The Tempest* and
the 'insubstantial pageant' of Prospero's island. I had
crossed the marshes from Sulina to Valcov, home of the famous
Russian religious sect of the Lipovani, in a little buggy cart
driven by a grumpy, bearded Russian and drawn by two horses
who were followed by a long-legged foal. . . . The road ran
in a straight line over a dead level waste of rushes, weeds and
water. I say road; but as we advanced the pools deepened
and closed together, until there was nothing but water under
our wheels. The horses dropped from their swift trot to an
amble, and splashed their way on ever more slowly, their
heads plunging up and down with the effort of the pull. The
little foal dawdled and got left behind, until a long anxious
whinny from the mare brought it level again, leaping friskily
in fountains of water and whinnying in answer. The rushes
seemed to grow taller, and shut out the earlier glimpses I had
had of the sea. Sulina lighthouse sank out of sight, the world
seemed to consist of rushes, water and the wild life that emerged

from them. Water-hens zig-zagged in and out of the lilies and
white-flowering weed at the edge of the road; wild duck, cur-
lews, snipe and many other kinds of bird I could not distinguish rose to left and right and vanished into the sky; occasionally a crane flapped heavily across, and settled invisibly
in the reedy jungle. Later on, we began to move out of the
water and into a forest of oaks and silver birches: nothing
could have been more unexpected in the middle of the Delta, at
the edge of the sea. We were soon deep in its silent, sedgy-
smelling undergrowth. Huge dragon-flies, red as pillar-
boxes, darted round us, bloodthirsty insects clotted in iridescent
masses on the wretched horses' flanks. Brilliant blue birds
flew among the branches: one glittering azure feather floated
down just beside the buggy, and an extravagant regret for not
having stopped to pick it up oppressed me for the rest of the
journey. Once we lost ourselves, and went round and round
in what I gradually recognized with dismay to be huge, slow
circles. Light was rapidly failing by the time we found the
overgrown track again. As if they knew the worst was over,
the horses broke into a trot and the foal, unwearied by so many
hours' wandering, galloped gaily ahead. In a few minutes we
were out of the forest, and then suddenly the enormous lake-
like river was in front of us: the northernmost arm of the
Danube, spreading down to a confusion of dark islands in the
west. A huge Russian Charon, with blazing eyes and matted
beard, emerged as if from nowhere, bundled our luggage into
the ferry-boat, and we pushed off for the lights of Valcov that
could just be seen twinkling down below, in the shadow of the
further bank.

All that now seemed like a dream, an episode entirely ab-
solved from time and necessity, as the memory came back to
me in my blacked-out bedroom in London; even more dream-
like my stay in Valcov, a little town that appeared to have been
over-run and captured by a reckless army of small boys.
Hardly had our ferry bumped into the quay-side, when a shrill,
excited Russian voice greeted us from out of the darkness, and
my suitcases were grabbed by diminutive and determined
hands. There was no chance for me to bargain or question.
My porter gave me a quick, urchin grin, and staggered off with

B

the suitcases that seemed as large as himself towards the
tourist inn, whose windows gleamed a hundred yards away
behind the trees.   When we reached it, I found in the hall
several other tourists, who had just come off the evening steamer
from Galatz: chattering deafeningly around them, caps in
hands, were clustered a dozen small boys like the one who had
taken charge of me.   In grubby, torn vests and even grubbier
trousers, with tousled hair and grins to split their cheeks, they
presented an astonishing spectacle against the rather self-
consciously modern furnishing of the hall.   The other tourists
looked almost as bewildered by this invasion as I did, though
one of them rather half-heartedly exclaimed: ' Aren't they
angels! '   The proprietor's young wife, an attractive dark
Rumanian girl, explained with a despairing smile that they
were all official guides appointed by the Municipality, and I
had better compound with the inevitable and engage Vanka—
who was now sitting firmly on my suitcases at the bottom of the
stairs—to show me round next day.   Vanka had kept his eyes
electrically fixed on me, and when I turned round pointed his
finger at his chest meaningly.   There was nothing for it but to
agree.   Vanka triumphantly hauled the suitcases upstairs to
my room.

I had hardly begun to unpack, when he reappeared, marching in without knocking, in the company of a stalwart adoles-
cent whom he introduced as Volodya, his special business associate and a peerless boatman.   Volodya would take me
through all the canals tomorrow morning, he was the best
gondolier in Valcov, I would of course prefer him?   That was
fixed then.   What time would I start?   5.30 a.m.?   My
bones still aching from the buggy ride, I refused flatly to be
ready before 8.30.   Volodya shook his head severely; but
thinking of other competitors lurking for me in hordes below,
had a hurried conversation with Vanka and gave in.   None
too soon; other Vankas and Volodyas were now padding to
and fro outside the half-open door, watching greedily; and
when I emerged again for dinner, I discovered several of them
squatting, eyes closely pressed to key-holes, outside the doors
of tourists who had lost their nerve and locked themselves in.

Next morning, the sun was rapidly growing hotter in a clean-swept blue sky as we slipped into the maze of tiny winding canals about which Valcov is built. These canals give it an extraordinary detachment and fascination of its own; the atmosphere is quite unlike any of the grander places built on water, and no comparison with them can illustrate the arcadian freshness Valcov derives from the web of willow-shaded stream-lets. We glided on, sometimes only just not scraping the bottom, between the lush grassy banks and under innumerable slender bridges made of planks. The willows arched over us in a trembling network of green, now and then the trailing branches brushed my ears; that rustling sound, or the gurgle of Volodya's paddle, would startle birds from their hiding-places, and away they flew upstream and out of sight. I was suddenly reminded of the circular backwaters at Bourne End, that wound through the Abbey Estate; my contentment, I realized, was in part a re-creation of boyhood pleasures in those long summer afternoons on the river. Over the palisades I could catch glimpses of luxuriant little gardens round the mud-built cottages, sunflowers and roses climbing higher than the doll's-house windows; and in a sudden clearing the white tower and copper green bulbous dome of one of Valcov's many churches. And now bands of even younger boys began to run along the banks beside us. They clasped nosegays of wild flowers in chubby fists and when they drew level would try to aim them at our feet. One was expected to throw a few *lei* back: Volodya cautioned me sternly against extravagance. We stopped now and then to take a drink at a waterside inn, Vanka not being allowed anything more than a *kvas* by the watchful Volodya. The sun burnt more fiercely through the frail shield of the willow leaves as we paddled on, and once or twice I noticed Vanka looking rather longingly at the water. And then gradually we began to leave the village behind, and with many twists and turns were approaching the wide, eddy-ing expanse of the Danube itself. At this point the temptation of the water grew too much for Vanka, and without warning he threw off his clothes and dived in. He shot ahead of us in the powerful stream, splashing and turning like a porpoise; then struggled into the more sluggish currents by the bank, and swung himself into the boat again as we manoeuvred near.

I rested in the heat of the afternoon in my room, watching as
the light turned to deep gold over the last reaches of the Danube,
just visible through the window from where I lay; Vienna,
with all its tragic conflicts and all the happiness it had meant
for me, seemed infinitely far away. I had a deep sense of
fulfilment, as if I had come to the end of some symbolic journey,
the meaning of which lay far back in my childhood, with roots
I could no longer discover. Among the bushy islands little
boats were creeping lazily hither and thither; the sea was indistinguishable, a presence only to be imagined out there where
the deep blue of the sky was sucked into the glowing rim of
haze beyond the furthest islands; the haze within which, far
away over the horizon, a memory within a memory, I pictured the acacias of Sevastopol dangling their sweet-scented
white flowers over the white-suited sailors who walked down
the avenues with their girls. Bells were ringing with a slow
beat from one of the white church towers in the village, and
nearer at hand a girl's voice rose and fell in the endless nostalgia
of some traditional peasant song, in this land caught up out of
time of a Russia that had vanished elsewhere. Again I had
the feeling of unreality that had come to me when I first saw
Sulina from the steamer's deck. I could imagine that all the
islands, the village itself, would suddenly dissolve into the air
and water that surrounded them, and

Leave not a rack behind. . . .

That evening, to while away the time before the boat left at
midnight, Volodya insisted on shepherding me on a moonlight
walk of exploration round the village; the accredited Muni-
cipal guide, Vanka, had been paid off and retired to gamble his
earnings with other small, but equally accredited guides in a
game played with chewed bits of cards under a willow. We
stopped in several small coffee-houses, peered into a hall where
local couples and sailors from the steamer were dancing to a
gramophone, and then struck out behind the cottages to where
the canals flowed into the main stream. It was then that,
twice, once by a bridge, once at the Danube's very edge, I all
but tripped over the prostrate form of a sentry. They were

lying absolutely still, their dull olive uniforms indistinguishable
from the grass and mud, with rifles in their hands pointed
down river. Every canal entrance was so guarded, Volodya
assured me. . . . It seemed unlikely that any little boat could
slip in or out without being observed and challenged. The
Soviet Union was so near. . . . No sharper reminder could
have been brought to me that Valcov, too, was in the real
world.

At last the steamer began to show signs of life, the time had
come for me to find my cabin. I asked Volodya whether I
could send him some present as a memento of the day. He
immediately replied that there was only one thing he wanted,
and that was a wrist-watch: it didn't matter how cheap it was,
how old, but if it worked and if he could fasten it round his
wrist, he'd be happy. So, a week or two later, back in Bucharest, I packed one carefully into a small parcel, and sent it off.
When I reached England eventually, I found a letter waiting
for me:

> I have received one o'clock that you have me expedied from
> Bukarest. Thank you very much for this jolly gest. Receive a
> goodbye from your boatman of the river Danube that gently
> flows to the sea.
>
> Volodya

On my way home I had stopped for a few days in Paris,
where I had met Beatrix. Together we had gone out to Ver-
sailles to visit the Chamsons, and my mind often returned to
the talk round the table that day. André, like so many honest
and far-seeing men in France at that time, was deeply divided
within himself about the political course his country had
followed, that had led to Munich, to the overthrow of the Czech
Protectorate and the situation in which we found ourselves in
that August of 1939. I had not, I realized, fully appreciated
the mark that had been made on him by his closeness to Daladier during the riots of February, 1934, shut up with him in
his Ministry while the mob howled for their blood outside.
' I am an officer,' André kept on saying, ' I am a French officer
and I am ready to go at once and fight for my country if it has

to be, but I'm not ready to say that it's right to plunge France into war against impossible odds.' Deeply disturbed and even shamed by the fate of the Czechs though he was, he asked what France could have done by herself, with England not ready and Russia—yes, he had seen the diplomatic exchanges —not willing to help? What could anyone have done in Daladier's shoes, especially with Bonnet pulling the strings so hard to prevent any stand? And he recalled how Daladier had said to him once: ' Did you want me utterly to annihilate this beautiful country of ours, to reduce it to a desert place where men would be eating roots? ' Now at least, over there in France, allied troops from England were beginning to disembark, while the French army settled into the forts of the Maginot Line, waiting, wondering when the fury that was consuming Poland would be turned on them.

André Chamson, fellow-editor, friend and admired author, represented for me, from old association, almost more than anyone else, the international side of *New Writing*, which now seemed broken beyond repair. And what else remained of the project at this time when the future was so obscure that no literary plans could be made? It looked as if it would soon become nothing more than a memory, especially as Christopher Isherwood and Wystan Auden were far away in America. The pattern, the impulse of the original conception no longer existed, and I had very few illusions about Christopher's optimistic suggestions that they would continue to contribute and collaborate from the other side of the Atlantic. How stupid I had been, I thought now, not to have seen what was coming the year before, at the time of Munich. I remembered how I had arranged with them, in order to help them with the money for their journey, that they should write a kind of travel book, successor to their *Journey to a War*, to be called *Address Not Known*; and how after Wystan and he had signed the contract in the Mecklenburgh Square office, Christopher had walked down the road with me to my still empty new flat, where I was to interview the builder. We had bought evening papers on the way and discussed dejectedly the final sell-out of the Czechs: and when I said: ' That's the end of Europe as *we* wanted it,' Christopher had replied: ' That's all

behind me now, I shall be in America.' I had thought
no more of this, because the tragedy of Munich occupied our
minds too exclusively: the same evening Rosamond and I
had confessed to one another at Fieldhead that the swing-
back from the tension had been so great that our arms and
legs had trembled from sheer psychic exhaustion. But
the idea of *Address Not Known* was soon abandoned, when
both Christopher and Wystan realized they were making a
mistake in committing themselves to a book that would be
little more than a repetition of something of which they had
already exhausted the possibilities, a collaboration that was
only keeping them both from the work that was more essentially
their own. Before Christmas the plan was dropped and in its
stead I made an agreement with Wystan that he should let me
publish his next book of poems; an agreement that was later
found to be incompatible with his long-term commitments to
Geoffrey Faber, creating an awkward problem that was amic-
ably settled through the shrewd and friendly offices of Tom
Eliot.

That decision was already many months in the past. And
now the last volume of the peace-time *New Writing*, posthumous
child of the collaboration that existed no more, was in the
press and about to be launched into a world at war and in
which already many of the beliefs and interests it reflected
seemed extraordinarily remote, overtaken by the roaring express of international events. The Spanish Civil War, represented by Bernard Gutteridge's poem *Spanish Earth* and John
Lepper's *Conscience is a Funny Thing*, seemed, in those early
September days, a tragic wrong turning where too many of
one's friends had suffered and died in vain. The belief in
Soviet Russia as ally of all democratic hopes throughout the
world and leader of the forces that wanted above all to resist
Hitler and everything he stood for, shaken by the final act of
the Spanish War and now shattered by the Nazi–Soviet pact,
still flourished in a section—planned far away in the Spring—
with illustrated articles on Mayakovsky by Aragon's wife,
Elsa Triolet, and on the Soviet Cinema by Basil Wright, and
two stories translated from the Russian. What a discouraging
irony of time it was to re-read Marina Raskova's account of a

Russian airwoman's experiences flying in a May Day parade
over the Red Square, while Russian bombers were preparing
to complete the destruction of our new ally, Poland.   The next
turn of the wheel, by which two years later we were to be toast-
ing the Red pilots as comrades in arms in the common struggle
against the Axis, was entirely unimaginable, as much to the
shocked and disillusioned Left as to the contemptuously told-
you-so Right.   Better it seemed for the moment, in the plight
in which we found ourselves, to meditate the paradoxes of
John Tessimond's poem on *England*, still uncertain whether its
final lines described a past that had been outlived:

> England of clever fool, mad genius,
>   Timorous lion and arrogant sheep,
> Half-hearted snob and shamefaced bully,
>   Of hands that wake and eyes that sleep. . . .
> England the snail that's shod with lightning. . . .
>   Shall we laugh or shall we weep?

That was only one of many remarkable poems in the
volume, a harvest that saddened me as I passed the proofs for
press.   Wystan Auden's *In Memoriam Ernst Toller* and *The Leaves
of Life*; George Barker's *Four Elegies*; Louis MacNeice's four
poems, including the beautiful *Meeting Point*; Stephen Spender's *The Vase of Tears* and *Ambitious Son*; William Plomer's
French Lisette, most skilful of all his comic ballads, and the
fragment from David Gascoyne's never-to-be-finished narrative poem *The Conspirators*; they saddened me because I felt,
in the ebb-tide mood of that Autumn, that they represented a
high-water mark, a meeting of young talents at their best
under a common impetus that was now lost forever.   No
doubt purely personal regret entered more into this feeling
than I realized at the time: these poems, V. S. Pritchett's
masterly story *The Sailor*, George Orwell's savagely prophetic
sketch *Marrakech*, and the scene from Rex Warner's work in
progress (soon to be published as *The Aerodrome*), seemed to me
to make this number in many ways the best of all, and I could
not without some anguish relinquish the idea of its being a
prelude to a long maturity rather than a final curtain-call.
    In the same number was a section I had called ' Workers

All ', a symposium of short sketches and stories of the kind
with which *New Writing* was perhaps most immediately associated in the mind of the public: stories of working-class life,
of miners, factory-workers and the unemployed, on the border-
line between fiction and reportage. None of them was bad,
in this characteristic genre of the thirties, and B. L. Coombes's
Twenty Tons of Coal was in fact outstanding; but none of them
could, for impact on the mind and imagination, hold a candle to
The Sailor at the beginning of the volume. The reason was
fairly clear: Pritchett's story was conceived first of all as a
work of art, for what it would yield in wit and the surprise of
novel human observation, while most of the others had as their
first object to inform you about conditions of life that were unfamiliar to you, to tell you what it felt like to be an exploited
mine-worker in Africa, a discharged prisoner under suspicion
in his first job after release, or a young boy arriving in Birmingham in search of a job at the worst of the slump. The aim of
this kind of story was to arouse pity and indignation; and yet
owing to a certain flatness and too monotonous an insistence on
dejection and misery the examples that had come my way all
too often failed to arouse any reaction except boredom. Not
always; I had, I believed, made some real discoveries of
writing talent whose natural material was working-class life,
but the limitations of the genre had become gradually more
obvious to me during the four years of *New Writing*'s life. Now
in any case, in a country where production would soon be
going all out for war supplies and where most of the unemployed who were not absorbed into the newly humming factories would be putting on uniforms, the conditions that had
brought this kind of writing to birth were fast disappearing.
I did not at that moment see what future the old impulses could
have under war conditions. I did not by any means feel that
the effort had been entirely wasted, but I was saddened by the
tiny proportion of authentic ore of literature that had been
found in all the dross; and saddened, too, by the feeling that
what I thought really worth-while as literature was so fragmentary. The decade we had been through seemed to me in
retrospect a period where promising beginnings had failed
again and again, among all the distractions of political causes

and the continual earthquake tremors that had been shaking
the old-established way of life, to come to *enough*; like a mag-
nolia-tree in a cold Spring that puts out a succession of blooms
but each time gets them nipped by the frost. Christopher
Isherwood's case was, I thought, the most spectacular example
of an experience that was typical: *Mr Norris Changes Trains*
and the stories of *Goodbye to Berlin* seemed to me far too inadequate an *oeuvre* for someone who had been tipped, for every
kind of good reason, as the most promising novelist of his
generation.

One day—it must have been in the first week of the war—
turning out the pockets of a summer jacket which I was putting away for the duration, I found an old, clipped railway
ticket to St. Gilgen: it brought back with almost unbearable
vividness the happiness of summer expeditions among the Austrian lakes and mountain forests. Such memories, after a
time, began to hurt so much, that I found myself trying to
avoid them. And yet they refused entirely to be clamped
away; objects as potent as the old railway ticket insinuated
themselves under my fingers as I was looking through writing-
table drawers, chests and wardrobes; photographs would fall
out of books as if lying in wait for me. Two suddenly am-
bushed me between the leaves of a blotter; one of my mother
and Toni at a picnic in the mountains, which I stared at in-
credulously, asking myself was it really as amusing, as easy, as
good as that? The other, of a walk through the pine forests
above the Attersee, with my sister Rosamond and my nephew
Hugo as a long-legged small boy in *lederhosen*, reminded me how
summer after summer I used to spend a week or two on the
Attersee, swimming and boating on the peacock-blue waters
and driving all over the surrounding country, visiting the great
baroque monasteries at St. Florian and Melk and following the
valley of the *Wachau* to Coeur-de-Lion's Durnstein through the
crowded vine-growing slopes. These are treasures, I said to
myself, as I put the photographs away, that I shall enjoy again
one day, if I am not killed, if when the guns fall silent again it
is not in a Nazi-ruled world; but they make no sense now. An
Austrian emigré asked me if I could lend him certain specimens

from my collection of illegal papers of the Dollfuss–Schuschnigg
era; opening the box and fingering through them, *Volkssport*,
Arbeiter Zeitung, Der Rote Trommel, and the little stickies with
Denkt an die Februaropfer! and *Wir Kommen Wieder!* cyclostyled
on them, I was stabbed by the recollection of the hope that had
buoyed us up then against the degradation of unemployment,
the insolence of the police, the constant sight of the bullet-
scarred walls of the Floridsdorf tenement-houses, the rumble
of tanks on the frontier—the hope that the dictatorships would
be defeated before it was too late and the insane destruction
and the killing be staved off. My godmother, Violet Hammersley, reminded me that we had lunched one day together
at the Lusthaus in the Prater, and afterwards had been strolling
down the long alley when suddenly a mounted party had
emerged from a side-path among the trees, among whom we
recognized Chancellor Schuschnigg, accompanied by one of
his A.D.C.s. Very erect and distinguished he looked, an Austrian aristocrat of the old school, embodiment of gentle and
humane authority: it was hard to equate this figure with the
monster master of repression who figured in the propaganda of
the underground parties, Nazi, Communist and Socialist; hard
to envisage him as the dictator of a police-state in the prisons
of which so many of my friends had suffered; easier at that
moment to think of the impossibly conflicting international
forces at whose centre he found himself, and to feel even a
stirring of pity for him. Often, since his regime had collapsed
and the comparatively mild Austro-Fascism had been swallowed up in the vaster, more demonic police-state of the Swastika, that image had come back to me, and in spite of my alle-
giances pity had deepened as I pictured him in some prison
prepared by his gloating and treacherous conqueror; where he
still remained while the anti-aircraft guns ringed the Vienna I
had loved so much, and my friends-transformed-into-enemies
turned to their sleep behind blacked-out windows and only
the moon lit the Danube as it lit the Thames where I was also
turning to my sleep behind blacked-out windows under the
guardian sentinel watch of our side's anti-aircraft guns.

II
TRANSFORMATION SCENE

I

LONDON had suddenly become two cities: the one, the
daytime city where we went about our business much as
before, worked in our offices and discussed what plans
we could make for the future, lunched with our friends, and
visited the shops to lay in what stores our consciences told us
were not so great as to be considered hoarding. Already
before the declaration of war many had disappeared into the
jobs in the war-machine which had been waiting for them
ever since the Munich crisis of the year before; others, who had
had some kind of training or experience in the regular forces or
the Territorials in the past, began to be called up and were off
at a few hours' notice after hurried telephone calls to their
closest friends; but as that first feeling of stunned shock wore
off and the days went by and the colossal air-raids we had
braced ourselves to meet failed to materialize, the rhythm of
life re-asserted itself with a remarkable steadiness.

The other London was the new, symbolic city of the black-
out, where one floundered about in the unaccustomed darkness of the streets, bumping into patrolling wardens or huddled
strangers, hailing taxis that crept along learning their new
element, admiring the gigantic criss-crossing arms of the
searchlights as they lit up the sudden silver bellies of the far
balloons or scurrying clouds on windy nights, and found new
beauty, when it was fine and still, in the fall of moonlight on
pavements and pillars and high window embrasures. Torches,
cigarette-lighters flashed their momentary, tiny illuminations,
the shuttered slits of the traffic lights winked their way through
red, amber, green; there were many accidents in the streets
those first days—a man heard moaning but not seen—a tin-
hatted policeman running into a pub to telephone for an ambulance—it seemed fantastic not to use light on such occasions,
but the discipline held everyone in its grip. Strangest of all

23

at night were the London terminus stations: King's Cross appeared like some weird imagining of John Martin, the long trains waiting like prehistoric beasts, smoking and hissing under the huge, gloomy caverns of the glass roofing only discernible by the rows of faint blue lights far above. Shadowy figures of porters and policemen moved round the bales and packages heaped in dark corners, a gang of plate-layers worked at the rails in a narrow circle of concentrated light at the far end between two platforms, and beyond them, in the vast indistinguishable mouth, a twinkling of red and green signals was all that indicated the beginning of houses, bridges, repair-sheds. The whole city was in a great conspiracy of secrecy, confusing yet curiously stimulating; when one went into a club or restaurant or drinking-place, one felt one had reached some beleaguered subterranean den or cave in the mountains, and one was conscious as never in daytime of airmen waiting by their hangars and soldiers by their camouflaged anti-aircraft guns, on guard to protect.

And yet it was difficult to imagine the war as a reality of violence. The pompous French communiqués from the Maginot Line announcing nothing, the R.A.F. raids over Germany merely to drop leaflets, the soberly factual reports of the German radio, all seemed part of some inexplicable game of nations only pretending to be at one another's throats. One evening, just before sunset, I went down to Hyde Park Corner, and walked up through the Park. So much was changed: and yet so much was the same. There was still a crowd promenading to and fro along the paths, though all the soldiers were in battledress; the booths at Marble Arch still had their preachers with the rings of sceptical listeners surrounding them, soldiers and sailors cracking jokes at the girls on the outskirts and shabby shufflers moving aimlessly between the groups, though just behind them a space had been railed off where a silver balloon was anchored, guarded by an R.A.F. unit. This was more like the rehearsal for some tournament, than the Real Thing we had been dreading for so long. I remember that, to occupy empty afternoons when the little publishing business that could be transacted was already done, I used to go round the London bookshops, to find out if any

The Author in 1939

The flat in the Invalidenstrasse

John Banting's mural

customers were creeping back. Some days the streets bathed
in the warmth of the late summer sun were so still, so empty
of uniforms, that only the sandbagged shop-fronts reminded
one that war was on. Behind one of these shop-fronts in
Oxford Street, J. G. Wilson, genial *maestro* among London's
booksellers, muttered darkly in the shadows: ' Terrible blow
for an institution like this, the war.' One morning, soon after
half-past six, there was an air-raid warning. The minutes
passed, and nothing happened. Finally, I left the shelter in the
basement, and went to the door of the house to see what was
going on. It was a hauntingly lovely September morning,
with a clear mother-of-pearl sky: the alarm had brought
almost dead silence, broken only by the echo of gunfire once,
very faint and far away, and then a few minutes later by the
muffled rumble of a train in the distance beyond King's Cross.
The soldiers on the gun-site nearby stood motionless in their
helmets and heavy greatcoats, watching the east. . . . Could
this really portend death and destruction? Only the news
from the other end of Europe, where the claws of the beast
were tearing Poland into bloody shreds, brought one back
again to the truth of one's place and time.

The mood of London was calmer than one had imagined
possible: a sense of tragic disaster was dominant, without the
slightest trace of terror or patriotic hysteria. Even the
melancholy fading wail of the sirens, like a dog in the ex-
tremities of misery or agony, gradually ceased to stir a queasy
feeling in the pit of the stomach. I tried to sum it all up in a
letter to Christopher in California, describing the impression
so many of us shared, that under the calm surface life was
changing very fast, like one shot fading quickly into another in
a silent film, that even if the war only lasted a few months it
would never be the same again. . . . And if it lasted for years,
how long would this mood of calm survive, against frayed nerves
and the clatter of guns and bombs, and the swelling casualty
lists? Meanwhile, until a finger beckoned from some window
slit in the vast fortress of the war bureaucracy, try to piece
together some of the fragments of one's old hopes and plans,
peer into the fog, find long books to absorb one's thoughts,
Gibbon or Proust or *Seven Pillars of Wisdom*.

c

It was inevitable that one of the questions that most deeply occupied those who had belonged to the pre-war anti-fascist movement, was the attitude of the Soviet Union to our war against Hitler. Disillusionment had set in for most of us many months before the Nazi–Soviet pact, but even after that pact had blown a huge hole through the myth of an idealistic revolutionary Russia leading the forces of resistance to Hitler, desperate hopes kept on bobbing up like shipwrecked men clinging to spars on the edge of an engulfing vortex. I mean for those who were not hypnotized by the farcical clap-trap of the new 'party line', who could still think for themselves; for the comrades, the war against Nazi Germany had suddenly become an imperialist war, with Russia in the role of far-sighted defender of peace, and now and then—incredible though it seemed—one actually came across sincere enthusiasts, fellow-travellers, who had made themselves believe this line. What fanatical twist in their minds made it possible for them to accept the topsy-turvy reasoning that found it suddenly respectable to shake hands with the Jew-baiters, the murderers of Guernica, the plunderers of Austria and Czechoslovakia? Certainly they got little or no support from the people whose interests they were supposed to be defending: Goronwy Rees, already transformed in battledress and forage cap, came in one evening to describe his job of guarding the docks, and confessed to us that all the dockers he had come across were for the war and dead against Hitler. Perhaps these dockers did not go all the way with Harold Nicolson, who declared that the British governing classes were committing suicide in the interests of humanity; but at least they had a sound view of the crucial moral question and of what national preservation implied. Nevertheless, the hopes still clung on, faint graspings at the idea that all might be well after all, and Hitler one morning be proved the biggest dupe of history. What happened one morning, however, was that we heard the shattering news that the Red Army had joined in the murder of Poland and was already sweeping across the Polish Ukraine to meet the victorious Reichswehr. It was little help to say that our own Government was reaping a well-deserved reward for seven years of bungled foreign policy, or that Stalin could not allow the Ukrainians to fall into Hitler's hands; both these reflections were true, but the inescapable fact remained that by cynical justification of aggression and violated contracts, the Soviet Union had lost in moral power what she had gained in material power. And yet, and yet, there were still pathetically obstinate hopes, castaways that refused to be sucked into the vortex: as the two armies approached one another, was it not possible to imagine that under the pretence of amity, Stalin was completing the first phase of a cunningly devised plan of *liberation*? . . . These last, icy-fingered hopes did not survive the Russian invasion of Finland.

The moral, it seemed, could not be evaded: I discussed it with Stephen Spender again and again during these weeks, and with many others who had been associated with us. Nothing that had happened made us feel that we had been wrong to stand openly for the ideas of liberty and justice, to show that we stood on the side of those parties and groups that appeared to be championing them most effectively in the political struggles of a political decade. Our general position, we still felt, had been right: poets, and other creative artists, cannot, if they are to remain fully living people, if they are to fulfil their function as interpreters of their time to their own generation, fail to interest themselves in the meaning behind political ideas and political power. It was our particular position that had probably been wrong: in the heat of the battle, to give our specific assent to a particular set of slogans, even if we did not actually join a particular party. We had at last learned what we ought to have tumbled to long before: that it is not only politicians of old and conservative parties who are unscrupulous, who in their scramble for power will use all means to gain sympathy, kudos, votes, who only pretend to respect creative artists, but also the new leaders the revolutionary situation throws up. Man may be a political animal, but a politician has to be a particular kind of man; and if politicians are necessary, because it is necessary to want power if the wheels of human society are to turn at all, it is not necessary for creative artists, however urgent the situation may seem, to turn themselves into half-baked and half-hearted politicians. Shades of our ancestors defend us against the

itch to sway multitudes with soul-lacerating periods from
some public platform—and (when it comes to poets of old-
fashioned Liberal ancestry) Heaven defend us from the shades
of our ancestors! Too easily poets are gulled into accepting
tactics, however shady, as necessary strategy in the political
battle, the day-to-day programme of a party as the equivalent
of the idealism it claims to represent. Too easily politicians
insist that loyalty to fundamental ideas and aspirations must
mean loyalty also to their own tactical manoeuvres of the
moment.

So our reasoning went in that first Autumn and Winter of
the war. Nor was it pride and arrogance that made us want
to distinguish ourselves from the contestants in the political
arena: we did not think that creative artists are necessarily
better (or for that matter worse) than politicians, but that it
was their business to remain true to their *different*, highly
specialized and difficult task.

That did not prove that all we had said and done was meaningless. Underneath even the most extreme political pam-
phleteering we had been guilty of, remained the humanist
impulse: to speak for justice, to reveal, through the power of
imaginative sympathy, what the action of 'impersonal historic forces' meant in terms of individual human experience.
That impulse was at least as important as before; perhaps, in
the agreed partial surrender of liberty that modern war-
making involved in a democratic country, more important
than ever. I felt myself that the purely human side of the
war would be far the most interesting and significant to me;
and I was aware of a growing need to understand the deeper
pattern of what was happening in order to grasp that human
side.

Meanwhile the practical problem remained of defending
liberty in whatever way was still open to us. The immediate
danger to guard against was censorship: the stifling, under
cover of 'military security', of opinions and attitudes that
were unpopular with the war bureaucracy for political or
narrow-mindedly patriotic reasons. Writers of every sort
had their eyes fixed on the Ministry of Information, into
which many of their kind had already disappeared to pursue

impenetrable activities that seemed to have no obvious results.
It did not, one thought, matter very much what they did
provided they left the rest of their tribe alone. The ' Big House
in Bloomsbury ' presented a façade of monolithic power, concentrated purpose and dignity to the mere denizens of neighbouring Squares creeping beneath its pile; but inside, to judge
from the stories that continually leaked out, and were passed
on with relish in every pub, restaurant and office frequented
by journalists and poets, chaos had come again. Making fun
of the Min. of Inf. became the favourite intellectual pastime
of the first year of the war; but the greater dangers never
materialized, opinion remained officially free, books were not
censored except by a voluntary—and eventually efficient—
pre-publication system on security grounds. No poet, as far as
I know, got into trouble with the civil authorities over the
expression of alarming or gloomy sentiments, though, when
they donned uniform, commanding officers were known on
certain occasions to have become apoplectic. The trouble,
however, was not by any means only the bureaucracy; editors
acting on their own hunch were often over-zealous, their
directors overcome by scruples the Big House seemed never to
have entertained. One afternoon I visited the *New Statesman*
office, to find Raymond Mortimer, Harold Laski and Desmond
MacCarthy there, engaged in a discussion about the chances of
an early armistice and the meaning of the Communist-led
peace campaigns. Raymond (rightly, it seemed to me) was
in bellicose mood, maintaining that the idea of peace was
absurd as long as Hitler was in power and triumphant; while
Harold Laski gaily explored the continuous contradictions in
the policy and statements of the C.P.G.B. and had to admit
himself defeated by them. Then the talk turned to the famous
Bernard Shaw ' peace ' letter. It was a typical example of
mischievous Shavian unreasoning, which advocated coming
to terms with Hitler as Poland, for whom we had gone to war,
no longer existed. The *New Statesman* had just published it,
but Raymond revealed that at a board meeting called to consider it, Keynes had been strongly in favour of refusing to print
it; a first-class row had broken out, and in the end the opening
paragraph was cut. This news incensed Desmond MacCarthy,

who exclaimed with some heat that it was utterly wrong, that
even to *think* of not publishing it was a denial of what our side
stood for.*

Desmond was one of the Old Guard of Bloomsbury who
showed himself most determined to prevent any kind of direct
or indirect gagging of opinion by the new bureaucracy. Soon
after the declaration of war, Lord Esher organized an informal
committee to help (behind the scenes) young writers and artists
of call-up age. The idea was, I think, not so much to prevent
a blind waste of talent, as to guard against the possibility that
those who held unpopular and unorthodox opinions might be
deliberately silenced by being drafted straight into the Forces.
Oliver Esher asked me if I would join, to give the committee
my advice about the younger writers. After some hesitation
I agreed, but, since I was technically of military age, only on
the definite understanding that my own name was not introduced. Desmond was also a member of this committee, and
after a provisional list had been drawn up of those whose gifts
were thought too valuable to be carelessly or maliciously
squandered, it was arranged that I should visit him one
evening in Wellington Square to go over it in detail. We
discussed every name at great length, Desmond showing the
most generously open mind about young writers who were
either unsympathetic or little known to him; the more we
argued the more difficult I felt it to discriminate or be certain
of my judgement in a matter of such importance. I had
visions of poets, whose works I was ignorant of, being thrown
into the early battles as mere privates and killed, their posthumous works being acclaimed as fruits of genius, and myself
guilt-ridden for the rest of my days. I need not have worried:
in the end the scheme was abandoned as impracticable, and
none of those whose names were considered ever knew anything about it (nor would they have known, even if the committee had succeeded).

The intellectuals of the 'thirties were by no means popular
at that time with Members of Parliament, influential Civil
Servants and Generals in authority. For some obscure reason

* Mr. Kingsley Martin has since revealed to me that the Foreign Office
shared Desmond MacCarthy's view.

we were held by many of these—or so it often seemed to us—
to be responsible for the mess the country had got itself into,
though in fact, of course, all our miserable efforts had been
directed towards preventing the mess. One sensed an only
just undivulged wish to put us in front of a firing squad, or at
least to clap us into prison for the duration under regulation
18B. The suppressed emotions of hostility broke violently
into the open over the ' Auden–Isherwood affair '. Christopher and Wystan were suddenly branded as traitors and
cowards in a campaign that was waged with the utmost fury
against them in dailies and weeklies, respectable as well as less
respectable; questions were asked in Parliament, scathing
judgements were passed on them under privilege by people who
may never have more than glanced at their works. They had,
these accusing voices thundered, called on their contemporaries
to fight fascism, and now that we were in fact at war with
Hitler they had run away to America and refused to return.
Flocks of wish-dream white feathers winged their way across
the Atlantic to them. It was in vain to try and point out that
they had left long before the invasion of Poland or even of
Czechoslovakia, that they had taken out papers for American
citizenship but had nevertheless registered with the British
Embassy in Washington and been told to stay put for the time
being. Their friends were dismayed: their position was difficult, because though they knew the campaign was unfair and,
privately, suspected that it was yet another, familiar outburst
of British official philistinism and had little to do with the
rights and wrongs of the victims' particular case, they themselves felt that their absence was painful. How often I was to
think in the coming years of all that had been lost by their not
sharing what the rest of us were experiencing in Britain under
siege: what treasures there would have been for us to lighten
the darkest days if the creator of *The Nowaks* and *Mr. Norris* had
cast his compassionate and humorous eye upon the ardent
follies of our wartime scene; if the spiritual physician of his
generation had been able to write of what it felt like to be still
alive after a night of heavy blitz, rather than offer us those
impeccably above-the-battle sentiments that appear in his
poem *September 1st, 1939*:

> There is no such thing as the State
> And no one exists alone;
> Hunger allows no choice
> To the citizen or the police;
> We must love one another or die.

During that first Autumn of the war, most of the writers I
knew, who had remained with us, seemed incapable of producing very much. Stunned by the catastrophe, oppressed
by a deep melancholy, totally uncertain about the kind of
future we were entering, their instinct was either to immerse
themselves in journals, to try and make sense of the changed
world around them and of their own thoughts in this pre-
Apocalyptic moment, or to plunge back into the past of childhood and youth, times which now stood out in memory with a
strange insulated intensity, an hallucinatory effulgence. Out
of this mood were to come such variously beautiful achievements as Henry Yorke's *Pack My Bag* with its ' cry of a hunts-
man on the hill a mile or more away '; my sister Rosamond's
story *The Red-Haired Miss Daintreys*, with its closing, nightfall
note ' there will be no more families in England like the
Daintrey family '; Cecil Day Lewis's sonnet sequence ' O
Dreams, O Destinations ', and Stephen Spender's novel *The
Backward Son*, with its centre-piece evocation of a childhood
Christmas, hauntingly poetic and humorously, unsentimentally
vivid at the same time, perhaps the most perfectly realized
scene in all his prose.

At the very beginning of the war Stephen had decided that,
until his call-up came, he must reduce expenditure to a
minimum, live in the country and bury himself in his writing.
Our meetings at first were half gloomy silences, half sudden
bursts of nostalgic recollections and random guesses at the
riddle in the crystal before us. Gradually, however, Stephen's
natural buoyancy re-asserted itself, his own private affairs
resumed their place in the foreground of his thought and conversation, and the old spice of affectionate malice returned to
his comments on the doings of friends and acquaintances.
Christopher and Wystan were not spared; Christopher's reported plan to reappear in Europe with an American Am-

bulance Unit, to soothe our dying moments among the ruins, caused him spasms of irritation, as it did me; there was even an unguarded moment at lunch in the Athenaeum when, his grin seeming to spread right across the huge dining-room, he referred to ' Christopher and Stalin, those great neutrals'.

On David Gascoyne, home from Paris and looking rather lost and ghost-like in London-at-war, the situation had, it seemed to me, the effect of spiritual revelation: I felt that he wanted to break out into prophecy, might at any moment or in any place do so—at noon on Westminster Bridge, or from the balcony of the Café Royal, or just as a train came in at Piccadilly station on the Bakerloo. We used to meet for lunch at my flat, or for dinner in Soho, or go pub-crawling in the black-out, and he would describe to me the new philosophy he was trying to work out, the new visionary poems he was writing, the old poems he was revising and which seemed to him to foretell symbolically what had actually taken place in the world; sometimes he would talk of the times in Paris when he was alone and penniless, when he lived on practically nothing for months together, plunged in a despair that bordered— so he thought as he looked back—on insanity. His central idea was that the war was nothing but a surface manifestation of some far deeper psychological disturbance in the world-mind that no one was really conscious of: an ' experience of the void ' were the only words he could find to describe it. One evening we went out with Michael Nelson, who was acting as my secretary at the time, and some younger friends, and in the midst of the noise and the crowds of the successive pubs, David, undeterred, continued to describe in detail six or seven books he was at work on, a new volume of prophetic poems, a play in verse, a philosophical inquiry, an annotated philoso-phical-religious anthology, a novel—these are all I can re-member, but there were more. Very little of all this pro-gramme, alas, was ever completed.

Virginia Woolf, too, was one of the writers who felt that the only thing that made sense was to devote oneself to one's work, to the inner world of order as the outer world collapsed in dis-order. One day, in the first week, she and Leonard came up from the country, and, while we ate sandwiches despondently in my flat, she confessed that the only way she could find to dispel the restless visions of anxiety that continually oppressed her was to force herself to carry on with the biography of Roger Fry she was preparing, and to re-create herself in her diary.

From time to time I went down to Rodmell, to discuss Hogarth affairs with her and Leonard. In theory, I had bought Virginia out of the Press, but in fact she continued to be as keenly interested in all its activities as ever before, and every evening we would settle down in the little sitting-room upstairs, where the shelves were filled with books in Virginia's own binding and the tables and window-sills covered with the begonias, gloxinias and rare giant lilies that Leonard raised in his greenhouses, and we would discuss books and authors and the opportunities that were open to us in the new situation. Leonard stretched out his feet towards the fire in his armchair on one side, and puffed at his pipe; Virginia on the other lit another home-rolled cigarette in her long holder. Occasional visitor though I was, I had come to be very fond of Monk's House, the old village cottage they had bought just after the first war and rebuilt to make an ideal home for two authors to live and work in: I loved the untidy, warm, informal atmosphere of the house, with books and magazines littered about the rooms, logs piled up by the fireplaces, painted furniture and low tables of tiles designed by the Bloomsbury artists, and writing done in sunny, flower-filled, messy studios. A smell of wood smoke and ripe apples lingered about it, mixed with the fainter under-perfume of old bindings and old paper. We ate our meals always at the stove end of the long kitchen-scullery. I remember one Autumn evening there, just after Leonard's book *Barbarians at the Gate* had come out: I had been moved by the persuasive force of the argument he developed, the lucidity of the style and the underlying warmth, and I told him so, and how important I felt his warning was at a time when people were all too easily allowing themselves to believe that any means were justified by the ends. Virginia was splashing gravy in large dollops over my plate as I talked, and joined in with her praise, ' You know, Leo, it's a wonderful book,' while Leonard himself sat in modest silence, with lowered eyes, like a schoolboy praised by the headmaster at an end-of-term prize-giving.

During those months Virginia alternated between cautious confidence and weary depression about the Roger Fry biography, very much as she always did when at work on a new book; but sometimes the depression seemed so deep that both Leonard and I encouraged her to leave it for a while, to put down on paper her objections to my generation of writers, and to prepare a third *Common Reader* collection of essays; the idea of a change nearly always lightened her mood. When *Roger Fry* was finished, however, just before Christmas, she was transformed: radiant and buoyant, full of teasing malice and the keenest interest in what her friends were doing, and finding a startling new beauty in London—the squares and side-streets in the black-out on a clear night—a transfigured look in the faces of the men and women she passed—the smartness of uniforms of every sort.

How grateful one was at that time for week-ends in the country; even before the air-raids one had a sense of escaping from an atmosphere of strain and tension, as the last suburbs gave way to the country fields and the yellowing Autumn trees outside one's carriage-window. Country houses seemed like islands of the pre-war life, all else had been submerged, perhaps for ever, and even the islands were hard-pressed by the encroaching seas. Evacuees were, of course, the great problem and endurance test at the beginning: no one likes his house to be invaded suddenly by strangers of unknown habits and unpredictable demands, but the communal emotion, the sense of national duty fortified hearts against the shock of privacy violated, squalor unmasked and property under siege. Only a sense of humour, however, could keep up the courage of their obligatory hosts until the grumbling hordes, who could never make themselves at home, began to trickle back to the still undamaged tenements they had expected to be reduced to rubble and ashes during the first few days of war. (The episode of the Connollys in Evelyn Waugh's *Put Out More Flags* remains the classic, unforgettable picture of this relationship.) My sister Rosamond had had her quota of evacuees at her

Berkshire home of Ipsden—eleven ragamuffins one of whom
promptly developed scarlet fever—but told tales of their say-
ings and doings as fantastically comic as Beatrix's description
of the porter's wife at the Highgate flats where she lived acting
as ' hostess ' in the air-raid shelter.   Rosamond had made up
her mind, as Virginia had, to treat the whole situation as a
challenge to her creative powers, and had settled to work at a
series of short stories, the first of which was *The Red-Haired
Miss Daintreys*.   Several times during that Autumn and Winter
I visited her at Ipsden, with an ill foreboding that I should not
know the old red-brick house set in its tree-circled lawns among
the gently rolling hills for much longer; it may have been
part of the general sense of imminent doom and ending that
lay at the back of all one's thoughts, but in fact Rosamond
left Ipsden not long after, and never returned to it.   Every
day she wrote for some hours, then read, while Wogan worked
at a bizarre portrait of her he had set up in the dining-room;
in the afternoons there were walks with the two children,
Hugo and Sally.   In the evenings we indulged in long discussions, about the kind of world that would come out of the
war, and the kind of literature too, about our chances of survival and my chances of war-service, what she wanted to write
in novels and I in poetry, and speculated about what had happened to all our many friends in France and Austria and
Germany.   Behind all our talk lay the sense of incalculable
danger, but also incalculable possibility as well: it was as if
we were slowly sailing up some great continental river into
unknown territory, where every bend might reveal rainbow
vistas of exotic bloom and tropical birds of the spirit, or rocks
and rapids that would fling us to quick destruction.   And day
and night the aeroplanes from the Berkshire and Oxfordshire
aerodromes roared overhead.

  At Fieldhead, where I spent at least every other week-end,
my mother had avoided the full tide of evacuees; Bourne End
was considered a little too close to London for safety, but a
few of them had nevertheless established themselves upstairs.
Before the war, Beatrix had invented a comic character called
Mrs. Boote-Smith, through whom she worked off all her remembered childhood resentments about the interference of

pious village busybodies with the free, amoral life of the young
—and dissolved them in laughter. One of her sketches devoted to this ' self-appointed Watch Committee ' of a slightly
distorted Bourne End, *Crisis in Our Village*, I had published in
New Writing. She now wrote a sequel, in which Mrs. Boote-
Smith attempted to cope with what, to the embarrassed surprise
of the English countryside, proved to be one of the chief problems of the child evacuees from the slums: their nocturnal
incontinence. (*Waterside* appeared in the *New Statesman* early
in 1940.) The problem was more acute in Rosamond's village
than at Fieldhead, which was mainly in use as an A.R.P.
point. Every night the floor of the hall was encumbered with
the drowsy forms of ambulance men and A.R.P. workers.
Later on, it became a hospital and we retreated into an even
more restricted inner fortress of rooms. We lived mainly in
the dining-room, a space in fact ample for all our downstair
needs. The old wine cellar, where the sinister magic lantern
and Helen's wonderful model railway had been stored in my
childhood, had been converted into an air-raid shelter, its
structure reinforced and emergency beds inserted. It gave, I
think, a certain sense of security to my elders, but seemed to
me as incapable of standing up to anything except flying glass
as most of the shelters that had been hurriedly constructed in
private houses.

My mother, though already in her middle sixties and given
to chronic anxiety, especially about her children—nothing delighted her more than their successes, but there was always at
least one she was convinced was on the road to ruin, in spite of
the efforts of those of us who had happened momentarily to
have escaped this sentence to persuade her to the contrary—
showed a wonderful fortitude in the face of the war. She
immersed herself at once in local Red Cross work as well as
carrying on with her many duties connected with the County
Council, of which she was an elected member, and the problems of the numerous schools of which she was a Governor.
One of the first things she said to me was that she knew I
would be confronted with very difficult decisions and she
wanted me to know that she would be ready to help me in any
way she could: I was not to think, even if I had to turn myself

into a soldier or sailor, that it was all up with my career as a
publisher, and if it were ever a question of expansion and more
capital, even during the war, she might be able to suggest ways
and means.   She wanted me also to hold on to *New Writing*,
to the foundation of which her help had contributed so much:
don't be discouraged, don't lose heart, was her message to me,
at a time when I felt she might well have been expected to want
moral support herself from her children.   Until her accident
in the Spring, when she fell in the Library and broke her thigh,
we used still to take walks together along the river, discussing
her favourite subject of history and parallels out of the past
with our own day, and the changing international situation.
Contemptuous as she often was of brash American attitudes
towards Europe, convinced that all too often ignorance and
arrogance mingled fatally in American handling of diplomatic
affairs, she nevertheless understood the deep moral currents
that united the two peoples underneath all differences and disagreements, and had an unshakable belief that her own countrymen would never let us in Britain starve, or, in the last
instance, allow our islands to be occupied by an enemy power.
This belief fortified her through the darkest days of the Battle
of Britain and the U-boat war: her comments, however, were
on the scathing side when food parcels began to arrive from
American relations who knew that the one thing Fieldhead
had was a large, well-stocked kitchen garden, and were found
to contain choice tins of concentrated onion-juice and other
remedies for vegetable deficiency.

    The house, the garden, was a haven of peace, where I settled
blissfully, on Saturdays and Sundays, into the mysterious,
sustaining compost of the happy past.   Through the tangle of
Autumn colours, the red and yellow apples falling from the
trees, Mr. Goodman the Head Gardener passed on his way,
prophesying, not without a certain exultation, black doom and
crimson revolution.

2

No one, in the early days of the war, had the slightest idea what the future of writing and book-publishing would be. It is easy to be wise after the event, and to say that the boom that developed in the course of the 1914–18 war should have been a precedent to give authors, publishers and booksellers confidence; but in fact, if air-bombardments had started at once and the main cities of Britain had found themselves under siege before industry, commerce, communications had adapted themselves to war conditions, it is very doubtful if the book trade would have flourished as it eventually did; and immediate, overwhelming attack was what seemed to everyone at first extremely likely. The bookshops were empty; and publishers cancelled their plans or postponed them indefinitely except for those with books already going through the press or preparing works of urgent topical significance. In The Hogarth Press basement in Mecklenburgh Square everything came to a standstill; all discussions about paper supplies and printing facilities seemed entirely academic, manuscripts lay on the shelves like orphans without prospects; and Leonard Woolf, coming in to work out an emergency skeleton scheme to keep the Press at least in being if raids came or if I were called up, commiserated with me on the ill-luck that seemed to dog my footsteps as a publisher.

Gradually, however, the lifeless body began to stir again; it was only concussion after all. After a few weeks, people began to feel that the German air-armadas were not coming just yet, perhaps had thought better of it, and to realize at the same time that they needed books and were going to have plenty of time to read them. Leonard and I began to look again at our stocks of The International Psycho-Analytical Library and Virginia's Uniform Edition, and to calculate how soon we should need reprints if the demand continued to recover. A little later, we brought out Henry Green's *Party Going*, which received an early batch of enthusiastic reviews,

and began to sell fast. Something could be done after all;
it was worth having a basic plan for the use of a paper ration
which threatened to be minuscule. I put in a plea for poetry:
if the 1914–18 war was any guide, I argued, people would
eventually want to read poetry, and books of poetry consumed
very little paper while keeping a flag flying over The Hogarth
Press—a flag which told young authors that we were still
keenly interested in them. Just before the war, I had started
a series of small anthologies of *new* poetry, called *Poets of Tomorrow*, and I now thought we might prepare beside it a
' library' of poetry in cheaply priced volumes, that would
offer selections of the poets the Press had already made a name
with, and allow room at the same time for new poets who
might come our way during the war. So it was that The New
Hogarth Library was born, which started off by producing
selections from the poems of Cecil Day Lewis, Vita Sackville-
West, William Plomer and J. B. Leishman's translations of
Rilke; and then as its popularity grew, went on to the first
volumes of Terence Tiller and Laurie Lee, the two volumes
Roy Fuller wrote while serving in the Navy, Norman Cameron's
translations from Rimbaud, the Spender–Gili translations
from Lorca, *Work in Hand* by Robert Graves, Norman Cameron
and Alan Hodge, and others. A small enough venture, but
I think the aesthetic vitamin-content was high, and it gave
me almost more pleasure than anything else the Press undertook during the war.

For me, however, the crucial question was still what was
going to happen to *New Writing*. As I have already mentioned,
I felt profoundly pessimistic about its future when the Autumn
number of the old *New Writing* came out: it did not
seem to me likely that I should have either the money—for
those packed volumes of 150,000 words each were becoming
rather expensive to produce—or the paper, or the opportunity
to go on with it as before; and it struck me as rather absurd
to pretend that the ' movement' had not been changed in
certain decisive ways by the outbreak of war, quite apart from
the fact that Wystan and Christopher had abdicated from it
(from us), and the old foreign contributors were mostly beyond reach. No more international conferences of angry and

Fieldhead, 1939

The lily pool at Fieldhead, 1939

militant and self-important writers for the duration; no more
clenched fists raised as one attacked one's typewriter in the
morning; but the silence of the monk's cell, the quiet, the
hopes of justification, the ' sighs for folly said and done '.
And yet my natural obstinacy and dislike of giving anything
up until it was finally proved to be hopeless, the little ember of
optimism that burned still under the ashes, was fanned by the
tone of the reviews. ' One hopes that war will not demolish
it,' said the *Manchester Guardian*; ' Now that the *Criterion* and
the *London Mercury* have gone the way of all literary reviews,
there is nothing left but *New Writing* to supply the demand for
good prose, good verse and good criticism ' was the opinion
of *The Listener*; and the *New Statesman* even more reassuringly
maintained that ' the task which Mr. Lehmann undertook in
1935 is by no means finished or even interrupted by the war '.
At the same time letters from some of my old contributors
began to reach me, in which there was a note almost of desperation at the idea that *New Writing* might come to an end.
The book trade was beginning to pick up, people were gradually distinguishing shapes and directions more clearly in the
darkness that had suddenly fallen. Perhaps after all there
was a chance; perhaps it would be foolish not to keep something going, less extravagant of paper, time and finance, which
would mean continuity and welcoming signals to the young
men who still believed, who had transferred their fountain-
pens and notebooks to the pockets of their battledress.

It seemed to me that the spirit of *New Writing* was in fact
very far from confined to the association of left-wing politics
and literature, whatever might be said by the detractors and
those who, silent in their hostility before, were now eagerly
gathering round the burial ground they had marked out for
it. The belief in literature as part of life, the belief in the
power of the creative imagination to give meaning to life;
these were surely going to be as important as ever in the times
we were about to enter. The reviews and the letters and
messages that were coming in hinted that once one had taken
on a responsibility towards young writers, it was not so easy
to put it down again without looking a little selfish, a little
cowardly (though I was aware of the ambuscade of vanity in

D

this argument). If *New Writing* was to go on, it must avoid
the political, yes, but emphasize the human, be committed
to the human scene even more completely; it could be a
laboratory, an experimental ground for the development of a
new consciousness; it would probably find itself moving towards something more lyrical and individual, burlesque and
satire too of a kind that represented the revolt of the free human
spirit against the prisons that the war with its imperatives and
its bureaucratic impersonality threatened to build up round
us . . . So my thoughts went, as I walked about London's
moonlit streets or leaned in pubs, deliberately alone, working
out practical schemes at the same time as I tried to clear my
mind about aims and values. I found the warmest support
from Leonard and Virginia when I explained to them what I
wanted to do; and it was not long before I had called for
estimates from the printers and was settling down with Leonard
to see if they worked out right. They looked just promising
enough; small changes but vital; there were to be 75,000
words instead of 150,000, the price would be five shillings
instead of seven and sixpence, and the volumes were to be
called, to distinguish them from what had gone before, *Folios
of New Writing*. And to cushion me against deficits on the
editorial side, my brother-in-law, Mouny Bradish-Ellames,
generously loaned me a sum of money which was to prove as
vitally useful as my mother's original help.

It was during the preparation of this scheme that calami-
tous disagreements broke out between Stephen Spender and
myself. They were connected with the birth of *Horizon*, which
happy event had just taken place. Ridiculously unimportant
though they may appear in retrospect, I find it difficult to
pass them over as if they had never existed, as they gave rise
to the quite unwarranted idea that some feud-to-the-death
existed between *New Writing* and *Horizon*, that Cyril Connolly
and I had snipers' guns trained on one another as long as our
two magazines existed side by side. Nothing could be further
from the truth; a friendly rivalry certainly existed, which
spurred us on (I hope) to greater efforts; I disagreed strongly
with the ' ivory tower ' attitude Cyril appeared to adopt at
first, his view that the only thing writers could do while the

war was going on was to concentrate on technique and shut
their ears; and I thought the sneers *Horizon* allowed to be
printed in its first number against Wystan and Christopher
were in bad taste; but I am quite prepared to believe that
Cyril, on his side, had equally decided criticisms of *New Writing*'s policy and judgement. That did not prevent Cyril and
myself remaining very good friends throughout the war.
Which of us could swear on all he holds most sacred that a
crack, edged with malice, did not escape his lips at the other's
expense between 1940 and 1945? And yet, as the war became more embittered and destructive and shortage of supplies threatened us both, we began, I believe, to hold one another's editorial existence as almost sacred. What caused the
disagreements was quite simply my belief that Stephen, with
whom I discussed all my plans in the frankest friendship from
the first day of the war, had agreed to come in, as associate
editor, on any scheme which I could realize for *New Writing*'s
future. It was for that reason that my dismay was so acute
when I heard one day, without any warning, that he was to be
co-editor with Cyril and Peter Watson on a new literary
magazine. No doubt I had assumed a great deal more than I
had any right to assume; but I imagined, in that moment of
shock, that Stephen would represent, on the *Horizon* board,
the policy that had made *New Writing*'s reputation; and,
equally wrongly as it turned out, that *Horizon*, off to a flying
start before *New Writing* could pick itself up and get going
again, would make the position of a rival literary magazine
untenable.

It must be admitted that there were some angry scenes and
exchanges of letters between Stephen and myself, while the
reverberations of the explosion spread over most of our literary
world. Sides were taken, and I was encouraged to find how
many strong partisans I had; but there were many who wished
to conciliate as well. The person who perhaps helped to
lower my temperature most effectively was the new young
secretary who came to me after John Lepper joined up,
Michael Nelson. As he had been recommended to me by
Stephen Spender, he had the ear, so to speak, of both camps;
and the vast amusement, openly expressed, which he derived

from the clash of the fell incensèd points, as a puppy may often
be seen to wag its tail while two older dogs are at one another's
throats, was difficult to resist. In the end peace was made and
sealed with the presentation to me by Stephen of an exceptionally splendid gift: the large, leather-bound ledger in which
he had written the whole of his play, *Trial of a Judge*, and the
greater number of the short lyrics composed at the same time.

One ironical result of this increased sense of competition
was that I turned all my spare energies to the nourishment
of my new baby, *Folios of New Writing*. Now, I said to myself,
it must not fail. Just before, I had begun to feel the impulse
to write poetry again; the contemplative, poetical-analysing
side of my nature was uppermost in those early weeks of the
war when the train of all one's pre-war activities was brought
to a sudden halt as if by a landslide on the line. Poems
were beginning to form in the back of my mind; but, as on so
many other crucial occasions in my life, a renewed challenge
to my career as editor-impresario made me turn away and
leave the poems to sink back again into the darkness. One
day I hope to understand whether this reaction was evidence
of weakness or strength.

The first volume of *Folios* came out in the Spring of 1940,
and was followed, as in the pre-war days of *New Writing*, by
another six months later. Many of the old names were still
there, and yet I think the change of mood could immediately
be felt. The old political assumptions had gone, except in
some of the foreign stories, and even the predominance of the
' victims of oppression ' had faded: the contributions by Henry
Green and my sister Rosamond, for instance, were about
upper middle-class childhoods; those by V. S. Pritchett and
Tom Hopkinson about class-levels just a little lower; those
by G. F. Green, B. L. Coombes and John Sommerfield about
working-class life—almost the whole stratification was there.
These volumes were, I believe, more ' miscellanies ' than any
of the pre-war volumes; for them I was trying to gather together the best prose and poetry I could find, without prejudice except for standards of intellectual integrity and artistic
craftsmanship; and yet they were given a certain unity by

the fact that so many of the contributors had been moved by the slogans of passion and idealism of the 'thirties, and now found them inadequate. Only an undertone, or even less— the faintest of implications—in some of the contributions, it becomes more articulate in André Chamson's *Liaison Officer's Notebook*—' we are at war, but in something much bigger than a war, we are in the midst of a metamorphosis of human existence '; in George Orwell's *My Country Right or Left* where he reveals (with some contemptuous side-thrusts at the' boiled rabbits of the Left ') that a dream on the night before the Russo-German pact was announced made him suddenly understand that he was patriotic at heart, if by patriotism was understood the ' devotion to something that is changing but is felt to be mystically the same '; and in Stephen Spender's article on *The Creative Imagination in the World Today*. Stephen attacked at the same time the blinkered Marxist view that all writers must side with a political party in their writing and the philistine patriotic view that all poetry in wartime must sound a clarion-call of heroism and defiance to the enemy, and asserted, with a more effective marshalling of arguments than ever before, that the essential and genuinely revolutionary task of the poet is to discover what is true and what is living in his own time below what is assumed to be true and what is only pretending to be alive.

It was by pure luck that Chamson's piece had come into my hands: it was the only prose contribution from Europe, which had previously provided me with such a large proportion of each volume. In the Spring *Folios* there were two poems by Pierre Jean Jouve, translated by David Gascoyne, and my own translation of Yura Soyfer's deeply moving *Song of the Austrians in Dachau* (the discovery of which I have already described in *The Whispering Gallery*); in the Autumn number nothing at all from Europe. The international character of *New Writing* was kept up, rather strangely, by the stories from China, India, America and New Zealand; strange, because this suggested a huge blasted area surrounding England, over which one had to make an oceanic leap to discover the activities of the spirit going on as before.

What gave me hope for the future was not so much that I

saw, from what I had been able to collect for those first two
volumes between the outbreak of war and the Battle of Britain,
that fresh developments could be expected from the writers
of my own generation, but that already new poets and story-
writers were beginning to appear. In the Spring *Folios* I
published some of the earliest poems of Nicholas Moore, son
of the Cambridge philosopher G. E. Moore, and of Terence
Tiller, who had just left Cambridge to take up an appointment
in the University of Cairo; and in the Autumn a group of
poems by Laurie Lee, a new poet of twenty-six, whose lively
Cotswold eye and vivid appreciation of landscape and life
in Spain gave his work an immediate appeal. The simplicity
and poignancy of feeling in Nick Moore's poems, the music
and evocative imagery in Terence Tiller's, the lyrical freshness of Laurie Lee's, gave the promise, I thought, of still-
flowing springs of inspiration and a poetic response to the life
of war far more full of meaning than any Rupert Brooke-ish
' war poems ' whose absence was so censoriously complained
of by some elderly pundits. And I had received from a young
Captain in the Signals, Ralph Elwell-Sutton, the first story to
reflect the mood of the new conscript Army, *The Deserter*:

. . . We talked about him being plumb scared of war. We
were all plumb scared of war, we reckoned. But it seemed to be
different with this chap. He couldn't stand anything to do with
war. He couldn't stand all the men in uniforms and the routine
and the rifles. It killed him inside and he went about in misery
and awful fear. Everything he saw and smelt and heard made it
worse, and some of us began to wonder if it would slowly drive
him mad.
   He stuck it for ten days. For ten days he went around the
tables serving out tea, and standing around in the Mess, generally
unshaven and always untidy, until he became a part of the place,
as much a part of it as the tables and the benches and the smell
of stale food. He hadn't any friends, but everyone was decent
with him, and he seemed to be getting along. Anyone who didn't
feel sympathetic left him alone. You couldn't make jokes at
him. You wouldn't have got anything out of it . . . The unit
was in improvised quarters at the time, and the men's mess was in
the disused part of a cotton-mill. It was a grey shabby building,
square as a prison, but neglected and decaying too, and you felt

cold looking at it. It was the same inside. I have never known anything so wrapped in gloom as that empty ill-lit machine-room, when the mess-tables were laid out.

To find out what the feeling about the future was among the booksellers outside London, I made a number of expeditions that Autumn, with Hogarth books and provisional lists in my bag, which gave me an opportunity to see what was happening beyond the narrow frontiers of my own existence. I remember one trip to the West Country, in a train filled with naval officers carrying important-looking brief-cases. Both Bath and Bristol seemed to have become extensions of the Admiralty: it struck me in Bath, as I watched the Admirals, Captains and Commanders stalking down the streets, and smoking in their arm-chairs after dinner with unruffled Nestorian dignity, that Jane Austen, if she could return to her favourite city, would not think that very much (except uniforms) had changed in a century and a quarter. Bristol, with the timber control as well as the Navy and a number of big firms evacuated there, was as busy and even more crowded. There the booksellers were already beginning to feel a little more optimistic, were even looking forward to a good Christmas, especially with the influx of students from London. But what, I wondered, prompted one bookseller to say to me: 'Time there was an air-raid—people need waking up'? It reminded me of the exasperated remark of a friend of mine only a few days before: 'Something definite must happen soon—the Germans must *do* something.' What curious train of subconscious impulses prompted such remarks? Was it the need to atone for obscure guilt, or the tension of the runner with his finger on the touch-line waiting for the crack of the starting-pistol? After all, as the presence of all those dark-blue uniforms reminded one, a gigantic naval war was in progress, invisible though it might be to us.

A week or two later, I went down to see the booksellers in Cambridge. Everything was looking its most beautiful in the late October sunlight, the great golden chestnut half obscuring the Senate House on King's Parade, and the yellow tumbling leaves on the Backs glimpsed through the iron gates of a newly scrubbed Neville's Court in Trinity. Confused and

painful emotions troubled me, not so much nostalgia, as regret
that so large a chunk of my life could slip away so easily, could
seem so far away on the other side of all that I had experienced
in the cities of Europe during the 'thirties.   Did I really spend
so many years of my life on this Pacific island, which now
appeared so extraordinarily blessed and remote from the
stormier waters of life, even though the young R.A.F. men
hurrying through the streets suggested the encroaching reality
of war?   Dining in King's with Dadie Rylands and Shephard,
I had the odd feeling of being like a man who had emigrated
to Australia and built up a sheep farm there: the nostalgia
was checked by the consciousness of being planted, spiritually,
elsewhere.   I kept on asking myself what I had learnt in
Cambridge; a great deal about books and art, but almost
nothing about life.

3

In spite of the fact that I had begun to change the focal point
of my life from Vienna back to London over a year before the
war broke out, and in spite of my impulse, after the blow fell,
to repress the too intimate, too painful memories, I could not
altogether resist a hankering to keep in touch with the Danube
world in some way or other, to do something, even if only of a
symbolic nature, for my Austrian friends.   I knew that the
sympathies of most of them were far more with England than
with the goose-stepping Third Reich that had absorbed
Austria, but I also knew something of the power of the Nazi
propaganda machine, and feared that gradually they might
come to believe in the distorted mask with which Goebbels
was concealing the true face of our country.   I could not think
of a single one who had ever expressed any bellicose sentiments
or any appetite for the military life, and it was horrible to me
to imagine them being trained to kill young Englishmen who—
so it seemed to me from my own circle of friends—had just as
little hatred of them and just as little zeal for killing.

No letters of course could get through, and I thought that even if I succeeded in sending something via America it might only cause them serious embarrassment with the Nazi authorities. I did ask an English friend in Italy, who had connections and acquaintances in many parts of South-Eastern Europe, to try and get news of my former secretary Toni, his wife and family, by devious means; but, not surprisingly, he failed. My life, that had grown its roots in two countries, thus brought home to me the cruel absurdity of modern war, the declaration of which immediately cuts off tens of millions of people on one side of the frontier from all contact with or knowledge of all the tens of millions of people on the other side of the frontier; and I thought with bitter envy of how in the past, right up to the Napoleonic wars, the artists and writers of one country could visit the capital of another with which they were at war, and be received in dignity and respect.

After a while, I began to immerse myself in books that would at least partly assuage the ache for the world from which I was now totally excluded. I took down again Hašek's marvellous *Schweik*, preferring to think that the immortal dodger more truly represented the attitude of my Austrian friends to army life than the massed fanatical warriors with whose pictures the Austrian papers had been filled since the Anschluss; I embarked on Joseph Roth's *Radetskymarsch*, I re-read Schnitzler's haunting story *Spiel im Morgengrauen*, which I had often thought of translating, and an anthology of modern Austrian lyrics I carried about with me. From time to time I saw my friends among the Austrian emigrés, who depressingly reported a hardy survival of dissensions between Social-Democrats, Communists and Monarchists: in France I gathered that only the Monarchists were favoured by the Government, and even in England there seemed to be, in Foreign Office circles, a strong hankering after a Habsburg solution to Austrian problems in the event of victory. This, I knew from of old, could only produce violent opposition among the Czechs and Slovaks (if not among the Hungarians) whom we had good reason to count among our potential friends behind the façade of Hitler's empire.

One day early in November surprising and rather exciting

news reached me. One of my closest friends in Slovakia, Marina Pauliny, a relation of the Slovak statesman Dr. Hodža, had reached London after an adventurous journey from Bratislava. It was strange to reflect, as we lunched together in the Café Royal, that only a few weeks before she had been in enemy territory; for a delusive moment, everything seemed possible, Toni or one of my other Viennese friends might walk in to join us as we drank our coffee, the old happiness start again on English territory. . . . Marina reported the inevitable squabbles behind the scenes in the various political parties in her homeland, and, worse, the continuing tension between Czechs and Slovaks, the rock on which so many hopes of a strong, democratic Central Europe had foundered. What struck me most, however, was her attitude —evidently reflecting a prevalent attitude in Czechoslovakia— towards the Russians. ' We are after all a proletarian people,' she said. ' We have nothing to fear from the Russians.' I had in the past heard similar sentiments on many sides in the Republic, but more rarely from the social stratum to which Marina belonged. Both the Czechs and the Slovaks, it seemed to me, had an *idée fixe* about the Russians as a great traditionally friendly Slav people, and not at all as ruthless ideological imperialists, a conception which would certainly not have been shared by their Slav neighbours, the Poles. A decade later, when they reaped the bitter harvest of this faith, the shock of reality was, I believe, far more severe for them than for the others, who expected no more than they got.

Marina encouraged me to maintain my interest in Central European affairs, and she very soon arranged an interview for me with the exiled Dr. Hodža, in order that I could present him with a copy of my book *Down River*, which had just come out. He hurried out of his room to the hall to receive me, just as I remembered him from our last meeting in Bratislava: the huge Slav peasant face, with the enormous cauliflower-nose embedded in deep folds of cheek, small slanting eyes behind strongly magnifying glasses, the curious overhanging upper lip. It was not, I thought again, a face that gave an impression of great intellectual force, but rather of deep, instinctive power. He was extremely friendly, and at once launched into a long discussion about the war and the future of Slovakia. He did not give me the impression of being entirely at his ease in London, nor as fully informed as he would have liked to be about all the behind-the-scenes intrigues that were going on. His mind was working in a kind of limbo, creating a shadowy edifice out of conjecture, rumour, confused secret information and hope. What use was it for him to say, with a dream determination, that the majority Slovak groups with whom he had been able to establish contact were now united in their belief that their post-war relationship with the Czechs must be on a federal basis? Did it matter if he had to admit that the miserable resentments and rivalries of the past were still alive, that he and his friends could not agree with the exiled Czechs nor with the secret leaders in the Protectorate, and that Beneš himself could still not be persuaded to abandon his obsessional hostility towards the Slovak claims for greater freedom? Two neighbouring villages on the slope of a volcano, half-ruined by a first eruption, quarrel about their future boundaries, while all the time the volcano is still rumbling and smoking, presaging total destruction and transformation of the whole mountain landscape. But I listened with affection and admiration, as he dilated again on his great idea of a Danubian federation without Bavaria—and without the Habsburgs. We argued for some time about Austria's place in such a federation: his idea was that Austria would gain far more than she would lose, because Vienna's importance as the natural trade and administrative centre would be immensely enhanced. I remembered how, in the last years before the Anschluss, Hodža's plans had seemed to offer the only real hope of peace and renewed prosperity in the Danube basin, and how his frequent unofficial visits to Austria and discussions with Schuschnigg had encouraged the belief that agreement between the two countries on such a basis was very close. He now told me that considerable progress had indeed been made during the meetings in Baden, but he had always been convinced that Schuschnigg had an unchangeable prejudice in favour of a restoration of the Habsburgs, however much he might conceal it for tactical reasons.

A few weeks later, I had an opportunity to discover for

myself how strong Dr. Beneš's resentment towards and suspicion
of the Slovaks remained. I made the pilgrimage down to
Putney, and rang the doorbell of a neat little villa in the row
of neat little villas, that had no external sign to show that it
was inhabited by the man who only a year before had ruled
over a huge country from the ancient castle of the Hradschin.
I had not met him before, and I was struck at once by his
smallness; I also found the curious shape and twisted movement of his mouth unexpected and disturbing. We talked—
or rather I suggested themes and he then held forth in his
forceful but imperfect English—about the revolt in the Protectorate, the future of Germany and Austria, the future
association of the Czechs and the Slovaks and the minority
problems that would arise when the frontiers were re-drawn.
From a man who had suffered so much at the hands of the
Germans, it was impressive to hear the opinion not only that
one could never expect Austria to follow an anti-German
policy, but also that it would be a mistake to break Germany
into small pieces again. I did not tell him that I had heard
only a few days before from a Foreign Office friend that all discussion about the problem was academic, because the French
were absolutely determined to smash the unity of the Reich,
and nothing would deter them. It was perhaps an unfortunate day for an interview, for the news of the mass-shootings of
Czech students by the Nazis had come through only the night
before. I went away with the tragic impression—Beneš's
lined and haggard face told as much as his words—that he
was a prisoner in a cage of bitterness, a mood, I realized, that
all Czechs were bound to share to some extent: bitterness
against the Germans, bitterness against the West for the
Munich betrayal, bitterness against the Slovaks for their
ambiguous attitude in the crises of the last few years, bitterness in fact against everyone—except the Russians.

Not unnaturally, my hope and aim was to be used by my
country in some sphere in which my special knowledge of the
Danubian countries would prove to be of some value. In the
first few weeks of the war, I foolishly believed that my applica-
tion of the previous year to be placed on the emergency register
would result in a rapid call to service: I had visions of myself

playing a small but crucial part in some military mission to a still neutral Balkan country, or being trained to be landed by submarine, my pockets stiff with false papers, on some Adriatic or Black Sea shore. It was not to be. Every week or so I would ring up the appropriate department of M.I.; every week the reply grew vaguer and more discouraging. I was finally told there was no hope: I was not told why, but the difficulties which some of my friends, who had been closely associated with the Spanish Republican cause, were experiencing in being taken on as volunteers led me to suspect that the same objections were working against me. By then, however, new suggestions and new ideas had come up, and at one moment possibilities were dangled before me of being taken on by three different outfits, one connected with the Foreign Office, one with the Ministry of Information and one with the European Commission of the Danube, which buoyed me up with the hope of being able to assuage my nostalgia for the countries I had left behind and serve my own country at the same time. The British representative on the European Commission told me that he personally very much wanted me to join him in some capacity, and over luncheon at the Athenaeum we swopped stories of Danube politics and Danube travel: he made me laugh with his description of the fantastic situation he still found himself in of having to sit at the conference table in Rumania with the German delegate and shake hands with him in the Council Chamber. In anticipation I saw the sunlit marshes of the Delta again more vividly than ever, I could almost smell the reeds and hear the cries of the birds. . . . All this was but a mirage, for the weeks turned into months, and still the fatal veto appeared to block my advance at all doors.

Finally, I forget how, an idea took shape that I should start a British bookshop in Yugoslavia or Rumania. The co-operation of the British Council with the Foreign Office appeared necessary for this project, and one day I went for an interview with one of the higher executives of the former body. I am astonished, on looking back, at the persistence which brought me to this point: my efforts by that time had something feverish and hallucinated about them, and I was quite unaware what a wild-goose-chase the whole scheme must have appeared in the eyes of a cautious and conventional civil servant. The Higher Executive was very polite, very F.O. with me; but it was quite clear he had no idea who I was nor what my qualifications really were, in spite of the briefing I was led to believe he had been given. He seemed much re-assured by observing that I wore an Old Etonian tie, but nevertheless betrayed acute anxiety as he posed *the* question: had I been to a University? Immense relief flooded his face when he heard the answer, but seeped away again as the de-sultory conversation proceeded. In desperation, and shame-lessly, I managed to mention as if in passing that my cousin happened to be Sir Ronald Campbell, who was British Mini-ster at Belgrade at the time: this provided a brief oasis of cheer for the Higher Executive, but dismay reigned again when I rather crossly explained that I wasn't looking for a job at all costs but wanted to be of use, if I could, in a way for which I felt myself specially fitted. . . . Yes, of course, if there were a British Book Exhibition somewhere down in the Balkans. . . . Exactly. . . . Very good of you, Mr. Lehmann. . . . Politely bowed out, I had the dubious satisfaction of knowing that I had been ' put on their files ', and the half-acknowledged inner conviction that precisely nothing would come of the interview.

Very soon after, however, while the idea of the Balkan book-shop was still being considered by the authorities, Rumania fell under Hitler's control, and I realized that it was too late. Nevertheless, as I had gathered that a large shipment of British books had arrived in Bucharest, in the restless hours of the night I conceived an even more extraordinary scheme: that I should open and take charge of a British cultural-propaganda centre, in the guise of a bookshop, in Moscow. I bombarded the long-suffering Leigh Ashton at the Ministry of Information with details of my latest project, proposing that the books in Rumania should be crated again and shipped to Odessa as a quick way of getting them into Russia; that as the Germans had staged a major cultural exhibition in Moscow we must do the same; and that special attention should be paid to the English classics and books about Shakespeare at the Old Vic, the Sadler's Wells Ballet, the Stratford Memorial Theatre and

English documentary films. I had a freakish hope that as I had worked in the past for Sir Stafford Cripps's paper *Tribune* he would be sympathetic to my proposals. In the end I went to discuss them with the Northern Division of the Foreign Office, and Fitzroy Maclean, who interviewed me, suggested chillingly that though they could not officially back me, they would have no objection to my having a shot on my own. When I had recovered—some days later—from the blow this bewildering method of turning me down had dealt me, I realized that I had been losing touch with reality. I thought no more about it. I knew that no one else was thinking about it. So why should I?

Meanwhile, publishing was rapidly recovering from the sharp frost of the previous September, and I was more and more engrossed with the problems of book-production which I thought I had left behind me at least for the duration. And yet one didn't quite believe in it all: for how could it survive the plunge over the Niagara one knew must be approaching?

4

I TRY to reconstruct the everyday life of those months from Winter to Spring, before the German swoop westwards, but, as if it were shattered by what came after, I only find fragments and cannot put them together again.

Voices from far away, from the past of *New Writing* and old friends: Frank Sargeson writes from Takapuna: ' I have only a dead sort of feeling about the war. I hear the intellectuals out here saying we'll have to let old man Europe just go to pot, and start culture all over again out here. But of course it wouldn't work. . . . Do ballet-dancers dance with their gasmasks on, or just carry them? ' And Bertold Brecht from Sweden: ' In the next few days I shall send you a copy of my *Svendberger Gedichte*, about which I've already written to you.

One request: can't you send me regularly a copy of each
number of *New Writing*? I'm always so pleased to see it, one
gets so few good things now.' And Anna Seghers from a Paris
become immensely remote: ' I go on with my literary work
in spite of every kind of worry and interruption. I've started
a grand essay on *Gewoenliches und Gefaehrliches Leben*. About the
questions that preoccupy us all at the moment. I expect the
title will tell you all you want to know about it. Do you know
of a review that would publish it? I've got to earn a living
for myself and my children somehow.' Madeleine from
Bucharest: ' The last time I saw you, we spoke about writing
as a means to get free from one's own obsessions. If that be
true, we need this sweet medicine (sweet for those who read it,
but somehow bitter for those who have to pour it) more than
ever. I am writing now—in my spare hours—something about
Sighisoara, oh! the most humble thing. I'll try to translate it
for you because you liked the spot and because we heard the
church organs there together.'

Voices from nearer home: from my Godmother Violet
Hammersley in the Isle of Wight, ' I agree with you that part
of the pain of this war, is an isolation from all one's accustomed
human contacts. Here, you can imagine what it's like. On
the Solent nowadays there's nothing to see save two or three
small yachts, painted grey, and flying strange flags proclaiming
them to be on scout duty of some kind. No other ships are
ever seen . . . I've been made very unhappy over various
Polish friends. It's all too long to tell, but several I knew, who
escaped from the Germans sought refuge in East Poland in a
friend's house, and were horribly massacred by the Russians,
one a boy of 17, the son of a very, very old friend who adored
him.' And from Victor Pritchett down in Berkshire, a glimpse
of the absurd difficulty of arranging even the simplest meetings
between friends in those days: ' Your letter horrified me because it sounds as though, not having received mine, you must
have sat in the Paddington snack bar hour after hour eating
snack after snack. A fate I would not wish you. I'm sure
I didn't call you a cad, but I wonder what the insult was?
Was it Com? Short for Communist? I get waves of rage

about the Party Line now and then, so perhaps I was wishing you are not of that persuasion; but like myself, a crypto-Tory anarchist free trade Liberal with strong Socialist bias. I'm not really any -ist because I don't like any good news that comes from On High straight from the lips of the Infallible. I'm a natural Protestant. . . . But I back myself to keep alive under any regime, even though I detested it—which is the nastiest kind of egoism, but it's like all the people you see going into the towns to get something cheap, on the country buses. Civilization was never built by people like me; we're the dead-weight, but sometimes an embellishment.'

Voices from young men under arms, poets and lovers of poetry, cramped into the discomforts of the creaking, grinding military omnibus: Robert Waller, now Gunner Waller, some-where in Somerset: ' Everything here is measured to suit the physique and character of the majority. If your feet, for example, are particularly tender or an odd shape, you will inevitably have to suffer discomfort. The same with the diet: I have no doubt eternal chunks of bread, potato pudding, pie, etc., is good for most men doing heavy exercise: it just blocks me up and gives me the stitch. . . . English youth is an in-dustrial product with a touch of Christian ethics (not religion): it knows a lot about machinery, nothing about good taste: it is ignorant of spiritual values but it is kind and considerate to others. The attitude of the whole place to soldiering is " professional ": it is another job: the officers are " bosses ": the soldiers are low paid manual workers. There is no sug-gestion of free men being led to victory in a great cause. For all I know this may create the best sort of armies—but it bores me stiff. Our 2nd Lieutenant is the most insolent, dissatis-fied youth I have ever encountered. The sergeants are friendly, delightful people, who though often guilty of uncon-scious cruelty, on the whole show surprising patience and humanity.' And from young John Irwin, enthusiast for all things artistic and (critical) fan of *New Writing*, now at an OCTU in Colchester: ' I feel exactly like the last movement of Mozart's G Minor Quintet (if that conveys anything to you) whilst the idle chatter, the ceaseless bawlings and the general ugliness eat into my brain all day. The work is very hard (in

E

the sense that the hours are long) and madly boring—so boring, in fact, that boredom down here becomes a mystical experience. . . . The enclosed verse was handed to me by a fellow-soldier (aged 20): read the enchanting letter which accompanies it and you'll see what he wants. I'm serious about it. I only ask you to do this because I know him to be so desperately concerned about his talents without ever having known anybody who can help him.'

Voices overheard in pubs, confidences over glasses of mild and bitter: one man, a stocky little signals despatch-rider from the North, forage cap askew on fuzzy head, a regular, says he joined up because of 'complications at home', but doesn't regret it because 'the boys are such a fine lot'. He talks of having had 'a grand time' on his own in town during his ten days' leave, only a day or two with his family, otherwise (with a wink to right and left) 'girls of *all sorts*'. Another night, a gunner overheard in violent monologue addressed to a fellow gunner and a callow-looking Scots Guardsman, ranting on about jobs abroad 'crying out for Englishmen, good jobs too—fifteen hundred a year—why anybody stops in this bloody country I don't know. And a government like this, bloody clever, but they don't look after their own people— six million a day they can find when the war comes—but they can't find a few thousands to send boys out to New Zealand. Now I'm telling you, New Zealand, that's a bloody fine country, fifteen hundred a year, etc., etc., etc.' Another, a regular Guardsman, seems bursting to talk about his experiences in Palestine, brings vividly before me the strain and nerviness of their work out there, the continual danger of land mines in the road by day and night, wrecked convoys, sudden ambushes and engagements, his best friend killed by his side. A crowded Friday night in a pub down by the river, a knot of soldiers arguing 'Don't tell me the Germans are down and out, that's all bloody rot, sheer propaganda, they're a fine lot, it'll be a long war '. . . . 'It's a machine-war '. . . . 'We shall all be broke anyway ' . . . . Voices rise and are gone like clouds on a windy Autumn day.

Day-dreams, forebodings, meditations and visions. . . . What is the prospect? A mad world after the war—or no

end to the war because the world has already gone mad?
Somehow or other, one must build a fortress for poetry, for
art. I must behave, think as if I'd died (and indeed I truly
feel like that sometimes). Signs begin to multiply that enormous slaughters may after all take place, by a sort of fatal
diseased compulsion, and the war spread East, down the
Danube, into Asia. Does anyone grasp that victory is as unlikely as defeat—victory in the old sense?

Reading a book about Diaghileff starts a long train of
thought. In spite of the war, if one could find the money,
one could work towards a great synthesis of writing talent, of
imagination and interpretation, creative and critical. One
could give hope and a field of activity to so many of the younger
writers who now seem lost, might discover new talents in danger
of being frozen out; bring the other arts into it, painting, sculp-
ture, music, dancing.

Lying in bed in the early morning, the stillness and the
stillness broken by the pouring song of blackbirds and soft
rou-couing of pigeons. The dangling water-quiet branches
of the plane-trees tufted with tiny pale explosions of green, the
primroses below. The pigeons go by into sunlight, Debussy
comes softly over the wireless. Debussy and Mozart the only
composers with the purity of art I need on this Spring morning,
while the war is holding its breath. Debussy's an art consisting
of hints only: as if he said—blue nights in June—alpine
meadows under snow—doves over a still sea—lips touching
and the sound of poplar leaves.

Now suffering, I thought as I watched my mother still in
distress in her hospital bed, is about to wash over us all like
a huge wave, and we must try to learn to live in it, a new
element.

Images of regret: goodbye to John Lepper, who joined up
one week-end without a word to me; John his usual unperturbed self, bringing out story after story over the bottle of
champagne; but a sense for me of guilt and frustration, of
not having done enough for him while he worked as my
secretary. Christopher Isherwood's room in London, as his
mother opens the door for me, with the windows closed, blinds
half down, and dust sheets over everything. A notebook filled

with the beginnings of poems, scribbled down in Austria, lines, half-finished stanzas; now impossible ever to complete.

Images of phantasmagoria: The centre of London on New Year's Eve. In some pubs there was little or no life, in others the Scots and the tarts between them were creating a pandemonium of sing-song; as one passed down the street outside, barbaric yells echoed from them; the dank streets, lightless in spite of the moon, chilly with thin, trailing fog. In the thickest darkness, in the thickest part of the crowds, at Piccadilly Circus where would-be revellers were grouped like swarming bees round the boxed lump that had taken the place of Eros, a group of Canadian soldiers suddenly began to shout at the tops of their voices, all faces indistinguishable. Later, as I walked home, two small sailor figures loomed up out of the blackness, and asked in obviously foreign accents where they were. I took them to the station, discovered they were Polish ratings on leave; a grin, a salute, and they were swallowed up again, leaving me with the strangeness of the war hanging in the air round me all of a sudden like a scent.

Images of pleasure; a visit with Cuthbert Worsley to the Westminster Theatre, to see Beatrix in *Desire Under the Elms*. A wonderful play, though dangerously near melodrama: because O'Neill's treatment of his terrific theme is far too brief and concentrated, a telegraphic treatment, for the emotional explosions he aims to set off. Beatrix gave one of her greatest performances: her unweakening intensity, her diamond-hard brilliance covered up the moments of melodrama, and made the love scenes an almost unbelievable discovery of joy and Spring.

This winter, ballet has started up again, tentatively, bravely; an iron-cold Winter night at the King's Theatre, Hammersmith, our fingers almost stick to the bars in the auditorium, the cold is so intense. The Three Arts Ballet: a new young Polish dancer from Paris, Alexis Rassine, showing in every movement the lyrical grace, the blood-sense of the dance that only the Slav peoples have. A world of pure art that still, incredibly, can exist in spite of the war.

Memories of parties run together: a last *New Writing* party, or was it more than one party? One when Rosamond helped to officiate, in my front room looking out over the Square.

John Banting in front of his mural, enlarging fantastically on
the themes and symbols in it to Robert Buhler and Julia
Strachey and Hester Chapman and a knot of young men in
battledress, and Guy Burgess making sardonic comments.
Poets: David Gascoyne pushing himself as if panic-stricken
into a corner, Nick Moore and Maurice Craig, owlish and pink-
cheeked, from Cambridge, Stephen and Rex Warner. William
Plomer and Joe Ackerley arriving like mischievous twins,
whispering malicious asides to me about their fellow-guests as
I passed with the bottles, closely followed by Roger Senhouse
and Tom Driberg, also George Orwell, full of friendliness and
stimulating talk. Short-story writers with their wives: John
Sommerfield, declaring obstinately that the events of the
Winter had not loosened the hold of communism on the fervent
core of comrades in the factories; Tom Hopkinson announcing
that *Picture Post* went roaring on, curiously unaffected by anything; Woodrow Wyatt, small, dark, talking excitedly, and
Dick (G. F.) Green pouring out compliments about *New
Writing* that became more incoherent as the bottles circulated,
then turning to Rosamond to make a grand declaration of
artistic homage which was beyond his powers of the moment,
for he slumped exhausted on the sofa. Goodbye, goodbye, a
dark bat in my bowels telling me it was goodbye for a long
time. Afterwards, a blur of restaurants and other people's
flats. John Irwin and an unknown boy in battledress trailing
around after me, while I held forth even more eloquently and
confusedly—or was it with the intuition that the morning after
can never recapture?—on poetry and life, poetry and war,
poetry the conqueror of all the demons that clustered in the
air around us.

And then voices, dreams, images were swept away, drowned
in a torrent that changed all our lives, that made them in a few
weeks as remote, as historic as they are today.

Let the Journal I kept at the time take over. . . .

5

Friday evening, May 10th, 1940

THE gathering storms of the Norway crisis dominated all minds,
I think, this week.   Everyone followed the debates in the House
as never before; and as they reached their climax, people held
their breath, scarcely believing it could be true that the outbreak of anger had come at last, that the Old Men of Munich
were slipping after years of obstinate, seemingly unshakable
grip on power. . . . And then, the next morning, the invasion
of the Low Countries.   The stationmaster at Bourne End told
me what had happened as I took my place in the 8.44: by the
time I was in London and more and more news began to come
through, I began to see what it meant, how enormous the
danger was, how many plans must go by the board.   By mid-
day most people, I think, had a slightly sick feeling in the pit of
their stomachs, with sudden visions reviving—after so many
quiet months—of air-raids and even parachute invasion.
Cuthbert and I discussed it anxiously at lunch; then began to
laugh about it and find absurd ideas; by evening with the
knowledge that the defence was working, there was a different
feeling growing up, a feeling that, well, after all, it was a good
thing if we could settle the beastly business this Summer once
and for all.

Tuesday, 14th

The strain of waiting on events becomes even greater, as the
news comes through of the gigantic thrust the Germans are
making. . . . It seemed impossible that the Spring day in
London could be so fresh and quiet and lovely, with death so
mercilessly at work only two or three hundred miles away. . . .
When one reads of the numbers of tanks and bombers employed
the world seems utterly and finally mad. . . . Only here, in
Southern England, one can refuse to believe it for just a little
longer.

New appointments to the Cabinet come through every few hours.   One can make all sorts of criticisms, but the decisive fact seems to be, without question, that a breach has at last been made in the concrete defences of the Old Gang.   As the war intensifies, especially if danger becomes greater, can they ever recover the ground they've lost?   Then at least it must prove to be the thin end of the wedge—of the power of the people.

Saturday, 18th

Still these glowing Spring days, these pure moonlit nights; and still this horrible, gigantic battle on the other side of the Channel, with news that presses on one's brain like the beginning of madness.   Leonard, coming up for the day to discuss urgent Hogarth business, tells me at lunch that hospital as well as refugee trains go through all day from the ports in the south.   He insists that the news is worse than the papers say, but sticks to his belief that we must win in the end: he agrees that we have only to hold the thing now, and in a few months all the production and power of the Americans will be at our side. . . . But right now, there are moments when it seems like a matter of days, not months.

A letter has arrived from my young boatman in Valcov, at the mouth of the Danube: strange intimation of a lost life:

> My dear Johnny, Your letter that I have received has produced me a great pleasure and I thank you very much for it.   I see that you have don't forgotten me and this thing is dearer than all for me.   Always I remember you and somebody with my friends I drink a glass of wine in your honour.   I should send you some things from Valcov, but I am not sure they should go up to London.   Give the God the peace, when you will come at us to enjoy and amuse us both.   With much love to you, yours truly, Volodya.

After which, feeling no doubt a little uncertain of his English, he added a translation in Russian.

Friday, 24th

The Germans have taken Boulogne, and England has adopted her own peculiar brand of totalitarianism: these two salient features of the last twenty-four hours, more or less incredible if suggested a year ago, are today simply in the accepted stream of events, and there is not even a trace of hysteria, now that the shock of last week-end has passed. And what a shock it was, with only too many people considering how best they should take their lives if the imminent became the real. . . . Only submerge slowly enough, and you will hardly feel the change from breathing fresh air to the beginnings of drowning. . . . Standing on Maidenhead platform a few days ago, I saw an enormous train of scrap-iron and raw materials roar through westwards, and it seemed a symbol of the new set of men in the control room, men who are at last going to put up a fight, and with the weapons of 1940, not 1914.

Leonard lost his usual and wonderful poise on Wednesday morning after Reynaud's speech. The evening before, when I sat with them late into the night, Virginia and Tom Eliot and William Plomer, we had agreed to avoid the subject, but he had been unnaturally silent; and when we talked the next morning, he seemed overcome.

I feel I can still have time, even if not in London, to devote June to my new book, and perhaps even get down in writing some of the things I still so passionately want to say about Vienna; but after that will have seriously to think whether I shouldn't try all over again to volunteer.

Roger Senhouse and I had lunch together, and after W. had gone and the arid discussion ended, we quickly found we were both feeling the same thing: overcome by the human element of the catastrophe, the suffering of soldiers and many young men we knew, we could hardly make the intellectual discussions —' does this mean a dialectical step to this, or that? '—of any importance to ourselves. . . . Echoes from a fading world.

I have been reading Wystan's *Another Time* which has just arrived for me from America; and find among many wonderful treasures (a large number of which appeared originally in *New Writing*) a terrible proportion of sententious, almost prosy stuff. And yet how superb some of the newest poems are.

Saturday, 25th

A letter has arrived from Christopher in Santa Monica, in which he says:

The news from Europe makes one feel unspeakably wretched—especially as many people here regard it as an exciting football game, in which they would rather like to play. It is strange to live amongst these psychically virgin Californians, with their sound teeth and intact nerves. Partly it is very stimulating; partly it makes you feel lonely. Sometimes I think that I must return to Europe, anyhow, at any price. But I'm afraid I should feel myself just as much of an outcast there. There are few people I could honestly agree with, about this war. You would understand, I think. . . . Believing what I do, there's simply no place for me in existing society—even in the opposition. And, not being a prophet, like Wystan, I can't raise my voice in the wilderness. The way things look now, I shall most likely end up in prison—or, if I'm lucky, the Red Cross. But enough of all this.

Berthold has gone to New York, as you doubtless know, to produce a play by Terence Rattigan—' Grey Farm ', or some such name. His departure was a scene of unspeakable excitement and confusion—after all these months of cloistered work and study—like a professor who is suddenly called upon to become Chancellor: a truly Austrian situation. . . . I am alone with the ocean, Gerald Heard and the Metro Lion. The weather is terrific—94 in the shade—and all the beaches crowded. Money swirls around me like Autumn leaves. I pick some of it up and throw it away again—there is really nothing to spend it on; except the books which remind me of England. I have quite a library. All the poets. I long to read Stephen's novel, and hope you'll send it in due course. . . . I saw Zorina the other day. She was wonderfully beautiful. Her face was pale violet. Rooney now looks like Hercules. He is so small you could get him into a large suitcase easily. This studio has just finished ' The Mortal Storm '—which will probably be good, but terribly funny, because the nice Germans are played by Americans, and the nasty ones by German refugees. I am just about to start a picture about Chopin, who is to be whitewashed for Robert Donat. Actually, I think he was the most unpleasant of all geniuses. Georges Sand was much too good for him. . . . First line of our picture: ' Hullo.' Last line: ' Let's hope and pray he is.' You can guess the rest.

Today I'm on the last lap of *Seven Pillars of Wisdom*. All along, I have been finding it difficult to read (a difficulty increased by the page), but the moment Lawrence stops describing minutiae of movement or landscape, my interest quickens; and for all the strain of his style (the very opposite of what I should like to achieve myself), superb in his account of his own self-questioning, of the highlights of action (the first triumphant bridge demolitions, for instance), and of scenes of glittering colour such as gatherings of chiefs in the desert, of the passage through the Valley of Rumm.

Sunday, 26th

An extraordinary situation for this country, in which one and the same Government can be sending a Conservative appeaser, Sam Hoare, as special envoy to Spain, at the same time as a left-wing Labour rebel, Stafford Cripps, to Moscow. Is this a passing, surface phenomenon, or a sign of a deep, geological change?

Thursday, 30th

In every street in Bloomsbury one meets men and boys, whose slightly out-of-the-ordinary clothes and looks show them to be Belgian or Dutch refugees. One hears from people back from the South coast that they're pouring across the whole time in fishing smacks, row-boats—any kind of boat.

Every day the battle leaps nearer. Lying awake at night, I'm surprised I can't hear the guns and bombs: for it's as if one of the greatest battles in history were going on as near as Yorkshire. And yet I believe that to most English people the Channel is a magic barrier that makes everything beyond it almost infinitely distant.

How can one's life ever be the same, whatever the outcome of the war, after this slaughter that has been going on for more than a month, a slaughter that's beginning to engulf so many of one's friends? Perhaps it's a good thing that I can only faintly imagine what the trapped men of the British Army are going through; imagination is not a thing to have these days if one means to survive and be sane.

The attack on England must come, and soon, and it will be one of the biggest events in history. I suddenly realize this as a fact, and am no longer shocked.

June 2nd

And I wake this morning, and am still alive and thirty-three years old, and still in the lush summer peace of the house where I was born. And I think of Toni, and wonder all day where he can be, on this our common birthday, for I am certain that if he's alive he's thinking of me. Is he in Norway? Is he in the advance columns of motor-bicyclists sent into Flanders? Or is he somewhere in Austria, stationed as anti-aircraft gunner, still out of danger, but for how long?

A.L., sitting out in the garden for the first time, smiling and fresh and wonderfully recovered, tells me how often she has thought of him and his family.

I motored over to Ipsden for tea, and found that the emotion of the epic withdrawal from Dunkirk, now reaching its last and most terrible stages, had almost overcome Rosamond. She had come back from Cambridge in a dark state of confused anxiety and depression; but as usual, as we talked, her spirits and gaiety were on the up-curve. She said that her train had passed train-loads of the returning B.E.F., almost every man of them sunk in a stupor of sleep.

Willy Goldman came to see me the other afternoon. As we parted, at the corner of the Square, he remarked how quickly a protective mechanism was developing itself in people's minds. When I said I thought imagination was a bad thing to have these days, he replied: ' Fatal, in fact,'—smiling his sardonic half-smile.

Johnny Banting arranged to meet me at the French Pub. He sailed in rather piano, but one pernod transformed him, he became exuberant and arch, pouring out fantastic stories, and finally having a long debate with himself aloud up and down Soho about whether he should take an obvious ' smart ' like myself to his ' secret ' negro dive. Caution was finally and dramatically conquered, and he led me down into a dark billiard hall, where a superb chicken pilaff was served to us and a melancholy young negro from the Gold Coast came up and discussed the war quietly and intelligently, and how conscription would affect him. I showed myself suitably impressed by the signed portraits of darkie celebrities on the walls.

Another letter from Christopher (dated May 13th), with a strange shaft of memory in it, an image I had forgotten: 'Today the news gets grimmer and grimmer, and a correspondent speaks over the radio from Amsterdam, and I remember how we discussed the first plans for *New Writing* walking around the sports-field, and stopping by the wire fence to watch the boxing. . . .' He adds that he believes the Americans will soon be taking more steps to help us—the President known to be in favour, and certain to run for a third term and be re-elected.

Tuesday, June 11th

One has tried to prepare oneself during the last few days for severe reverses, even up to the capture of Paris; so Italy's entry into the war did not come as the shock it might have been. And the voice of Roosevelt over the wireless last night, a voice made symbolic by the roaring of the atmospherics, calling out the New World to our aid, was one of the most dramatic and hope-inspiring things I have ever heard.

I have forced myself to get ahead with my book this week. Each day I found it hard to get into it, but the work formed a sort of protective case around me once I was absorbed.

The soldiers from Dunkirk seem to be stirring up a violence of opinion in the country against the Old Men of Munich, that must burst soon: a more effective army of revolutionary agitators, penetrating to the furthest villages, could not be imagined —could not have been organized by the cleverest political party.

Last Friday night: London streets may be quiet nowadays, even in the growing light, but I have never seen such a scene of vigour and high spirits as in the pubs round Victoria way. Pay night, but even so: soldiers and sailors and civilians packed tight, a roar of conversation, animated groups and grins, some singing; and amongst all of them, soldiers deeply sun-tanned back from France, Guardsmen still on London duties, sailors from the Low Countries, girls of every age and description, not a trace of despondency.

Saturday, 15th

A letter from John Lepper, now deep in his training up in Nottinghamshire: 'We have left our camp, and for the past few weeks have been bivouacing " somewhere in Lincoln-shire ", sleeping in haystacks, barns and open fields. The whole regiment has to be ready at fifteen minutes notice to rush off and deal with any paratroops who may decide to pay us a visit. Among our many duties is the task of providing a patrol to scour the countryside at night looking for lights flashed by Fifth Columnists. This is facetiously known as " The Glowworm Patrol ".' He ends up ' Is it possible to obtain a second-hand copy of Garcia Lorca's poems (the recent translation) ? '

As the Nazis go on pouring through France—and nothing seems to be able to stop them for long—the constriction of one's heart grows tighter and tighter. It is still possible to believe that not merely this island but also France will survive; but sometimes it's as if one couldn't breathe.

In Brighton to see Beatrix's play again. Her performance more polished even than before, deeply, terribly moving. Lifting the curtain in the morning, the hazy, unbroken expanse of the sea revealed, faintly blue in the rising sun: how impossible to think there's a war on. . . . That across that smiling water, only a few miles away, the Nazi Empire is already established, and Paris opening her gates to the marching columns. . . . Something utterly incredible a year ago.

Saturday, 29th

The end of an extraordinary week of despair and recovery; now, in incredibly few days, people's mood has changed again. In spite of the fact that it becomes clearer and clearer that what has happened in France is a Putsch by the Right (though obviously the Army was beaten), now that all our troops are home, people's spirits rise: if we die, we shall die in our own fields and near our families and friends, and we need only consider ourselves. All our English obstinacy and xenophobia comes into its own. One gnawing question nevertheless: are there Petains here too, among our own Government ranks?

Sunday, 30th

I saw Marina Pauliny and Fedor Hodža again: Fedor had escaped from Paris and Bordeaux, and returned in a Dutch cargo boat, very bitter and disillusioned. I said: but you have no need to worry, your friends the Russians are at your gates, and will always get there first. And they both agreed that from their point of view there might be something in it. Fedor said he thought Russia was going to get Warsaw in the end. He also said he'd been with General Prchala at Czech H.Q., and all the time he'd pointed out how hopeless the position was after the breakthrough.

I begin to see the war in a new light: as an European experience, quite independently of sides and winners, with my Austrian friends for instance in it just as I am in it. And this is in some curious way comforting and strengthening.

One of the most poignant things I have experienced, that brought the war home to me more than anything else, was hearing the French wounded in this country send their messages across the wireless to those at home.

Saturday

Dined with Tom Wintringham last night at the Madrid, together with his wife, Montagu Slater and two Comm. friends who came in. A fierce argument develops about whether the L.D.V.s are an embryo fascist force, and about revolutionary tactics at the moment. One friend attacks Tom for ' co-operating ' (he seemed to be whirling around in an entirely airtight compartment like all ' party members ' now), and Tom coolly but vigorously defends himself.

London is an extraordinary place in this pause between battles. On the streets and in the pubs you see Canadian, Australian, New Zealand soldiers; French sailors, air-officers, legionnaires; Dutch officers, Norwegian and Dutch sailors; Poles and Czechs. . . . It quickens one's interest and excitement in the moment: it seems almost impossible to contemplate that one should fail them all.

Leonard, up in London for a few days and obviously in a more optimistic mood, produced a wonderful story of Virginia insisting in a stage-whisper that an innocent and embarrassed nun who got into their carriage was a German spy.

Mlle. X comes to see me, with the story of how she joined de Gaulle. It's difficult to get a picture through it all of what's really going on there, but she assures me that at present the movement is ' purely military ', politics are frowned on, that more and more influential people are rallying to the General, and also that an important French colony has definitely declared its support. She lets slip that de G. used to be associated with the Action Française, though he left it in disgust.

If obscurity reigns there, it is even thicker around the Czech National Committee. I asked Fedor Hodža out to lunch at the Café Royal—I find him more sympathetic each time I meet him—and managed to persuade him to give me some picture of what is going on. It is a gloomy picture, and he is profoundly *déçu*. He asserts (I am still uncertain what part he and his father are really playing) that Beneš and those around him still refuse to make the Committee properly representative, and that the Slovaks are still very badly treated. He accuses Beneš of *idées fixes* and vanity, and fears that the Committee cannot command much respect in the Protectorate itself until it is radically reorganized. He's lenient towards Hacha; and maintains that stories I've heard about Czech officers not commanding the confidence of their men are in many cases true. Finally, he promises me some literary stuff from Czech authors already over here or very soon to arrive.

Reading Palme Dutt's analysis of the war situation in the *Labour Monthly* the other day, I was struck by three things. First, he definitely believes that British capitalism means to smash its rival as the French never did. Second, that his line that the war is a supreme struggle of British, German and American capitalism has importance—it's an element anyway, an element too much obscured in the ordinary analysis. But, third, that there's no sign of him even remotely recognizing that there can be any difference between British and German imperialism, that it matters in the least whether Churchill or Hitler runs us.

Later that same day, I wrote a long letter to G. in reply to his, saying that I too felt inclined to weep when I observed (1) the Dean of Canterbury school of thought still believing that the U.S.S.R. was something like a super-charity organization, (2) the bright intellectuals of the weeklies maintaining that the U.S.S.R. and Nazi Germany are one and the same because they've signed a pact, (3) the hundred-per-cent-party-liners believing (or pretending to believe) that they can identify the varying needs of the U.S.S.R.'s foreign policy with a revolutionary programme for this country.

To be ' indestructible ': that is still my search, and I believe I see the end clearer now. Walking down the Embankment today, it occurred to me that Toni's stepfather Stangl was the most completely indestructible person I've ever been in contact with: because he had absolutely no worldly baggage, didn't care what happened to him, and yet had a pretty clear idea of what was what. And I thought of the passage I have been reading in bed of Henry Miller (who strikes me as a mixture of a really powerful writer and something a good deal less) aiming at the same thing: the character who suddenly accepted death, and became at once immensely alive.

July 23rd

Yesterday Fedor brought a young Czech writer, by the name of Mucha, in for a drink. He is now in the Czech forces here: he gave a fascinating account of Paris life just before the end. I asked him about the French writers, and he said: One didn't realize how decadent (!) France really was, a great writer was apt to be respected as a great artist whatever his political past. . . . Malraux was said to be in the south and unmolested. Gide and Mauriac were together at Mauriac's chateau in the south, getting on one another's nerves. Romain Rolland was dying, too ill to care. Giono had formed a party ' de la paix honteuse ' at the last moment. Jules Romains had slipped away to Lisbon with all the PEN Club records. He knew nothing of Chamson, and I fear he may only too easily have been submerged, either at the Front or in the Daladier debacle.

Later in the evening I fell in with some French sailors, both merchant marine and navy. How bitterly they talked of the way their officers had sold them, how lost they seemed, in spite of their determination to ' vaincre ou mourir ', not knowing what had happened, what would happen to their wives and sweethearts, not certain that the English would play fair with them. One boy from Bordeaux, half Spanish, was almost in tears as he described how he'd never heard from his girl whom he'd left in May seven months gone with a baby from him. At one moment he was saying that the English were far more kindly than the French, far less each one out for himself, and the next he was suspecting that the English themselves were torpedoing the shiploads of returning sailors . . . and absolutely certain he could never endure to go back.

Friday, 26th

Yesterday Desmond MacCarthy came to tea. Beatrix was there, with Ahmed Ali and Willy Goldman. Desmond in great form, discussing Shaw. He said he had become very disappointed with him in recent years, especially his irresponsible admiration for ' power in action '—now he sees it was always latent in him, and understands why the Germans are so fond of him. And yet such generous and likeable traits in him. He told a story of how Shaw once advised him to buy some Irish tweed and have it made up at his own (Shaw's) little tailor. D. did this, and of course didn't pay the bill. Some months later he received a letter from Shaw, saying he hoped very much he wouldn't mind but he'd paid the bill himself, as he didn't think the little tailor could afford to wait. D. choked with amusement at his own behaviour, adding that poor old Shaw had had to wait two years to get his money back.

I want to understand the anatomy of this war, to penetrate right to the heart of it where one can see the deeper shape and direction. My feeling that I must keep away from all public activity (apart from whatever service I have to do) is not merely because I see that such activity now attracts too many self-advertisers, double-dealers and frenzied innocents, but also comes from my conviction that the war's far more complex than it seems and we have far less data than ever to go on. I want intensely to understand it, but it's the thing behind that is supremely interesting—the taking form of what's to come.

The supreme lesson of the past seven years, if one has been in the thick of it in one way or another, is that the most difficult, and at the same time the most important thing for a writer or artist is to maintain integrity as an artist and to make no concessions where truth is at stake.

F

A letter from Virginia about her ' Leaning Tower ' lecture, in which she says:

> I handed on your message to Leonard, and we are both very sorry you couldn't come to Monk's House, and that your mother's ill again: please give her my sympathy. We could have offered you a great variety of air-raid alarms, distant bombs, reports by Mrs Bleach who brought a stirrup pump (installed, needless to say, in my bedroom), of battles out at sea. Indeed its rather lovely about 2 in the morning to see the lights stalking the Germans over the marshes. But this remains on tap, so you must propose yourself later. And let me know if you want to meet the Major and hear about—what was it?—why the crab walks sideways?
>
> Leonard's tackling Mrs. N. downstairs—showers of confidences and complaints, also children's letters make the room almost uninhabitable, he says; and he's teaching Miss Griffiths how to mark off. I'm quite pleased with the sales of Roger Fry so far— L. is binding more. Don't bother to read it now, but some day I should value your opinion very much. . . . I'd like you to print the Leaning Tower, if I can bring myself to revise it, which I loathe. Also, when would you want it—also, what about America? I mean can I print simultaneously there? But at the moment I can't stop reading Coleridge—thanks to you, I'm lured back to the ancients, and read a William Morris, Chants for Socialists, with immense pleasure. So I can't bring myself to do anything I ought to do. Forgive this long letter.

Friday, August 9th

Yesterday I finished my Pelican,* and sent it off to Lane. I find myself hardly able to believe it's been possible to get it done, with invasion and the Rumanian (or Russian?) job still vaguely lurking in the background. And now, I have to admit, the war is sometimes narrowed down for me to the question: will it be published in time? Which is vile, I fear, but natural, I hope.

Monday, August 12th

' I couldn't stop laughing,' said the grinning young Cold-streamer, recounting his experiences at Dunkirk in broad

* *New Writing in Europe* (see p. 100).

Yorkshire. ' I didn't like seeing the lads popped off, under-neath it all I was sorry, of course, but I couldn't stop laughing. I was scared of being killed all right, scared stiff I was, but what the f—— hell, I thought. And when I saw all the lads who'd talked so big pushing me aside on the beach in their hurry to get into the boats, I just couldn't stop laughing.' Some day I must try and get down on paper his whole story of how he and thirty others held a barrier on the road, let what seemed to be a refugee car through and were machine-gunned by the occu-pants immediately afterwards, twenty-seven of them being killed. And how he tried to take some loot—wine-glasses—back for his sister's sideboard, and how it was all blown to pieces . . . and how he couldn't stop laughing through all this. And how the guns of the destroyer made the whole ship quiver and shake, and how that made him laugh too.

A letter from John Sommerfield, now in the R.A.F., in remotest Cumberland, in which he says:

> The scenery is very beautiful, but at least ten miles away, and obscured by aviation. Life is a combination of public school and concentration camp—this isn't meant as a crack, it is an exact description. . . . It really does seem odd from here to be con-cerning myself with the literature trade—there are no books, no radio, and about one newspaper to fifty men, usually read in the urinal—which when freshly dug has a six-foot drop. I have ideas for writing, but little time and less opportunity to carry them out in. What is happening about *New Writing*? I do hope that you will manage to carry it on. Let me know will you, and it will be nice to hear from you anyway. The planes themselves are very lovely, and incredibly civilized, but nothing else in this life is.

September 3rd, 1940

A year has passed since the beginning of the war: it seems quite extraordinary that I should be sitting out in the garden at Fieldhead, reading my books and fairly at ease. Did one ever imagine one would come to accept so much so quickly? The nightly, daily danger of death from the skies? The defeat and subjugation of beloved France? The whole of Europe ranged against us? And no word, no sign for twelve months from all my friends in Vienna? And the narrowing of the shutter of one's response into accepting the hourly toll of victims and destruction on both sides as the key of one's life? London bombed—Berlin bombed—picking up any day's paper, if one could have had it shown to one two years ago, wouldn't one have thought: No, this can never be, this is too mad? Yet it *is*, and one has been in it, and one goes on—if one is one of the lucky and older like myself—with one's own pursuits—I even go on with *New Writing*.

But the bombing of London hasn't been nice, I won't pretend that, nor will what is still to come be nice. Only one finds one adapts oneself so much more easily than one thought possible. And some instinctive mechanism in oneself prevents one thinking too much of the worst: prevents me remembering Vienna too often—prevents me realizing too logically that I also can be wiped out any day, with so much unfinished and unattempted—prevents me following too far in imagination the lines of destiny of all my many friends in uniform.

I have been thinking much of them recently, and seeing quite a lot of them too, as well as having a number of letters. Young writers in the Air Force—Gully writing of the unapproachable heroic world of the pilots; John Sommerfield of the fantastic no-culture of the remote stations. And bookseller Roy coming back from France longing for more Auden and *New Writing*, but bursting above all to tell me of his first French girl-friend; John L. uncertain of himself in the civvy world, more firmly convinced than ever of ' England's destiny ', tough yet rather pathetically lost in a way, breaking down when he finds his girl has left him; Jackie subtly changed, growing rapidly into something stronger inside as well as outside; they are all going through a transformation, deeper even than those who control the machine know.

That night at X's when T. and the two boys came in, giggling and blowing kisses and chirruping away, discussing who they'd met at the Café Royal, what C.'s or B.'s latest *bon mot* was, where the new night-club was and who'd be dancing there: I have to admit I was shocked at such a world still existing, and I don't think it was my latent puritanism coming out by a back door as I wouldn't have cared two hoots in peacetime; but this world existing now, so utterly out of touch with what's happening in the world all round us, so horribly unaesthetic to set beside the world of the Irish and Scottish soldiers I knew who vanished in Narvik and Dunkirk—and John and Jackie and Gully and Roy.

Another very odd transformation of war: the young Czech novelist Mucha, sitting in my flat in a private's uniform of the free Czech Army, discussing something to write for N.W.; and Fedor at Fieldhead, planning the new Slovakia from this country. How much water has flowed under the bridges since we first met in Bratislava, and yet how natural it already seemed that he should be here and preparing for Den Tag—*Our Day.*

One incident of these air-raid nights sticks in my mind. Alexis had arranged to look in some time during the evening, was delayed by friends and caught by the sirens. Hours passed and still he didn't come; and night came down and the searchlights swept the sky and raiders zoomed like angry bluebottles overhead. . . . Then it was quiet again, and suddenly down the road in the utter darkness and silence I heard a well-known step and the clicking fingers like castanets for a Spanish dance—and a minute later he arrived in the highest spirits, bursting with news, not of the raid or anything to do with it, but of the Polish Ballet being started.

Saturday, 7th

Motored down yesterday from Fieldhead to Lake with Helen in her car, after a night of air-raid alarms in London and seeing the film of Marie Walewska. The country round Salisbury seemed enormously peaceful and gentle after London and Bourne End so near London, in spite of huge aerodromes among the hills and circling aircraft. . . . The desire to have a small cottage somewhere in the hills possessed me again, though I know it's really impracticable until after the war—or at any rate until my part in it has been settled somehow.

As I was in the front office of The Hogarth Press signing some letters, Stephen burst in with his proofs. I turned round, and saw to my astonishment that he was just about to rush out with a look of rage on his flushed features. He turned when I called

—and grinned at once.   Afterwards he explained that Cyril
had just refused a story written by a protégé of his, and when he
saw my back turned his immediate reaction had been: ' Just
another of these—Etonians! '

Sunday, September 8th, 1940

Last night (in Wiltshire) Helen was at the canteen and
Mounty and I were talking hard together after dinner, when
the telephone rang and a military priority call came through—
but it turned out to be for the real (and absent) owner of the
house.   Both of us thought the same thing, but we said nothing;
then only a few minutes later the call from the A-Striking Force
came through for Mounty.   He rushed up to put on his battledress and pack, and I rushed round picking up field-glasses,
cigarettes and anything else I could think of for him.   In the
middle of it a confirming call came through, and then Helen
returned from the canteen.   We rushed Mounty into the car,
splashed some petrol wastefully into the tank by the light of a
torch, wished him good luck—and off he went.   Directly after,
a third confirming call came through.   The night was deadly
still, no sound of aircraft.   It seemed impossible to doubt that
something big had begun.   When we heard at midnight that
gigantic raids were taking place on London, we felt absolutely
certain.   Yet no church bells had been rung, and the stillness
was unbroken.   It was an odd feeling, really something impossible to credit, that the enemy was at last at hand, here and
now, yet the feeling was more of dramatic excitement than of
alarm, or confusion, or even anger.

Later, we heard that church bells *had* been rung in some
places in England. . . .   But Mounty came back for luncheon,
and said the whole thing appeared to have been just a flap.

Wednesday, 11th

I am writing this at Fieldhead, after three of the most extraordinary days of my life.   Yesterday I was ordered to evacuate
my flat, and came down to Bourne End after looking Beatrix
up at her new flat (Julia Strachey's) in Charlotte Street, to
make certain she was leaving for the country.   She told me the

strangest of stories, how she had wandered through London in the early morning, trying to find out what had become of me.

Mecklenburgh Square was a pretty sight when I left it. Broken glass everywhere, half the garden scorched with incendiary bombs, and two houses of Byron Court on the east side nothing but a pile of rubble. Clouds of steam were pouring out of one side, firemen still clambering over it and ambulances and blood-transfusion units standing by with A.R.P. workers and police. The road was filled with a mess of rubble muddied by the firemen's hoses, but the light-grey powder that had covered the bushes at dawn had been washed off by the drizzle. The time bomb in the Square garden sat in its earth crater, coyly waiting. The tabby persian cat from No. 40 picked her way daintily and dishevelledly among the splinters of glass on her favourite porch.

The night of Sunday was my first intimate contact with war. What surprised me was not to have been frightened, but to have been frightened so little; also that the actual noise of the bombs exploding was not nearly so bad as I'd expected. At the same time I felt rather ashamed not to be among the A.R.P. workers and firemen: they were really magnificent. . . . I left Salisbury in the afternoon. About 5.30 p.m. the train ran plumb into an air-raid. Blinds down, we went slowly on, then stopped: overhead a battle was going on, with sudden zooms and the rattle of machine-gun fire distinctly audible. People rushed to the windows in spite of all warnings, shouted that they could see the battling machines—but against the dazzling blue I certainly couldn't. Then the all-clear went, and the girl next to me sighed with relief and giggled. We went slowly on, then stopped at a signal outside Clapham Junction. Time dragged on, still we waited there, light began to fade. Passengers began to think of their lost appointments—the soldier of his date in a pub at Gravesend—the little fuzzy man of his work at 9 p.m.—but also of darkness and raids and being caught there. The fuzzy man's fat wife began to show signs of hysteria, the girl of pathetic agitation. Then soldiers began to jump off the train and slip through people's backyards into the road for buses: the old, very irate guard tried to stop them—nothing like it had been known in his fifty

years' service with the company—but they went on, and
civilians with their luggage began to follow them. At eight
o'clock the signal light was still at red against us, though electric trains for London Bridge were still roaring by. I decided
to make a dash for London. Luckily a 77 bus stopped only a
few yards away, and I packed into it with a young R.N.V.R.
officer. Only a few minutes later the inevitable sirens went
again—but the bus sped on through the moonlit streets. Over
the Thames and up into Kingsway it raced, and still there was
no gunfire to be heard: I had an eerie, tense feeling after the
weekend reports, eerier still when I jumped off the bus to get
to my flat and saw the glow of fires in Holborn. But I got
home, and dined off half a bottle of wine and an apple and some
chocolate biscuits in my shuttered bedroom. Then I lay down,
fully dressed, on my bed, and began to read *Père Goriot*.

I didn't get far. Gunfire began to rumble in the distance,
and now it seemed to get nearer, with the persistent, maddening
sound of aircraft overhead. Then I could distinguish bombs
dropping. Then suddenly three whistling, ripping noises in
the air, as if directly overhead, getting closer, and each time
violent concussions followed by the sound of tinkling glass. . . .
When the noise of the aeroplanes seemed to be getting fainter
again, I went to the window and looked out on the Square:
I found—underneath the black curtains—that some of my
panes had been smashed, incendiary bombs were burning
merrily in the garden, and an enormous blaze was developing
beyond the Balloon station in the Foundling grounds. My
first feeling was: how curious and almost incredible it was that
this should have happened so near me. There was no searchlight: when I went downstairs the man from No. 46, who was
just getting out of his car, said he thought the searchlight had
had it. Then I went to shout to my landlord in the basement
shelter, but he only answered sleepily and I left him. I hung
about the ground floor for some time, a little dazed, went to the
door again and heard the shouts of the A.F.S. men as they
tackled the blaze beyond the Balloon site: suddenly it struck
me that it looked alarmingly close to Stephen's flat over on the
other side. 'Well, poor old Stephen's the first to go '—was
the odd, sad, resigned thought that went through my mind. A

little later, as I was standing by the stairs, there was another tremendous explosion, the house seemed to clench itself like a fist for a moment, then silence. It struck me as strange that I had heard no whizz of a descending bomb, and I went to the door again and peered out: the sight that met my eye was an enormous bellying cloud of grey dust advancing down the road towards me like a living thing, and a man in pyjamas curiously walking across it to his flat. There was dead silence; but it struck me that it might be as well now to go to a shelter. Hardly had I got myself ready when I heard a crowd of people moving out of the garden: I opened the door, and met the man from No. 46 again, now in a tin helmet, who said there was an unexploded time-bomb in the garden and they were evacuating the shelter there, also that the houses on our side had rocked badly—he advised me to go. When I turned round I thought part of Byron Court looked rather odd: it was only a few seconds later that I realized I was looking at a tree beyond —Byron Court had simply been blown to bits.

As I passed it on the way to the shelter, the presence of death and murder seemed very vivid to me, to fill the atmosphere, as a thing now at last *perceived* in this war behind ' the furious words ' and all the stories I'd heard. The Guildford Street fire was still very violent, but seemed to be more under control, there was a red haze away in the direction of the City—but our searchlight sword was striking across the sky again.

And in the shelter: the hours passed by and one longed for the dawn, knowing the Nazis would retreat from it and our ascending daylight fighters. I sat on a step, scarcely under shelter, and talked to an A.T.S. girl in uniform, on and on. Girls lay sleeping clasped by their young husbands, women and children were down below, someone produced a Dostoevsky novel, a group of young women huddled in an angle of the stairs with what looked like powdered hair—but they had just been rescued from the ruins of Byron Court and it was rubble dust. Then more bombs whistled by—and the banging of the lavatory door sounded like bombs too—incendiaries were dropped outside—a warden came in and whispered to us that a flare had been dropped. . . . At last, in the grey light of morning, the all-clear went.

When the evacuation order came, the first place I went to was the Athenaeum, asked for a bath and then breakfast. Soon it was round the Club that I had been bombed out, and so many waiters and other Club servants came to condole with me that I was surprised and moved. Air Marshal Joubert passed by on his way to breakfast, looking very preoccupied. I telephoned to a great many friends, sent off some letters and telegrams dealing as best I could with the problems of The Hogarth Press, then went down to A.'s flat in Bayswater as he had suggested. To my relief, I found it was a basement flat, with a steel girder running through the ceiling. He said he could not leave, as he was rehearsing: the job as usual came first with him.

Paddington in the evening was packed tight with families evacuating once more from the East End, a pitiful sight, but in spite of an air-raid warning that came on for a short while, order astonishingly prevailed and the trains were moving off on time.

How long is this to go on? When the end comes, it will seem something incredibly blessed.

Sunday, September 15th, at Fieldhead

It is nearly three o'clock, and an air-raid warning has just gone. Each time it goes now, one can't help wondering whether it's the prelude to the so long threatened, so long delayed invasion. The A.R.P. workers and their ambulances are gathering below, and the sky is overcast with rainy clouds. When the warning went, I began to think of my friends, waiting at their posts scattered over England. There's a feeling that if it were to come now probably the whole war would be decided one way or the other, and that's a good thing; and also a feeling that vies with it, that if only this Winter the war would shift to the East, one would be ready for anything next Spring.

But this is the epoch of surprises, of bombs that crash not merely through ancient buildings, but carefully built-up systems of thought and belief.

And now the all-clear has gone again.

Just after lunch I finished *The Good Soldier Schweik* at last. I don't think I've ever read a book so fast, or with such continuous enjoyment. Not merely because it made me laugh the whole way through, but also because it steeped me again in the Austrian atmosphere; and perhaps even more because Schweik seems somehow the final answer to war—to the State and Authority and all the other horrors that batten on human life.

On Thursday I went back to London to try and get back to my flat, but in vain: it was still cordoned off. I met Willy, who told me that what the East End had been through was indescribable: he had been down himself and seen the ruins of Stepney and Commercial Road, and knew several people who had been killed; there was scarcely a Jewish family that hadn't lost someone. Then I suddenly met Stephen with Peter Watson and Cyril C., who came up later; it was a relief, after my fears, to see Stephen as well and as wild-looking as ever. They told us nothing had been spoilt in the flat except one pane of glass—a miracle considering how close the bomb and the fire had been. Both Stephen and Willy said the terrific new A.A. barrage the night before had put astonishing heart into people. Cuthbert, who came later to have coffee with me at the Athenaeum, said that its din was greater than anything he'd heard before, but so comforting that he fell asleep. Lunch with S., and a friend of his, at the practically deserted Café Royal—bombs had fallen in Regent Street and it was cordoned off just above. Like all the rest of us, he seemed a little piano, a little bit at a loss. I think we were all wondering how much of London would soon be left standing.

Up on Friday again: a far worse day, which showed that low clouds—we were all longing for the weather to change—gave the raiders a devilish chance to dodge and make a nuisance of themselves. The first air-raid warning started while the train was waiting outside Paddington, and it didn't finish till after lunch. All that time, intermittently, you could hear aeroplanes overhead, occasional crashes of bombs or bursts of A.A. fire, and suddenly catch a glimpse of a bomber as the clouds parted, sailing cool and high overhead. In spite of all official threats, people just stayed in the Underground stations, piled up with their newspapers against the walls: the dislocation of ordinary life seemed complete. In the middle of it I met L.S.W. and Virginia wandering along Guildford Street

in their car after a fantastic journey from Rodmell. Leonard
rather agitated with the confusion of everything, also in a mood
of rather unhelpful bravado that slightly annoyed me when we
were discussing plans for starting up the wheels of The Hogarth
Press again. Virginia very smiling and apparently collected,
the only gesture she allowed herself being later on; while we
were viewing the Mecklenburgh Square damage from afar, she
touched Leonard's arm and said quietly: ' Leo, there are aeroplanes overhead, don't you think we'd better take cover? '

That was the day they bombed Buckingham Palace. But
the worst was in the afternoon. I was about to round off my
day by a quick visit to Charlotte Street, to see if I could get in
and inspect the rooms below Beatrix's. There had been no air-
raid warning; there was no sound of aeroplane engines; but
suddenly, directly ahead of us, three screeching noises from the
clouds and bombs burst—it can't have been more than twenty-
five yards away in Howland Street. Window glass flew
splintering in all directions; dense black smoke arose covering
the whole area of the hits; people ran in all directions and the
trolley buses piled up against one another; my taxi skidded
violently from side to side and then drew up in a side-street.
The astonishing thing was that in that side-street people were
gazing quietly and curiously out of their doors to see what was
happening. . . . After wandering, slightly dazed, in search of
a shelter, I finally jumped into another taxi and made for
Paddington. The sirens, incidentally, went about one minute
after the attack was made.

Later, on reaching home, I discovered that Beatrix had by
chance been in town and had an equally nasty experience at the
same moment in the Euston Road. She rang up from Rosamond's, rather shaken.

September 19th

A couple of days ago, when we were at last let into M.
Square, we found that the exploding of the time-bomb had
caused further damage, smashing the Hogarth's windows and
bringing down part of the ceiling of the basement front room.
Everything was covered with dust and plaster and splinters;
Miss P. and I went round collecting things, dusting and sorting,

while more sirens wailed outside. My flat has a chalk cross on the door to mark it unsafe—I thought of the Plague Year—but I got in, and found that though the shutter fasteners had been split and more front windows broken, there was no other damage. Yet it was uninhabitable, like the Press: and I suddenly felt very sad, standing by the windows and looking out on the ruin of the lovely old Square—and what had been for me a happy life there.

6

THE plan that Leonard and I discussed after the bombing of Mecklenburgh Square—we had had it in mind for some time—was to remove the operations of The Hogarth Press to our chief printers, The Garden City Press in Letchworth, a town which seemed an adequate distance out of London and not likely to be a target for a bomb. I therefore arranged to have the minimum of necessary files put on to the van, and went down to supervise the move-in.

A couple of excellent rooms at the top of the works were put at our disposal, and we soon made ourselves reasonably comfortable. The situation, though inconvenient from the point of view of getting there, had the enormous advantage, at a time when communications were constantly being interrupted and mail itself sometimes going up in flames, of putting the actual production of our books under the same roof as our own publishing work: we had only to walk across the factory to give our instructions, get our estimates, and eventually keep each stage in the making of the books under watch. The works were never bombed, and from there all the publishing of The Hogarth Press was directed until the end of the war, though during the long interval between the end of the blitz and the beginning of the tip-and-run night raids and the attacks by V1s and V2s I did most of the work from the new flat I had by then acquired in London.

I spent most of the first night in Letchworth under the table in the dining-room of the works manager's house. He had kindly offered me a bed on as many nights as I wished, and equally kindly insisted on my taking shelter, when the sirens went, with his whole family under that table. It was a tight fit and seemed to me—though I did not say so for fear of offending him—ludicrously insufficient protection. At intervals between an all-clear and the next warning I walked out into the garden, from which the progress of the nightly bombardment of London, thirty-five miles away, could be observed to strange effect. The barrage shells burst like coloured rockets in a Fourth of June display in the clear sky, and the great lateral flashes of bombs exploding flickered like electricity; but all the time not a sound was to be heard, not even a faraway thump. I resisted the impulse to put on a bravado act, and tell my friend that, having experienced the real thing, I preferred sleeping in my own bed until the swish of bombs approached—if it ever did. I decided, however, that if I felt obliged to spend several nights a week in Letchworth, I would try to find a house of my own. I spent some time next day exploring the place, but like all garden cities, it seemed to suffer from a miasma of smug comfort and petty respectability; I quickly came to the conclusion that one of the ugly little cottages down one of its tidy little roads was the very last refuge I would be driven to, and only if all alternatives failed.

The plan I eventually adopted, and kept to for the next six months with some regularity, was to spend two or three nights in the middle of each week in Cambridge, forty minutes further down the line, stop off in London with a friend or at the Athenaeum for one night going and one or two nights returning, and make my base and week-end refuge at Fieldhead. This may sound complicated, but it worked extraordinarily well and gave me the agreeable opportunity to renew friendships in Cambridge and get to know what the undergraduates were thinking and writing. Dadie Rylands was immediately helpful, and produced, as if by magic, a little room in St. Edward's Passage, opposite the Arts Theatre, which belonged to King's. There I was entirely on my own, and could come and go as I pleased, with the excellent restaurant of the Arts only a few yards away.　And every now and then I was able to enjoy the Wili-like apparition of Lydia Lopokova, who kept the room above mine for her rare visits to Cambridge.

Thus were the bounds of my wartime world drawn, though I did not then foresee how constant they were to remain, and for how long.　As, by a piece of luck, my lease of the Mecklenburgh Square flat only ran to the end of September, I decided to evacuate it at once and take my books and furniture down to Fieldhead, as soon as I had removed The Hogarth Press to Letchworth.　I shall never forget the faces of the removal men. They had, I suppose, been at work without pause and probably with little or no sleep ever since the raids started, ignoring sirens and bombs and making as much haste as they could through cordoned-off roads that changed every day: they had the trance-like expression of utter exhaustion as they went mechanically through the movements of packing and loading. I have always thought they were among the unremembered heroes of the blitz.　I felt ashamed to hurry them, though I was that morning acutely conscious of the vulnerability of human chattels and human bodies, having been caught in my bath at the top of the Athenaeum by an unexpected raid and violent barrage, with the prospect, so I pictured it, of cascading naked in a torrent of soap-suds down the grand staircase if the august building were hit.　I wondered whether Air-Marshal Joubert, familiar imperturbable figure in the Club at this time, would even have lifted his head from *The Times* as this fleshly bomb landed in front of him.　Only a week later clubland *was* hit, and it was with a shocked sense that this time the Nazis had definitely gone too far, that I arrived at the Athenaeum to find the liveried staff sweeping away debris while disconcerted Bishops stepped as delicately as cats over the litter of broken glass.

It was a relief to unpack everything into the comparative calm and shelter of Fieldhead.　I considered myself remarkably lucky not to have lost anything, luckier still as the months went by and the casualties to my friends' dwellings mounted, while many who had managed to send everything they possessed overseas had scarcely ceased to congratulate themselves before they heard that a torpedo had sent the lot to the bottom of the ocean.

Days of perfect early Autumn weather succeeded one another in the valley: the skies were clear, there was an idyllic stillness among the yellowing leaves and on the glassy water, a fresh sweet tang in the air and a faint mist that never entirely cleared. The memory of bombed London might have faded in such surroundings, if this very beauty had not turned to treachery every night. The moon, that ' lucid friend to aerial raiders, the brilliant pilot moon ', was bringing the bombers overhead every night, and as the sirens went my mother's pekinese, who had acquired air-raid sense with astonishing speed, jumped up to lead the procession to the old wine-cellar. One night a stick of bombs fell a mile or two down river near Cookham gasworks, and the reverberations in the valley made it sound as if they had fallen in our kitchen garden. I dressed and ran out, and saw one of the raiders drop a flare, so pretty in the moonlight that one could not believe it signalled danger: softly it floated down, while the only noise that now disturbed the night was the familiar roar and clanking of the mill away in Cores End, so loud in the dead hush that I thought at first there had been an accident there.

One week-end Cuthbert Worsley came down to rest from the air-raids. We took a walk that has always remained in my mind: down through the rain-softened garden, heavy with ripe apples and already looking a little untidy-autumnal with the ragged dahlias flopping over the beds and the leaves scattered over the lawn, and along the river basking in the late September sun to Marlow island. We were both under the feeling, half melancholy, half exhilarating, that the events of the past few weeks had marked a great divide between our lives as they had been and as the war would now shape them. Our friends across the Atlantic, Christopher and Wystan and others, seemed to have grown far more remote, as if they had suddenly gone out of hearing; and the old days of the Spanish War and the early enthusiasms of *New Writing* seemed to have become at last definitively the past. We talked of the shape of society after the war, and the spiritual thinness of politics and political slogans; of the need for a total reassessment, a new kind of philosophy evolving from artistic and religious experience;

everything, both within and without, seemed at the beginning of a great transformation scene.

One result of my spending week-ends at Fieldhead was that I began to take a more active part in the local Home Guard, which I had joined in the Summer while the L.D.V.s were being formed. My responsibilities consisted in little more than parading on Sunday mornings, with instruction in the fantastic spigot mortar which was supposed to lob grenades at the advancing tanks of the invaders, but was so primitive and slow —so it seemed to me—that it would have been spotted and smashed to pieces by a tank's guns long before it could have taken a second aim. There were also guard duties on Sunday or Monday nights to fit in with my week-end routine. Absurd it all may seem in retrospect; but we were, in fact, an essential part of the delaying tactics envisaged if the enemy actually were to land in England, and we were uneasily conscious at the back of our minds that, with our totally inadequate equipment, there would be precious few survivors if the Nazi armour were to thrust up from the west, in spite of concrete road blocks and gun-emplacements disguised as cow-byres and pig-sties. The guards were generally mounted at the H.Q. in a little converted shop between the local branch of Lloyds Bank and the cinema. I took a volume of poems or a novel by Conrad with me, but there was little chance of either reading or sleep with the electric light and the electric fire blazing and the local characters gossiping and arguing away without pause. I learnt, however, a great deal about the village that would hardly have come my way through any other activity. Cars and motor bikes and radios and the various ways of growing vegetables were exhaustively discussed by the carpenter, the plumber, the builder and the owner of the sweet-shop down the road, but the fortunes of the war and political alignments scarcely ever. Lying wrapped up in an army blanket on the floor, I would listen with innocent amazement to dramatic details of the more intimate side of village life that had been shrewdly and silently observed by the carpenter or builder in the course of their work; I began to wonder with a slightly anxious amusement how much they had noted of our own family life at Fieldhead through the years, while mending bell-wires or painting

G

window-frames with apparently total absorption in their work. Gradually, the quiet, humdrum respectable façade of the neighbourhood dropped away, and I had glimpses of violent passions working to tragic ends in boathouses, appalling vices flourishing on the further side of cabbage-patches, reckless ambitions thwarted in diabolical intrigues behind ribbon counters, and innumerable fantastic evasions of the law: one of the village mechanics confessed to having a secret bootlegging tobacco farm, on which he grew Virginian, Turkish and Egyptian varieties of the leaf and smoked the raw, exotic products in cellar orgies with a few chosen confederates. Sometimes, too, I was detailed for guard duty on the railway bridge with a young locomotive fireman: I remember how one still, moonlit night, the river smooth as a looking-glass reflecting the softly irradiated sky through a sleeper's open window, the drone of aircraft passing far overhead rose and fell in regular rhythm for several hours, though no siren sounded: in the morning we learnt of the destruction of Coventry.

On rare occasions only an urgent, unexpected assignment took me out of the circle of Fieldhead–London–Letchworth–Cambridge, which became for me the theatre of my war. One day in the early Spring I had to go to Blackpool, and spend two nights there. The north had always been strange to me, and by now the seaside had also become remote, something I missed as much as bananas and Viennese cigarettes. It was therefore an exhilarating and curiously releasing experience, to get off the train and arrive at once in a warm world of Spring sun and clear skies over a sparkling sea that sent its ripples of foam up to the distant edge of the beaches, a white, restlessly unchanging ripple and return on the rim of the copper sheet of sand; and to find the one-time city of pleasure-seeking trippers and holiday conferences spinning to its keen, new-found rhythm of war activity. Airmen passed along the esplanade in endless streams, English boys with their cheery, pink-and-white looks, and Polish boys with their long straight noses in square faces and fiercely glancing eyes; and all the morning groups of them went marching and drilling and singing along the sea-front, or down on the sands performed the staccato ballet of their physical jerks in singlets and shorts; the vast deserted piers with their closed halls and galleries slept in the distance, while the air was filled with the unremitting hum of aeroplanes from the airfield down the coast. It was a scene of aspiration and promise, strength coiling into a spring for the action of the future.

7

MEANWHILE, during these months of tension and violence, an event of some importance had taken place in my career as editor. One day, in the fatal May of 1940, I received a letter from Allen Lane asking if I would be interested to follow up my Pelican *New Writing in Europe* with a selection of the best contributions from *New Writing* for the Penguin series. I immediately saw the possibilities in this suggestion for reviving the influence and usefulness of *New Writing*. I wrote back enthusiastically agreeing, and at the beginning of June Lane informed me that his Editorial Committee were keen to back the idea and that he would come and see me about it. The following Wednesday he arrived in my office in Mecklenburgh Square, very much on top of the wave, announcing that the sales of the Penguins were steadily increasing, that he had confidence they would go on increasing even if the war got worse, and that he had a scheme for opening an office in Canada —just in case. His sanguine mood made our discussions extremely harmonious, and the very next day a draft contract was sent off to me. I had persuaded him that I could as easily produce two selections as one, out of the abundant riches of the old volumes of *New Writing*, and by the time the contract arrived I had already sketched out a provisional contents-list for both of them. The selections pleased him, and I had little more to do than write to the authors and explain the terms that Lane was offering them. All agreed, and a few weeks later all the MSS., with my own introduction and brief history of *New Writing*, were in the printer's hands.

The publication of the first volume was fixed for the first week in November. I had been anxious, in the early Summer,

to work on the selections as fast as possible, partly from fear
that the threatened invasion would begin and the Penguins
be forced to take wing for Canada, partly because it seemed
likely that one of the war-jobs I had been discussing with
the authorities would materialize and I would have to go
abroad any moment.   ' Perhaps,' observed Julia Strachey in a
letter to me at this time, ' even as I write you will be sitting with
your curly Balkan hat on, upon the hotel terrace at Sarajevo.'
But as the months went by and the Battle of Britain was won,
and the mooted job and the curly Balkan hat receded even
further into improbability, and the bombardments by night
took the place of the battles by day, one began to anticipate a
long period of siege and staying put.   At the beginning of
October, an idea that Allen Lane had put into my head during
a conversation, in which he had talked of the possibility of
Penguin Books sponsoring a monthly magazine, suddenly
crystallized.   Why shouldn't the Penguin selections from *New
Writing* be continued?   Why shouldn't they appear monthly,
with half of each number entirely *new* material, stories, poems,
articles about books and discussions?

I wrote off to Lane at once, and was happily surprised to get
an immediate answer telling me to go ahead with the scheme
as fast as I liked.   The details were settled with what—considering the difficulties that were cropping up on all sides from the
intensification of the attack on Britain—seems to me now
incredible speed, and a new contract for six numbers of a
monthly *Penguin New Writing* was signed by the end of October.

This was a signal that I felt I had long been waiting for
without being entirely aware of it.   The book volumes of *New
Writing* had never been read as widely as I would have liked,
and I believed that in its sixpenny format it would carry its
message to thousands who had never heard of it before but in
whose minds, especially in the revolutionary circumstances of
the war, it would almost certainly strike a responsive chord.
First of all, however, its contents had to be redesigned to make
it more of a monthly, and to allow space for several regular
features it seemed to me the times demanded.   I set to work
with an elation I had not known since the early days at The
Hogarth Press: the new venture occupied most of my thoughts

on my continual train journeys, on walks by the Thames and
along the Backs at Cambridge, and I discussed it at every
opportunity with the friends who had been closest to me in the
old days of *New Writing*.   I think the air-raids and the appalling
precariousness of the country's situation would have shaken
me much more deeply if my hopeful schemes had not dominated
my mind.   I began by writing a series of letters to the contributors I valued most, such as George Orwell, V. S. Pritchett,
Tom Hopkinson, William Plomer and the poets, telling them
what was planned and asking them not to sign away any second
serial rights in their old contributions without letting me know.
(I had heard that several commercial magazines, in the dearth
of new stories at the time, had been carefully scanning the files of
New Writing for material they could use.)   At the same time I
reminded them how anxious I was to have new contributions
from them.   George Orwell I had already written to about
this, and received a self-revelatory reply from him in July:

I am very sorry I have written nothing for you after promising I
would.   I began something, then the war began to get serious.
I just can't write with this kind of thing going on.   I have written
nothing except book reviews etc. for a long time past, and also my
time has been rather filled up with helping with the L.D.V.
What is so terrible about this kind of situation is to be able to do
nothing.   The gov't won't use me in any capacity, not even a
clerk, and I have failed to get into the army because of my lungs.
It is a terrible thing to feel oneself useless and at the same time on
every side to see halfwits and profascists filling important jobs.
However, things *are* moving a little.   I was informed at the W.O.
that it is no longer held against a man to have fought in the
Spanish Civil War.   Of course you can use the elephant sketch
again if you like.   Two guineas would be very handsome.   As
to the photo referred to in your other letter, does it have to be a
real portrait or will a snap do?   I don't photograph well as a
rule. . . . I have been living in London because I am now doing
theatre criticism for *Time and Tide*.

The reply I had from Victor Pritchett put me in good heart.
'A monthly issue is just the sort of thing that ought to catch
on,' he wrote to me at the beginning of November.   'I imagine
the shortage of creative writing will gradually go as we adjust

ourselves to the war. The blitz has been a good thing in a way, because it is decisive in making everyone part of the war. One of the difficulties I have felt in writing is that I had the feeling of writing against the current of events. However the past despondency caused by the blitz seems to have passed; so it appears to me when I go to London. I don't even react with great horror when lovely things are destroyed, for the house-breakers in the last twenty years destroyed far more beautiful things for loathely profit than the blitz has done. At any rate, though often sick with disgust and gloomy with forebodings, I think the paralysis of the last years is passing. One *feels*. I had felt nothing for a year, had been a mere telegraph exchange for ubiquitous anxiety. I say all this with caution. One can only observe day by day.'

One of the first people I approached was Stephen Spender, who was teaching at a school in Devon at the time, and had had some difference with the other editors of *Horizon* which made me feel it might be possible to enrol him as a regular contributor to *Penguin New Writing*. After some thought, I had chosen him as the first person to ask to do the monthly article about books, which I envisaged as an essential feature: my idea was that it should not be the usual ' middle ' about books in general, though current books would occasionally be reviewed in it, but rather a continuing discussion on the relations between litera-ture (and the other arts) and life, especially those aspects which the war made to seem so important. I believed that such a series of articles could provide food for the thoughts that were stirring—as I had already discovered—in the minds of innumerable people who had hardly taken literature seriously before, or felt any need to go to the great poets and novelists for answers to the problems that now obsessed them, and at the same time could be valuable and interesting for the highbrows and professionals; and I believed that Stephen was one of the few writers of our generation who could undertake them success-fully. I found him very eager to tackle the job, and after some discussions with Cyril Connolly and Peter Watson, in which a frontier line was drawn between the work he would do for *Penguin New Writing* and the work he would after all continue to do for *Horizon*, he agreed.

Another feature, which the manuscripts that had recently been coming in for *Folios of New Writing* made me believe might answer a growing need, was a series of articles, part reportage, part story, based on personal experiences of people plunged into new circumstances by the upheavals of the war. For this, which I decided to call ' The Way We Live Now ', I wrote to several of my old contributors; but as the war went on my ' hunch ' proved right and contributions arrived increasingly from quite unknown writers. Indeed a great many of the first-person-singular war stories that we published without including them in the series, would have suited it almost as well. And to balance these, I felt I needed fairly regular, rather personal stories that came out of the deep exploration of the past that so many people had found since the war broke out gave meaning and spiritual fortification to the dissolving present. My sister Rosamond's perfectly evoked story *The Red-Haired Miss Daintreys* had been so warmly received when I published it in *Folios*, was to me so exactly what I had in mind at its best, that I persuaded her to write several more stories for the Penguin in the same vein. Each story was a difficult birth, Rosamond being one of those complex imaginative artists whose whole creative being wilts at the merest hint of the regular production-line obligations of the journalist, as surely as a dahlia at the first touch of frost; but I was rewarded for my persistence and more than adequately consoled for the disfavour I frequently found myself in as merciless editorial slave-master, by the eventual appearance of those beautiful stories *When the Waters Came*, *A Dream of Winter*, *The Gypsy's Baby* and *Wonderful Holidays*, which were at a later date collected in one volume with *The Red-Haired Miss Daintreys*.

It was very soon clear that Rosamond's methods of work would not allow her to produce one a month, as originally projected, and I realised that I could not count on these contributions coming very frequently. In order, therefore, to be certain of being able to strike this note fairly regularly—for the confusions of the war made me feel it vital to plan well ahead— I took a step for which I was sharply criticized on some sides, though I never regretted it myself as it led to an unexpected and exciting discovery. I had been an eager admirer of Dylan

Thomas's early poems, but rather less so of those (with certain outstanding exceptions) which had followed them, as their obscurity and over-elaboration seemed to me to be leading him into a cul-de-sac; when, however, I received *Portrait of the Artist as a Young Dog* to review for *Tribune*, I realised with a shock of delight that Dylan was a wonderful prose artist as well as poet.   I wrote at once to ask him whether he was at work on any more stories or sketches such as he had included in the *Portrait*.   He wrote back:

> I'll be very glad to be a contributor to the Penguin *New Writing*. Thank you for writing.   I haven't finished any new stories yet, but I hope I will have by the time you've finished the publishing details.
>
> I'm glad you liked my *Portrait of the Artist as a Young Dog*.   I'm going to start soon to write a continuation of it: one long story about London.

The months passed, however, and no new stories appeared. I therefore thought of another plan.   I knew from conversations with Dick Church (whose persistent advocacy and encouragement of Dylan's work can never be praised too highly) that sales were small and that these stories of genius were not reaching the public I felt was there for them.   So it was that I suggested to Dylan and his publishers that I should reprint some of the stories from the *Portrait* in *Penguin New Writing*; at the same time I urged him to let me see as much as he had written of the new long story as soon as possible.   He wrote back from Bishopston at the beginning of March 1941:

> Thank you for writing, and for wanting to know about my new book.   I'm afraid I haven't got anything much of it done; I'm still looking for somewhere to live on extremely little—do you know of anywhere?—and have been so homeless and penniless and uncertain lately that I've only been able to write little bits of the story; I hope very soon to find a place to live in, really to live in for perhaps even two months, and then I can get it going. I'll let you know as soon as there's enough to print.   I'm very glad you want it for *New Writing*.   Staying, on sufferance, with parents and unfortunate friends, wanting to get away but quite unable, it's hard, I find, to settle to writing anything continuous.
>
> And I'm very glad that you want to print some of the stories

from *Portrait of the Artist as a Young Dog*. I wish I had sent
some of them to you in the first place. I'd like, a lot, to see them
come out in *New Writing*. Will you let me know which ones
you're thinking of printing? I'm sure Dent won't raise any
objection. The book sold hardly at all. Three or four hundred
copies, I think. And if Dent do agree, any chance of a few quid
soon?

I don't know when I'll be in town next, but I'll drop a line to
Athenaeum Court when I do come. I'd like to see you.

After a good deal of coaxing, I managed to persuade him to
let me see the sections of the ' long story about London ' which
he had finished, and to which he had tentatively given the
title of *Adventures in the Skin Trade*. I was enchanted with them
when they came: they seemed to me to promise an entirely
original work, with an unique mixture of humour and fantasy,
and a strong vein of Dylanesque poetry running through it.
How freshly it read, how alive it was compared with some
of the more earnest ' reports on war experience ', authentic
though they might be, that were beginning to come into the
New Writing office at the time. I was a little worried that some
of the passages in the version he showed me might be thought
by a printer to be too obscene, but I decided to print the opening section at once in *Folios of New Writing*: it appeared in the
Autumn 1941 volume as *A Fine Beginning*. And from that
moment I decided to make it one of my main objectives to get
Dylan to finish it. If only he could be assured of a small regular income, he said, the thing was in the bag. I therefore
agreed to pay him a few pounds every week. And every week
we met in a Shepherd Market pub, Dylan generally bringing
with him a silent, good-looking young man in a London Irish
kilt who seemed to be assuming the office of personal body-
guard; and to the accompaniment of drinks, general gaiety and
many vivid descriptions of how the work was progressing, the
notes were handed over. The work, however, did *not* progress;
I began to realize that Dylan was treating all my cajolings and
homilies as a huge joke (to which I was privy), and that while
he was getting more deeply involved in war work or scripts for
documentary films, the writing of *Adventures in the Skin Trade*
was running down like a clockwork toy. Or was it that the

experiences of the blitz made him feel it impossible to carry on with this innocent vision of a pre-war London? Gradually our meetings grew rarer. Eventually my letters remained without an answer. I deeply regretted this, not only for the loss of *Adventures in the Skin Trade* but also because it put a spoke of embarrassment into our relationship for many years, during which I should only have been too happy to publish his poems.

That was all in the future. Meanwhile, I felt that another feature was necessary: something in rather lighter vein, part commentary on the war-scene, but allowing full play for fantasy, humour and imagination. I first of all turned to William Plomer, whose descriptions, in conversation, of people he had come across and remarks he had overheard since the beginning of the war had delighted me with their feeling for the touching and the eccentric, their humour and their sharp observation of basic traits of the national character revealing themselves under stress of war. I suggested to him that he should write a series of articles in a form loose enough to admit any of these stories, any moral he wished to draw and any satire on England-under-bombardment he wished to indulge in. He finally agreed to this suggestion, but proposed that as he was now a (temporary) Civil Servant in an important Service Ministry, he should write them under the pseudonym of Robert Pagan. The secret was, I believe, well kept, and only an extremely small handful of intimates and initiates were told or guessed who the real author of the articles was. Even in our correspondence we kept up the pretence: I was always urging William to tell Bob Pagan that I was in a hurry for his next article, and William reported that Bob had just had a new idea, and did I think it was suited to the odd fellow's talents, etc. All the new series started in No. 2, William's very gaily with *You Must Have Two Hats*, a satire on Civil Service bureaucracy and a tongue-in-the-cheek defence of anarchism, which struck, in my opinion, exactly the right note to prevent *Penguin New Writing* falling into the sins of gloomy routine bitterness and the over-earnest attitudes of may-light-break-through-our-darkness. The Pagan contributions were extremely varied, evocations of the past and reminiscences of childhood as well as vivid glimpses of the extraordinary present, but through them all ran the sense of living in a revolution that gave them a kind of unity and common perspective. Looking back on them, I see that one might have thought *A Dodo in Every Bus*, for instance, to have been written by a spirited new writer who knew how to grind an axe without losing his sense of humour, but I find it almost impossible to understand how any-one who had rejoiced in the unique Plomer touch in the past failed to spot it in, say, *Happy Days* or *Pas Avant*.

At the same time, I wanted another lighter feature, some-thing in a purely fantastic vein, as nonsensical (and yet as pertinent) as the columns of Timothy Shy and Beachcomber and Nat Gubbins, and written by somebody with a fastidious sense of style. I hit on the idea of asking George Stonier, and thought that the Penguin was indeed going to have a lucky start when I found that the plan appealed to him. He immediately created the mask of ' Fanfarlo ', and a whole world of imaginary blitz-bound London characters began to take shape in his mind with astonishing speed: I felt as if I had pressed the lever—a lever that had been waiting to be pressed for a long time—of one of those cunning miniature musical boxes which immedi-ately perform a series of airy, entrancing tunes. *Shaving Through the Blitz* became one of the favourite features of *Penguin New Writing*, and if Fanfarlo missed a number I would get anxious enquiries at once about the fate of Bob and his Lizzie, Captain Spandrill and the inimitable Mrs. Greenbaum (and her land-mine). To treat the bombardment as something inconvenient but somehow absurd, a settled background for inconsequential comedy, was too sophisticated for certain minds, and no doubt would have been incomprehensible to the young Teutons up aloft who were the cause of it all, but it just suited a mood of the time:

There it is, the Blitz, all night and half the day, mooching round, coming and going, sniffing, grunting, throwing up showers of gravel against the windows, as though one had accommodated too big a dog in the garden. When you step outside it has an unpleasant surprise for you; it follows you down the street and into the tobacconist's; you can't go to the movies or make love without it being there, too. ' How about a little dinner in town tonight? ' someone asks hopefully. ' What about the Blitz? ' is the invariable response. And two years ago few of us could have imagined putting up with even a Blitzlet! But at least there's the consolation that everyone else has it, too, a big, shaggy Blitz he can't get rid of or excuse. Your worst enemy (in the peace sense) stops his ears and shudders when you do.

Fanfarlo catered for a wartime mood with perfect judgement, but re-reading the sketches in the volume in which they were eventually collected, it seems to me that they continue to exist in their own right, preserved from the fate of most of even the best topical journalism by their qualities of wit and style.

While these preparations for the monthly were going forward, I was correcting the page proofs of my Pelican *New Writing in Europe*. This had been commissioned at the beginning of January, long before even the first *Penguin New Writing* had been conceived, but as it took me some months to write, it appeared at the turn of the year, at the same time as No. 2, the first of the monthly series; a useful conjunction, but not part of a wicked commercial plan to boost the new series, as some hostile critics immediately imagined.

New Writing in Europe was an attempt to give a bird's-eye view of the whole new movement that had grown up in the 'thirties, to analyse the impulses that had set it in motion, and to suggest what might happen to it after the disillusionments of 1939. Parts of it seem to me now absurdly simplified, some authors, inevitably, over-estimated, some misinterpreted or unfairly neglected; but there are many passages that I would not want to change now, except in the shift of emphasis that must occur as an author's *œuvre* reveals itself more completely. For some years I continued to receive letters about it which showed in a most interesting way the varying reflections that such a history of a movement can stimulate in the minds of those who took part in it, or observed it at fairly close quarters: I felt that I had helped them to clarify their judgement while trying to get my own clear, and reading their letters my understanding was in its turn deepened, my judgement slightly altered. One of the first, and one of the most entertaining that reached me was from V. S. Pritchett:

> I've just been reading the Pelican, a most gratifying book. You have made the 30's blush with pleasure. . . . It's hard to

imagine what will become of the poets but I suppose the future has always been their enemy, which only a few have surmounted. Prose writers rise and fall like the waves of the sea; unless some catastrophe or aberration strikes one, one goes on like a cork on the waves, sometimes in a trough, sometimes on a crest, but still going on. Of course I suppose poets go on too—Sturge Moore sturged more and more as the years went by—but prose writers do not have to suffer so much from the contempt of the public. Poets, like sopranos, are supposed never to sing flat. I'm on the outside of the Auden–Spender family circle, and am not racked by its inner ecstasies and storms. Among them I feel like some coarse taxi-driver who has picked up a lot of eccentric fares who are all going to different places. This letter is going to be full of similes and there must be one more. You, I see as a sort of Simon Legree of letters, the slave-master, whip in hand, who drives us all to work with an air both flattering and threatening. Editors must threaten. I don't know how you manage your own writing—do you threaten yourself?

But seriously, I've been glad to be published by *New Writing*. No one else would publish me consistently and the idea of belonging to a ' generation ' or ' school ' has been very helpful to me. Being a few years older than most of the *New Writing* contributors I was too young for the war lot, and was quite homeless and isolated as a writer. Something has crystallized in *New Writing*. I loved the photographs. Wm. Plomer was frightening. There was a real writer at work, pen in hand, paper, blotter and desk. But what a fraud—for he never writes!—I thought.

Another letter which I valued particularly, full of sound criticism of ' proletarian ' writing as it had been practised in the 'thirties, came from E. M. Forster, who had from the beginning shown a sympathetic interest in *New Writing*:

It struck me as a real clearing up of the matter for the benefit of some future chronicler of the decade, or indeed for yourself if you take on that job sometime, and you are well qualified to do this. And it also helped to clear up *me*, and I now see better than last week where I stand in relation to all this left-wing stuff. I'm very glad the relation isn't a remote one, and I thank you very much for what you say about me. My difficulty with working-class writers is that they don't make the working-class come alive —Leslie Halward is an exception. . . . They give one information as they give their comrades gratification, but that's all:

gloom, indignation, aspiration in plenty, and plenty of stains on the table-cloth and coal-dust in the milk—but no living beings to experience them. Consequently I find a lot of what you have (very rightly) published dull. Or put it another way: I find that we middle-class do demand that people in fiction should seem to be alive, and I realize too that this demand may not be as important as I think, and that there may be a fiction I am not conditioned to appreciate, in which Ted at the table, Ed in the mine and Bert at the works need not be differentiated. But I can't look at them in that way myself, and the working-class people I know don't seem so to look at them either, though their judgements are different from mine because it is more important to them than to me whether a man has money or not.

What's so good—among other things—is the way you relate the literature to the heaving political background. In connection with this, Christopher's *The Lost* stands out as it didn't before. Something lost for us, I fear, no one'll ever mirror the whole flux now—it's splashed too much of the mirror. A certain awareness (nice word, yes) is possible, though, and you help one to exercise it.

Many small points occur to me. Auden and Wm. Plomer are the poets I like best, and I particularly like what Auden wrote in the China book, which I think you don't mention. . . . Don't Marx and Engels like Balzac because he gives them so much material appropriate to a decaying society?—A section needed on the Conference spirit?—the only sort of literary life these new little international authors had access to. I wish I had been to more conferences. They were very strange things.

You'll make me read some new people—particularly J. Gibbon whose letter was splendid. Also John Lepper, who wrote very kindly to me once. . . .

In connection with this little book, the old row about Auden and Isherwood blew up again in an unexpected way. Sir Hugh Walpole was at that time writing regular literary reviews for the *Daily Sketch*, which had considerable influence with the reading public. Hugh had always prided himself on showing a generous sympathy towards the young, and had before the war written many appreciative reviews of *New Writing* and the authors who were associated with it. He could not, however, stomach the absence of Wystan and Christopher in America, and when *New Writing in Europe* came

out he wrote in the *Daily Sketch*: ' This is a wonderfully com-
pact summary, generous and appreciative, and I feel that it is
ungrateful to criticize it. But the harsh fact is that time
relentlessly moves on. The leaders of John Lehmann's *New
Writing* are no longer new at all. The leaders are all well
over thirty. They are already old-fashioned. There is a new
generation of new writing, and it disregards Auden, Isherwood,
and the others altogether. The fact is that this war has, at one
stroke, deprived most of Lehmann's " New Writers " of their
contemporaneity. They belong to an earlier age, with their
pessimism, their cynicism, their apprehensions, their despair.
After Dunkirk new poets were born.' I had sent him a copy of
the book, and at the same time as the review appeared Hugh
wrote me a letter in which he said: ' I'm afraid you will be
cross with me after yesterday's *Sketch* but I have to write what I
feel. I don't think you realize the harm done by Auden,
Isherwood, MacNeice fleeing to America. I'm not blaming
them but it has *killed* their influence here. The men you
write of seem to me to belong in the main to the Spanish War.
The young writers of this war have an outlook quite different.
Anyway that's what I feel.'

It was clear to me that what stuck in Hugh's gullet was the
famous imaginary ' flight' to America. He was determined to
prove that the three writers (and the rest of their 'group' as well)
were old-fashioned, dead, without influence, because he didn't
like what he fancied they'd done. The new poets who were
born ' after Dunkirk '—only six months back—were a fiction of
Hugh's imagination. Perhaps it was a pity that there were no
rousing backs-to-the-wall singers in England, but the more
interesting young poets who had appeared since the beginning
of the war showed no signs of filling the role: too many, for one
thing, were deeply absorbed in what Auden had been doing.
I wrote and told Hugh what I thought, and suggested that he
was a little premature in sketching the poetic character of
the 'forties in such bold outlines. (If he had lived to see that
character emerge he would have been truly dismayed; and fancy
boggles at what he would have made of Wystan's triumphant
return fifteen years later as Oxford Professor of Poetry.) I
also said I would not go over the whole dreary question of

whether Wystan and Christopher did actually ' flee ' again, but pointed out that Louis MacNeice was in fact back in England, as he had always intimated that he would be.

Hugh, however, was not to be moved so easily, and Hugh evidently had the ear of this young generation of post-Dunkirk poets I had not heard of, to whom—he retorted—' Auden, Isherwood and Co. seem infinitely ancient '. This ' flight ', he went on, had ' damaged their whole school in the eyes of all artists '. He ended gaily by sending me ' all the best wishes of a typical *Daily Sketch* reader (*and* writer) whom you scornfully abuse and deride in your little book while at the same time asking me to give it publicity in the said *Daily Sketch* '. He was, I saw, torn between the conflicting desire to punish my friends for being in America on the one hand and to admit that they were good writers who gave him pleasure on the other. The correspondence went on, livened by various exchanges in the newspapers. ' I am not attacking anybody,' he wrote a few weeks later. ' Far from it. I am almost the only critic, save MacCarthy, who is widely known, who is constantly mentioning your new writers. . . . I believe more in Auden, Spender, etc., than anyone else of *my* nearly sixty years. . . . I fully believe that Auden, Isherwood and Spender will do great work in the future.' And then a few lines further on: ' Your whole group are *pre* this war in spirit. Still Stephen and the rest go on writing lugubrious articles, still you permit miserable little realist stories about boys who clout their mothers, kick their fathers and steal from the baker's shop. . . . As to the under *thirties*—Auden seems to them an ancient schoolboy-joking pedant.'

I remembered that a year before I had had a long talk with Hugh in his Piccadilly flat, where every inch of wall-space in all the rooms was covered with exquisite water-colours and drawings, a large number of them precious Old Master sketches of the male figure. He had been at his most amiable, and full of compliments for *New Writing*, but extremely indignant about the ' flight '. I had tried to persuade him then that he was being unfair to Wystan and Christopher, whom he had always admired and liked personally. I could, however, see from this correspondence that my attempt to put the other side of the argument had been in vain: he had sensed, I am inclined to think, that I, too, bitterly regretted their absence, and believed that it would be a loss as much to them as to ourselves that they should not experience what we were experiencing—what we were going to experience; and took the rest of my attempted justification as loyalty to friends. I never saw him again.

By the time No. 2 of the *Penguin New Writing* came out, in the new year of 1941, the first number had already had a start-lingly swift success—and that was before the real wartime run on books began. By the end of March two printings had been sold out, making 80,000 copies in all; and Nos. 2 and 3, the first two of the re-planned monthly series, had also exhausted their first printings of 55,000 each. Allen Lane was as jubilant as I was, having found that what he had originally envisaged to some extent as a ' prestige ' publication was in fact making him a profit. Very soon he agreed to increase the advances to me, so that I could pay out more money to the contributors and engage a regular reader to help with the ever-rising flood of manuscripts that were arriving: my sister Rosamond became that first reader. Nevertheless, there were difficulties about the monthly plan: difficulties of production, which the blitz had been making more and more hazardous and more liable to delay, and difficulties of paper-rationing which had begun to make itself felt. I passed some anxious weeks in which it looked as if the new monthly was going to die almost as soon as born. I bombarded Lane with letters, and in the end my advocacy—and the growing evidence of *P.N.W.*'s success and popularity—won the day. It was a near thing: before going down to Harmondsworth for the crucial interview I passed a sleepless night on Home Guard duty, rehearsing all the argu-ments I could muster while the guns banged away almost without pause and the door rattled to every reverberation. We decided to carry on, and five tons of paper a month (at that time roughly the whole ration of paper for The Hogarth Press in a year) was set aside to produce approximately 75,000 copies of each number.

This meeting took place the day before Stephen Spender's marriage to Natasha Litvin, an occasion which, in reuniting our literary world, painfully marked the absence of Christopher

H

and Wystan. William Plomer and Joe Ackerley were there, acting once more the part of satiric chorus in undertones which grew disturbingly merrier as the alcohol began to work, Cecil Day Lewis and Louis MacNeice, Julian and Juliette Huxley with their son Anthony, Rose Macaulay, Stephen's fellow-editors on *Horizon* Cyril Connolly and Peter Watson, and Tambimuttu, who had just started his career as editor of *Poetry London*. Tambi, I remember, appeared rather confused and lachrymose among a host of Stephen's more elderly female relations, and after several glasses of champagne bewildered them by appealing for reassurance about the intellectual mission of his magazine. I had bought an edition of Schiller for Stephen in David's bookshop in Cambridge, and announcing its imminent arrival to him on the telephone some days before had teasingly warned him that I wouldn't promise to send anything for his third wedding. He only paused for a second before replying: ' Will you send something to my funeral, then, John? '

My recollection of those early months of *Penguin New Writing* is of continual train-journeys accompanied by a suitcase full of manuscripts and proofs which I worked through; of frequent halts on the line during an alert, the progress in and out of King's Cross or Paddington sometimes being as slow as the game of Grandmother's Steps we used to play in front of the Pavilion at Fieldhead, sudden spurts while the Nazis weren't looking, dead stops when aerial eyes were upon us; sometimes dusk fell over the darkened train and reading had to be abandoned, and passengers in silent gloom reflected that their plans to arrive—or leave—before the evening blitz were going to be in vain; guns started to bark and the faraway thump of bombs changed, disagreeably, to the swish-swish-swish of a stick of them swooping down close by. Also I remember blissfully peaceful nights in Cambridge, where my secretary, Michael Nelson, would often join me, typewriter in hand; and of trips to the works where the Penguin was being printed, sometimes to find there had been a raid the night before and a tarpaulin was being hurriedly stretched over jagged holes in the roof under which the machining of the next number miraculously proceeded. And all the time the letters and manuscripts poured in, chests of drawers at Fieldhead were desperately requisitioned, old rowing vests, mountain-shoes, lederhosen and anti-fascist newspapers, maps of Prague and Vienna and A.A. itineraries of long-ago car trips across Europe flung out, to make room for the ever-increasing offerings of every day's post. More and more were coming in from young authors who had been drafted into the Army, or the Navy, or the Air Force, and some of them so interesting that before long I began to see that it would be possible gradually to reduce the proportion of contributions reprinted from the old *New Writing*, and make the Penguin a completely contemporary magazine.

One of the most interesting of the new authors who came my way in those early days was Alun Lewis. He had sent me some of his poems in the Spring of 1940, none of which I liked as much as the poem—his first to be published in London— which had appeared in the *New Statesman*. He had, however, let out that he was writing short stories at the same time, and I managed to persuade him to let me see some of them. I was struck at once, not so much by his technical skill, which was still, I felt, immature, but by the warmth of feeling and by the atmosphere in which they were soaked, the atmosphere of the recruits in the ranks in the months of waiting which I had believed must eventually find its poet. My letter telling him that I wanted to publish *The Farewell Binge* followed him from camp to camp, and after some weeks he wrote back:

I am delighted you like my *Farewell Binge* enough to use it for *New Writing*. It's an honour I don't undervalue. Especially now, when I find myself under a regime which is so hostile to everything it is fighting to preserve. It's odd, the mixture there is in the Army. Centralized and socialized in distribution and pro-duction of goods, monastic in its celibacy and its veto on private property, communal as hell: and yet absolutely crucified by repression, regimentation, precedence and the taboos of hierarchy. I have been trying incessantly to humanize and fire the unit I'm with: I've started a weekly magazine, a debating society that holds mock parliaments and peace conferences: I've put forward a scheme of lectures in nineteenth and twentieth century world affairs: and all I have earned is suspicion, resentment, a petty charge and reduction to the ranks. *Tiens!*

Excuse this divagation: actually it was your review of Beneš' life in the *Statesman* that made me say this. *C'est la même chose*, Chamberlain's yawn and the Colonel's distrust.

Will you mark the passages in the story which you want altering? I'm no judge of my own work. And best wishes from me and my likes to you who are doing so much to achieve what we desire.

His letters to me after this all sounded the same note: boredom, restlessness, impatience to make the war the first act in a social revolution. ' The staleness of this particular unit is my most immediate enemy and I've been doing a lot of educational work, building up a library, getting decent weeklies and monthlies and Penguins and Pelicans included in it, and trying to persuade soldiers to read intelligent stuff in cinema and canteen,' he wrote in March 1941. ' It's hard work! Fighting will be easier.' And again, a few days later, ' I have been in trouble with the diehards at the top here, serious trouble. But I think I am winning my case. I was called a liar by a colonel when I was lecturing to 500 recruits on Germany and war. He promises now to apologize before the same 500 next time I lecture—on the League of Nations and war. *Enfin, c'est dur ici.*' While he was struggling to make enlightened crusaders out of his fellow-soldiers, he was hard at work at his stories and poems, and finding a sympathetic response among editors and publishers. What gave me such a strong belief in his future as a writer were the glimpses of passionate devotion to his art that came through the letters: ' The story I'm sending you now I *must* send it. Will you please read it and tell me it's much too big a theme for such a little writer, and then I'll pipe down and go to bed at lights out instead of staying up hidden behind black-outs trying to write better and better, feeling for the truth, and not being able to sleep when I do go to bed.' In the end I sent this particular story back to him, feeling that he had indeed tackled a job too big for his equipment at that stage; but my conviction was already forming that, moving though many of his poems were, his real originality and power as a writer were going to show themselves in prose—in short stories.

One of the more unexpected centres of literary and artistic

activity, as the war got under way, was in the Fire Service.
Easy enough to foresee that, sooner or later, stories and
poems would be written out of the experiences of the new,
articulate soldiers, sailors and airmen, born from the shock of
hitherto intellectual lives suddenly thrust into the alien environment of barrack and airfield, the mix-up of all social
classes, and a great, shrouded adventure beginning—as if our
whole civilization was a giant liner that had left its berth and
was slowly sailing into unknown waters under a thickening fog;
but that in the fighting of the fires in the target cities, an
adventure to prove as dramatic as any that the war provided,
so many writers and painters should find the material through
which to express the strangeness of this journey we were all
embarked upon, was one of the surprise developments that had
no precedent in any previous war. It appeared also a lucky
chance (lucky that is in terms of the vitality of art) that one of
the most subtle and complex literary personalities of our
generation, Henry Green, should have volunteered for the
A.F.S. at the very beginning of the war, and plunged into all the
arduous dangers of the London blitz, should nevertheless have
succeeded in keeping a detached creator's eye alert in his inmost being to record his experiences and turn them, even
while the raids were in full swing, into the art of his unique
rococo prose. He began to write out of his A.F.S. experiences
in the late Autumn of 1940, working with extraordinary speed,
first at the opening chapters of his novel *Caught* and then at
several short sketches or episodes. He sent me *The Rescue* early
in January and followed it with *Mr. Jonas* very soon after.
When I look back on it, it seems to me even more astonishing
than it did then, that a fireman liable to be called out any
night and at all times of the night, drained as he must have
been by the sheer physical effort of tackling vast conflagrations
among collapsing buildings with bombers still overhead, not to
mention the nervous tension, could have produced a piece
of descriptive writing as elaborately wrought as *Mr. Jonas*:

What I saw, a pile of wreckage like vast blocks of slate, the slabs
of wet masonry piled high across this passage, was hidden by a
fresh cloud of steam and smoke, warm, limitless, dirty cotton

wool, disabling in that it tight bandaged the eyes. Each billow, and steam rolls unevenly in air, islanding a man in the way that he can, to others, be isolated asleep in blankets. Nor did the light of a torch do more than make my sudden blindness visible to me in a white shine below the waist. There was nothing for it but to go on towards voices out in front, but climbing, slipping up, while unrolling the hose, I felt that I was not a participant, that all this must have been imagined, until, in another instant, a puff of wind, perhaps something in the wreckage which was alight below the surface, left me out in the clear as though in, and among, the wet indigo reflecting planes of shattered tombs deep in a tumulus the men coughing ahead had just finished blasting . . .

The idiosyncratic twists and flourishes of Henry Green's style seem in this passage cunningly manipulated to add to the sense of struggle and bafflement in what he is describing; and the skill with which the end of this short piece, only two or three thousand words long, makes its triumphant impact on the reader's mind, leads one to reflect not only how often it is found to be untrue that dead-pan reporting of terrible happenings produces the maximum effect, but also how much was lost when Henry Green all but abandoned such descriptive writing to explore his (nevertheless ingenious and enlivening) theory that novels should consist almost entirely of dialogue:

> After twelve hours we were relieved, at half past nine in the morning. When the other crew took over we had fought our way back to exactly the same spot above that hole out of which, unassisted once he had been released, out of unreality into something temporarily worse, apparently unhurt, but now in all probability suffering from shock, had risen, to live again whoever he might be, this Mr. Jonas.

When he sent me *Mr. Jonas*, Henry wrote: ' I have just let a girl read it and she laughed herself into a state of tears she thought it so bad. . . . In fact she laughed so much at the first page that she put it into her mouth as you can see from the lipstick on the first page. . . . On the other hand another one three days ago liked it. Anyway I thought I'd put some commas in this time. I've tried to do it in a more spectacular way to suit the more spectacular blaze. It's true, of course, as the other one was.'

By the time *Mr. Jonas* appeared in *Penguin New Writing*, another regular feature had been added. I had persuaded Cecil Day Lewis, who also found himself on the crest of this curious wave of creative energy that had begun to gather, carrying so many writers and painters with it since the Battle of Britain, to let me have one of his new poems every month. We had just published his famous retort to the still repeated cry ' Where are the war poets? ' with its lines so exactly express-ing the mood of the ' anti-fascist ' intellectuals of the 'thirties, a mood that was already giving way—as Cecil's own poetry showed—to something more positive though no doubt very different from what the clamourers expected and thought proper:

> It is the logic of our times,
> No subject for immortal verse,
> That we who lived by honest dreams
> Defend the bad against the worse.

8

Since the bombing of Mecklenburgh Square and the final evacuation of their belongings to Rodmell, Leonard and Virginia had left the running of The Hogarth Press almost entirely to me. We worked in greater harmony than ever before, and all problems which we discussed in our letters seemed to settle themselves with miraculous ease. From time to time Leonard would arrange to meet me in London, to exchange views about manuscripts and devise the best publish-ing plans for the future that we could envisage on our extremely minute paper ration. Virginia I rarely saw, but one day to-wards the middle of March they both came up for the day, and we all met for lunch at St. Stephen's Tavern. We had a table in the window on the first floor, looking out on Parliament Square and Big Ben, and I can clearly remember how brilliant the Spring sunshine was in which the whole scene was steeped.

The week before, I had sent them Terence Tiller's first book of poems, with a strong recommendation that we should publish it. They had brought it with them: Virginia liked it, and declared that in her opinion the Press should accept it. Leonard grumbled about the obscurity of the young poets, and taking a sheet here and there out of the folder, challenged me: ' But parse this poem, John, *parse* it! ' Virginia came to my rescue, maintaining that he was being too logical, that there was music and imagination in the poetry that was rare for a first book. Leonard's objections, however, were only a rear-guard feint, and I soon saw that he had made up his mind to yield to our majority opinion—that in fact he agreed with us more than he had been prepared to admit at first. This was the last book Virginia was to read and approve for the Press.

During our argument I noticed that she seemed in a state of unusual nervous tension, her hand shaking slightly now and then. I began to feel that there was some awkward subject they intended to bring up. I had been aware for some time that Virginia was at work on a new book, but I had no inkling what it was, and knew her well enough not to press for details she was clearly reluctant to give. Then Leonard revealed the secret: she had written a new novel, which had been given the tentative title of *Between the Acts*. This was exciting news for the Press as well as for me as a devotee of her work, but when I turned to congratulate her she began to talk about the book in great agitation, trying to damp down my enthusiasm and saying that it was no good at all and obviously couldn't be published. Leonard rebuked her gently, telling her that she ought to know that it was one of the best things she had written. They went on arguing for some time, Leonard trying to calm her with the firmness of his conviction, until I pleaded to be allowed to read it and give my opinion. I could not believe that under any circumstances a new novel by Virginia, particularly after her triumph with *Roger Fry*, could be ' no good '. Finally she agreed to think it over when she got back to Rodmell, and let me see the typescript if she was in any doubt.

Before we left, she suddenly said she had nothing to do now, and could I send her some reading. I told her I would gladly pick out some manuscripts from the latest batch that had arrived for *Folios of New Writing*, if she really meant it. She eagerly agreed. Looking back on that request afterwards, when the tragedy was over, I realized that her need to have something to occupy and steady her mind was desperate.

A few days later the typescript of *Between the Acts* arrived at Fieldhead, where I had gone for my Home Guard night duty. With it came a letter, dated March 20th:

> Dear John: I've just read my so-called novel over; and I really don't think it does. It's much too slight and sketchy. Leonard doesn't agree. So we've decided to ask you if you'd mind reading it and give your casting vote? Meanwhile, don't take any steps.
>
> I'm sorry to trouble you, but I feel fairly certain it would be a mistake from all points of view to publish it. But as we both differ about this, your opinion would be a great help.
>
> Yours
> Virginia
>
> I hope you're sending the manuscripts—I should like to do them.

I plunged into the book at once, and finished it before I went off into the night with my rifle and tin hat.   The typing—even the spelling—was more eccentric than in any of her typescripts I had seen before: that, and the corrections with which each page was splashed, communicated an extraordinary impression, as if a high-voltage electric current had been running through her fingers. But I was deeply moved: it seemed to me to have a quite extraordinary imaginative power, pushing prose to the extreme limits of the communicable, further than *To the Lighthouse*, to be filled with a poetry more disturbing than anything she had written before. I sent off a telegram the next morning, and followed it with a letter telling her that as far as I was concerned there was no question at all: *Between the Acts* must be published.

Her reply came at the week-end. It wasn't at all what I had hoped; and it was enclosed in a letter from Leonard that shocked and dismayed me, in spite of all the warning signs I had seen. Virginia, he told me, was on the verge of a complete nervous breakdown; she was so seriously ill that she could not possibly revise the book; we must therefore put it off indefinitely. He asked me to send the typescript back to her, with a letter to say how sorry we were that we could not publish it in the Spring, but would hope for the Autumn. I was touched that even in the midst of this terrible personal crisis he could add a few words to say what bad luck it was for me as a publisher. This was the letter he enclosed:

> Dear John: I'd decided, before your letter came, that I can't publish that novel as it stands—it's too silly and trivial.
>
> What I will do is to revise it, and see if I can pull it together and so publish it in the Autumn. If published as it is, it would certainly mean a financial loss; which we don't want. I am sure I am right about this.
>
> I needn't say how sorry I am to have troubled you. The fact is it was written in the intervals of doing Roger with my brain half asleep. And I didn't realize how bad it was till I read it over.
>
> Please forgive me, and believe I'm only doing what is best.
>
> I'm sending back the MSS. with my notes.
>
> Again I apologise profoundly.
>
> Yours
> Virginia.

By the time this letter reached me it was all over. On the Monday I had another letter from Leonard, breaking the incredible news of her suicide. He had taken her to a doctor against her will, as many of the old symptoms that had in the past preceded one of her attacks were returning. They had already started the precautions that had become routine with them, even though, strangely enough, the nightmarish headaches from which I remembered her suffering when she was finishing *The Waves* had been absent. On the day after the visit to the doctor she told Leonard that she was going for a short walk. The walk seemed to take a long time. Disturbed, he went down to her room, and discovered a note on her desk addressed to him: in it she said she knew she was going mad and had decided to kill herself. He ran out in the hope of overtaking and preventing her at the last minute; but all he succeeded in finding was her walking-stick lying on the river bank. Just after she disappeared the tide had turned and poured out to sea. Her body was not found for several weeks.

The news broke in the papers on the Thursday, as Leonard

had decided that the best thing to do was to give the facts to Geoffrey Dawson at *The Times*: he had delayed a few days in the hope that the body might be found. In the last letter he wrote to me on the subject he said, apropos *Between the Acts*: ' She was very pleased when she got your letter about it. I still think it a very remarkable book. I had expected from what she said and feared to find a loss of vigour. I may be wrong, but it seemed to me the opposite, to be more vigorous and pulled together than most of her other books, to have more depth and to be very moving. I also thought that the strange symbolism gave it an almost terrifying profundity and beauty.'

About a fortnight later, Leonard came up to town and lunched with me at the Athenaeum. I was struck by his fortitude in discussing all that had happened, and the changes Virginia's death would make in his own life and our future as publishers, though it was perfectly clear from one glance at him how much he had suffered. It relieved me, for his sake and for my own sake too, to hear him speak with such decision: everything was to go on as before, he looked to me to manage the affairs of the Press from London and Letchworth, while he went on working mainly at Rodmell. He already saw there would be a great deal of work for him to do as Virginia's literary executor: she had scarcely ever stopped writing, when it was not a long work it was essays or articles or short stories, and in addition to all such manuscripts left in finished or half-finished state in her desk there were many volumes of her diary and her enormous correspondence. First of all, he would do his best to get *Between the Acts* into shape, and he would then publish it as soon as war conditions allowed. We talked a little about her illness, and he confirmed the conclusion I had already come to myself: that the air-raids and the tide of war that had been flowing so long against us were far from being the main cause of her breakdown. Once again, and this time fatally, in her labour of imaginative creation she had strained the delicate mechanism of her mind beyond what it could endure.

When Leonard described all the posthumous works of Virginia that he intended to bring out, a programme that would obviously extend over a long period of years, I had a curious feeling of solace, as if Virginia the writer was still to be with us; but the prospect was only a small consolation for the absence of Virginia herself from the activities of the Press. Apart from my grief at her death as the loss of a friend, I was oppressed with melancholy at the thought that she who had seemed as essential a part of the spirit of the Press as Leonard, and whose retirement from partnership in the early months of the war had been little more than a formality, would no longer be there to discuss the manuscripts and their authors, to plan new anthologies and new series with us, and to laugh over the day-to-day alarums and excursions in our business life. It seemed to be yet another nail in the coffin of the hopes I had had when I started my publishing career, the worst discouragement yet.

I had the opportunity to write something about her attitude to young authors almost at once, as she had just been involved in a controversy in the pages of *Folios of New Writing*. In the Spring of 1940 she had read a paper to the Workers' Educational Association in Brighton, called *The Leaning Tower*; and as the main weight of it was an attack on the writers of my generation I thought they should read it, and I persuaded her to let me publish it. In spite of some finely characteristic passages, it was not, I think, one of her best papers: her attack was biased and a little ungenerous and her argument full of holes which her victims were quick to expose. The truth was, she had long been irritated by the rather hectoring tone of some of the political verse written by the *New Signatures* poets; and in reacting sharply, and justly, to that she made it seem she was blind to their other and far more positive qualities. Also, I think her hackles instinctively went up when it appeared to her that writers were organizing themselves into groups and counter-groups: she had already made that clear in her *Letter to a Young Poet*. When *The Leaning Tower* came out, in the Autumn 1940 number of *Folios*, I asked Edward Upward, B. L. Coombes and Louis MacNeice to reply. By the time these replies were in my hands, Virginia's death had already taken place; but I decided to publish them nevertheless, as together they seemed to me to shed such interesting light on the aims and achievements of a movement that was already part of history: Edward Upward's on the strict, marxist, party-line attitude, Coombes' on the aspirations and difficulties of working-class writers, and Louis MacNeice on the ideals of the young middle-class poets who had formed the core of the movement. Louis's was the most effective reply, and it seemed to me that he easily got the better of the argument; but as his point-by-point refutations inevitably left the impression that Virginia was entirely unsympathetic to the work of younger writers, I felt it necessary to add a *Postscript* myself, in which I described how keen—in my experience of working with her—she had always been to encourage any sign of imagination or wit or original thought which she discovered in the manuscripts that came to The Hogarth Press. I also pointed out that in controversial writing of this sort, as in her conversation, she liked to fire off provocative opinions, but that she never insisted on them, as her mind was too active, too fond of exploring and experimenting with ideas ever to be satisfied with one dialectical position for long. Had she not written to me, when we were having an argument by post about her *Letter to a Young Poet*, that she was not in the least satisfied with it ' and would like to tear up, or entirely re-write '? I felt that her tongue was a little more in her cheek than it might seem when one read in cold print what one should have been present to hear her say in person. One curious inconsistency in *The Leaning Tower* was that she appeared to maintain at one point that a middle-class writer's advantage of expensive education was something that he dared not, should not at any cost throw away; and yet, that unless he threw it away he could not come into any sympathetic or fertilizing contact with those who had not had that advantage. Coombes, in his sincere and deeply felt reply—a reply without any bitterness—took her to task about this, saying that it was precisely because of such advantages of education that the middle-class writer could be of help to working-class writers. And that in fact is precisely what Virginia herself had said some years before, in her ' Introductory Letter ' to a volume of reminiscences of working women called *Life as We Have Known it*. She had on that occasion even approved the mixing of language which she seemed to object to in *The Leaning Tower*. It was, I believe, a far truer expression of Virginia's deepest convictions when she wrote: 'If it were possible to meet them not as masters or customers with a counter between us, but over a washtub or in the parlour casually and congenially as fellow-beings with the same wants and ends in view, a great liberation would follow, and perhaps friendship and sympathy. How many words must lurk in those women's vocabularies that have faded from ours! How many scenes must lie dormant in their eyes which are unseen by ours! . . . And they remain equally deprived. For we have as much to give them as they to give us—wit and detachment, learning and poetry, and all those good gifts which those who have never answered bells or minded machines enjoy by right.'

Only a few years later, however, a request to write for a special English number of *Fontaine*, the French review that Max-Pol Fouchet had founded in Algiers, gave me a much more complete opportunity to crystallize all my thoughts and feelings about the wonderful person who had meant so much to me, and whose genius—when all that was of purely topical and polemical interest, all that was written to amuse friends or tease the fashion of the moment has been winnowed away—will stand out as one of the important events of the English spirit in the first half of this century.

9

ONE of the consequences of the arrangement I had made to spend part of each week in Cambridge, was meeting the young Greek poet and critic, Demetrios Capetanakis: for that alone I should hold it one of the most fortunate decisions I ever made.

I have written about Demetrios elsewhere, and have tried to give some idea of his remarkable appearance and personality, and to assess what is still to me one of the most extraordinary literary phenomena of the war-years: the poems and critical essays he began to write in English soon after I came to know him. We were only friends for three and a half years

in the middle of a war, a time when people are apt to embark
on friendships which fade away when more normal times return; but I cannot conceive that Demetrios could ever have
ceased to be my friend if he had survived into the peace, because he had a genius for friendship such as I have never known.
If he wanted to be your friend, he entered into your mind and
heart with an uncanny power of imaginative understanding
that he never allowed to become jealously possessive. His
tact was as unique as his perceptiveness, and because he had
certain very profound and unusual feelings about the meaning
of life and what was valuable in it, he would read your behaviour and the pattern of your existence as if interpreting a
secret language that revealed a far deeper significance than it
had been possible for you to see before. If he saw you dis-
heartened or confused, he could restore your faith in yourself
in the course of a brief conversation. So it was that being
with him was almost always an astonishingly stimulating experience: he would, as it were, hold up a looking-glass in front
of you in which you saw, not the face you had become accustomed to accepting as your own for so long, but a new face
with all sorts of potentialities you had allowed yourself to
ignore or forget, or had been discouraged into disbelieving, and
perhaps with scars on it you had long ceased to be aware of,
clues which explained many things that had puzzled you in
your relations with the world. And he would talk of mutual
friends in the same way, so that you saw them in a new light
too. It sometimes happened that the clarity of this strange
X-ray power of his was clouded by temporary infatuations
and repulsions; but this was rare, and again and again I found
—and I think his other English friends had the same experience
—that if I tested these intuitions of his, they proved accurate
and capable of transforming the climate of a life.

I had not been established in my little room in St. Edward's
Passage long, before I began to collect a small group of young
men interested in writing, who would come and talk over
drinks before dinner during my weekly sojourn. One of these,
Adrian Liddell-Hart, a freshman from Eton and son of the distinguished military historian, I had met in the rooms of George

Rylands, whose pupil he was; and one evening he appeared
at my door in his sky-blue polo jersey with Demetrios in tow.
He introduced him as a fellow-pupil of Dadie's, a fabulous
connoisseur of modern literature and a fan of *New Writing*. As
far as I remember, Demetrios did not say very much that first
evening, contenting himself with sitting quietly amongst us,
his enigmatic smile playing over his strangely mobile features
and giving them the look of an archaic Greek statue, and
occasionally breaking in with an absurdly humorous or enthusiastic observation that would immediately evoke Adrian's
convulsive laugh. It was not long, however, before we began
to see a great deal of one another, and his tongue was loosened
to discuss every conceivable aspect of books and their authors,
mutual friends and Cambridge figures about whom he could
be extremely amusing and malicious in the most unwounding
of ways, his experiences in Germany as a pupil of Jaspers and
among the disciples of Stefan George, modern Greece and
Greek civilization, and the meaning of the war for his own hard-
pressed countrymen. He used often to come up to the evening
gatherings of the young poets in St. Edward's Passage; sometimes we would meet for dinner at the Arts Theatre Restaurant,
or go to see a particularly interesting play that was on. When
he came to live in London about a year later, and to work for
the exiled Greek Government, I saw even more of him, and
scarcely a day passed when, if we did not actually see one another, we failed to ring one another up.

From the very first he showed an immense interest in *New
Writing*, the back numbers of which he had managed somehow
to swallow whole since his arrival in England the year before.
The enthusiasm and passionate curiosity which he lavished on
every detail connected with it buoyed me up and gave me fresh
confidence at times when practical difficulties, emotional complications and jangled nerves seemed about to overcome me.
He was always keenly ready to discuss general plans or special
contributions for coming numbers, and I cannot remember a
single occasion on which he failed me when I asked for his
advice or assistance. He was particularly helpful in connection with the European contributions, as his knowledge of
the European literature and thought of our time was enormous,

and disciplined; and, of course, above all in connection with
Greek literature. He it was who first introduced me to the
great achievements of modern Greek poetry. He would talk
for hours about Cavafy, about that noble sage of Athens,
Angelos Sikelianos, and George Seferis, who was a close personal friend of his and happened at that time to be Greek
Consul in Cape Town; and I persuaded him to translate some
of the poems of these poets, and others such as Pantelis Prevelakis and Odysseus Elytis, which I could publish in *New
Writing*. Thus began an association with Greek poetry which
lasted all through the war and into the first years of peace, one
of the features of *New Writing* that gives me the greatest pleasure
to look back on; and one of its results was that Demetrios
himself began to write poems and articles for *New Writing*.
Fascinated by the way he talked about Rimbaud, Dostoevsky,
Rilke and other ' ancestor ' figures, I persuaded him to write
studies of them which would reveal the extraordinary quality
of his thought. *Rimbaud* was the first; like everything else he
wrote at this time, it was the fruit of long, arduous struggles
of mind and spirit, more the resolution of problems of philosophy and belief, projected by personal experience, than the
detached study of a literary expert. Indeed, he could not
during these last years of his life write with any such detachment, and the quality of intimate engagement with his subject
which all his *New Writing* studies possess was precisely what
struck his readers, and made them feel that someone had at last
got away from the kind of polished, superior *causerie* that so
much literary criticism seems—in this country at least—so easily
to slip into. Just before he finished *Rimbaud*, he wrote me a
revealing letter from Cambridge:

I have thought and am still thinking of all the interesting things
you said the other evening. I reread *To the Lighthouse* and I was
so surprised to see how much better I understood its secret language this time. I kept some notes—perhaps they will help me
to understand better her other works and to find out if she is
really the woman of whom Rimbaud speaks in his famous letter
about ' le voyant '. . . . I am just writing the last lines of my
Rimbaud. I have worked on it these last days with almost
no interruptions—I was so frightened of interruptions!—and I

I

am rather satisfied with it.   I believe that no one else understood him.   I put everything I have to say in it.   It was the only
subject that would save me from madness or death.   Tomorrow I
shall start revising, correcting, completing, typing it out.—But
what shall I do when I shall have finished with it?   I am so
frightened.—Fortunately I have just had a very vague answer
from the British Council saying that they sent my particulars to
the Ministry of Labour and the B.B.C.   That means I shall have
a few days of respite—to finish Rimbaud.   That is all I want.

Then came the day when he brought me, out of the blue,
his first poem in English, *Detective Story*, which under the de-
ceptive simplicity of its form and statement, concealed some
of his deepest philosophical speculations:

> The stranger left the house in the small hours;
> A neighbour heard his steps between two dreams;
> The body was discovered strewn with flowers;
> Their evenings were too passionate, it seems.
>
> They used to be together quite a lot;
> The friend was dressed in black, distinguished looking
> The porter said; his wife had always thought
> They were so nice and interested in cooking.
>
> And this was true perhaps.   The other night
> They made a soup that was a great success;
> They drank some lager too and all was right.
> The talk, the kisses and at last the chess.
>
> ' It was great fun! ' they said; yet their true love
> Throbbed in their breasts like pus that must be freed.
> The porter found the weapon and the glove,
> But only our despair can find the creed.

The easy, conversational tone worked into a tight stanza
pattern was an altogether astonishing achievement for a
foreigner whose intimacy with our language was little more
than a year old; the dramatic concentration, the metaphysical
overtones in a poem of only sixteen lines something that very
few English poets of the time, straining as they were after far-
fetched effects, were capable of; it made a deep impression on

all who read it, and seemed to me to offer the promise of a new break, of infinite possibility, in the poetry of our time.

The appearance of his poems and articles in *New Writing*, however, troubled Demetrios as much as it delighted him. He wanted our friendship to be so entirely without a shadow, that the thought of my professional, editorial self bent over them, blue pencil in hand, agitated him. He had, I suppose, carefully noted my obstinacy and what he called my ' ruthlessness ' in dealing with the contributions of even very close friends, and he dreaded the tension that might arise between us over his own work. Some months before he actually started writing for me, he sent me the beginning of a (never finished) novel, and said: ' I want you to read it as a friend—not as a critic or a publisher. I hope you will never be a publisher to me. It is perhaps ridiculous to make such distinctions, but I shall always be only your friend and nothing but your friend.'

As it turned out, his fears were unjustified and some of the most delightful times we spent together were in discussing possible modifications and developments to poems and articles he wrote for *New Writing*. Partly this came from the fact that I was genuinely excited about them, partly because I had started writing poetry again myself, and found him the most acute and stimulating of advisers—though a great deal too indulgent to my faults. So the criticism was mutual; and I am convinced that if it had not been for his endless, insistent coaxing and enthusiasm, his absolute rejection of my own doubts about my very minor gifts as a poet, his habit of ringing up and reporting to me the favourable things he had heard other people say about my work, I might never have found the power to go back to poetry in the middle of all the strains and responsibilities of life in London under siege. That he was a dangerous flatterer to those whose work he admired, other people can testify besides myself; but perhaps even the humblest artist needs the kind of faith and encouragement to work his tiny territory that Demetrios gave me; that breathes from his letters to me when I told him that I had some new poems of my own ready: ' I hope I will be one of the first people who will read them. Don't forget that, please! I believe I have the right to ask for this privilege, because I feel that I understand your work so well.'

Among the other young poets I used to see during these mid-week sojourns in Cambridge were Donald Bain, Maurice James Craig, Mark Holloway, Nicholas Moore, occasionally Anthony Huxley, Julian's son, and Alex Comfort. The last-named joined us as a travel-writer, for I had accepted for *The Geographical Magazine* an extremely fresh and vividly written sketch he had sent in without any personal information, and discovered only afterwards that he was an undergraduate. He sat with us smiling, saying hardly anything, while his fellow undergraduates argued hotly about Yeats, Auden, Spender, Rimbaud and Rilke. I felt rather embarrassed, imagining that the polite smile concealed a tough young adventurer's contempt for all this intellectual theorizing and sissy chatter about poetry, and perhaps even a desire to chuck one or two of my guests into a college fountain. . . . It was an entertaining irony, therefore, when he emerged a year or two later as one of the most intellectual of the poets of his generation, the most fiercely given to controversy, the most determined to question the claims of the poets of the 'thirties to continuing respect. It is good for an editor to receive such shocks to remind him how wrong he can go in his first judgements; and when Alex Comfort's poems began to pour into the magazines I remembered an occasion of equal shock in the early 'thirties when I was editing *The Year's Poetry* with Denys Kilham Roberts. I discovered among the MSS. sent in a batch of what seemed to me quite remarkable nature poems by a new young poet—by the name of Andrew Young. I wrote him a rather patronizing letter of encouragement: my face was red, when I discovered from his reply that he was a middle-aged cleric of the Church of England, who had been writing poetry for years.

Maurice Craig struck me at that time as the most gifted of the group, with an aggressively forceful personality. He had an Irishman's love of argument for the sake of argument, and would often vigorously attack some proposition which he had defended equally vigorously the week before. His patriotic feelings were ardent, and he would not allow anyone to say a slighting word about Eire's neutrality, from which we were all suffering rather more than trifling inconvenience at the time. When it was suggested to him that his country's invulnerability was a fiction sustained by the British Navy, without the presence of which Hitler could invade his country any time he chose, he replied hotly that Ireland had a fine Navy of its own, capable of routing any invaders. On being asked to give some details of this Navy, he thought for a moment and then proudly declared: 'There's that gunboat we bought from Britain the other day, a ship to strike terror into the enemy's breast when manned by Irish boys.' He, Donald Bain and Nicholas Moore were very keen to follow up *Cambridge Poetry*, which we were about to publish in the *Poets of Tomorrow* series, by a revival of the undergraduate literary magazine *Cambridge Front*. I promised to give it my support, and many discussions went on about who was to edit and who to be invited to contribute: these discussions illustrated the fact that the war had not yet made deep enough inroads to destroy the intensity of the politics of undergraduate life. I could almost feel myself back again in the exciting world of literary faction and counter-faction which had produced *The Venture* and *Experiment* ten years before. And yet the impression grew, as I got to know this generation of undergraduates more intimately, that they were in some important way very different from my own generation or those who followed us—with John Cornford among their leaders—a few years later. My own contemporaries had not, while at Cambridge, been political as Cornford's generation, with the discovery of anti-fascist faith and a Spanish cause to die for; but, like them, we had at least a positive belief in the value of public as well as private activity. Maurice Craig's generation (though of course there were individual exceptions) struck me as being without any faith or spiritual impulse. Deep down, I began to feel with increasing dismay, there was an emptiness that reminded me of the Germans of the same generation I had known before war broke out. In pessimistic moments I became convinced that the inevitable result would be, as it had been in Germany, that the emptiness could only be filled by one thing: the impulse to destroy. And I remembered my long conversation with David Gascoyne, one evening the winter before, in which he had maintained that the war in reality was nothing but a gigantic extension of the modern world craving to experience the void. No doubt my intuition went too far; the course of the war was to prove that in Britain's case the cement of our civilization held against this assault of nothingness; but there were times when the truth seemed to lie in Demetrios's lines:

> And all mankind's despair becomes one cry:
>
> ' O look at us! how nothingness has preyed
> Upon our faces full of cracks and holes
> Opening to the void that will invade
> Even the core of our deserted souls! '

10

THE new turn of the war provided another revelation of spiritual change in our familiar world. All kinds of people, especially young people, were continually astonishing one by displaying qualities of endurance and stoic fortitude that one had not suspected, that one had never thought likely they possessed.

A young man whom a casual label-fixer might have written off as a ' sissy ', an enthusiastic follower of *New Writing* and the left-wing writers' movement, an adoring gallery fan of anyone with ' glamour ' in the world of the theatre and ballet, gentle-voiced, sensitive and shy, worked as a doctor's assistant on rescue parties all through the raids, was witness of the most nerve-shattering scenes of suffering and mutilation while in constant danger of falling bombs and collapsing buildings himself, and yet seemed cool and quite unshaken by it all and spoke of his experiences with a quiet objectivity that disclosed only as an undertone how deeply he had been moved.

One day, in the train between Letchworth and King's Cross, I found myself alone with a night-fighter sergeant-pilot, a stocky pleasant-smiling boy of twenty-one. He immediately got into conversation with me, and told me that he had already had one crash and had also had to bale out on another occasion. It had shaken his nerve, yes, but he was O.K. now: pilots often lost their nerve for a time after a bad experience, but generally recovered it fairly soon. He warmed to the subject of the class distinctions between officer-pilots and sergeant-pilots in the R.A.F., so rigidly insisted on by the hierarchy and yet so absurd when they were both doing the same job. He told me how difficult it was to get on to the track of the enemy at all at night, and how they all prayed for bad weather to keep the Germans away. There were no false heroics about his story. I found it difficult to believe that such an unaffected, frank and even awkwardly schoolboyish type was actually one of the intrepid pilots whom we civilians looked up to with such humble respect as our guardians and avengers. His remark that death became very matter-of-fact, not to be worried about too much, haunted me for a long time after he had said good-bye to me at King's Cross.

Some weeks later, I had to make a journey to the North, and I noticed on the platform at Euston a shabbily dressed boy with a big, round face, and a woman who was evidently his mother beside him, dressed in black, with the same big, round face, rather tear stained. When the train was about to move off, he got into my carriage and very soon began talking; it was clear that he *had* to talk to someone. In a rapid Cockney patter he poured out the grim story behind that farewell scene, and all with the same simple, innocently friendly expression on his big face. His father had been killed by a bomb only the week before, while he was on Home Guard duty somewhere in London. Their house had been wrecked in the blitz, and now he himself had been called up: his mother was left on her own to look after his younger brother and sister, and he didn't know how she'd manage. There was no trace of bitterness in his voice, even when he described how it was only because of a piece of bureaucratic bungling that his father had been on guard at all the night he was killed. He wrung my hand warmly when he got out at the junction to find the train to his unit; leaving me to wonder how many other tragedies of the

same sort lay behind the uncomplaining, friendly faces of the
recruits one saw milling about the platforms at every station
the train drew into.

Among one's own circle of friends and acquaintances too
the same heart-warming surprises lay in wait for one: younger
friends, for instance, who volunteered for military service before their time came, and though of highly strung imaginative
temperament, or more bookish and artistic than athletic, decided that the plunge, however icy, was better taken in freedom than under compulsion; sometimes discovering unexpected rewards—especially I think in the naval training estab-
lishments—in the gaiety, kindliness and adventurous confidence
of their fellow volunteers and conscripts gathered from all
classes.   But fortitude was not the privilege only of those who
left for the battles.   Pip Dyer, artistic in feeling through and
through, whom I had got to know by chance through his love
of Austria and keen interest in *New Writing*, had been turned
into a pacifist by the tragic experiences of his father in the
first world war, and came to the conclusion that he could not
kill anyone whatever the uniform he wore, and must therefore
be a Conscientious Objector.   From the point of view of the
tribunals and their categories, his case was flimsy; but he
stuck to his convictions and went to gaol, and even a long
succession of nights of blitz while he was locked in a cell on the
top floor of a London prison failed to make him ' repent ' or
retract.   No gentle and sensitive person could fail to suffer
abominably under such circumstances; but his letters were as
unruffled and uncomplaining as if he had been in a monastic
retreat a thousand miles away from the war.

The scientists tell us that during this period we were all
doped with self-secreted adrenalin, that marvellously helped
us to endure things that had appeared totally unendurable in
prospect.   For me, and for many of my friends still carrying
on professionally or assimilated into the war bureaucracy, I
think work was the real adrenalin.   To have to answer letters,
to have to go on reading manuscripts, to have to go on making
one's business plans and calculations, whether bombs were
falling in the distance or not, prevented the imagination from
straying too far and steadied the nerve quite remarkably.

Actors and dancers found, I believe, the same; in fact, if the sirens went, it was more difficult to remain unconcerned when one was a spectator in front than while one was performing on the stage; and I remember marvelling at the coolness with which a group of dancers pursued their precise and delicate evolutions one evening when a bomb happened to fall quite close to the theatre—and shook me as well as the walls of the building.

I was particularly buoyed up myself by the feeling that grew in me, that the work I was doing with *Folios* and *Penguin New Writing*, and believed I could extend through my direction of The Hogarth Press, had something more than a marginal importance in the revolution through which we were going. It induced a curious confidence in spite of all that was so uncertain in the future, and this confidence was reinforced by many of the multitude of letters that were reaching me, and by many chance remarks made by friends and even scarcely known people I met. Like all other fervent creeds, it was, I suppose, a kind of drug; though I did not go so far as to believe that I should immediately be translated to Paradise if killed while working on the next number.

Again, I found extraordinary comfort and refreshment, as I believe many other people did, from reading the longer classics of poetry or fiction, books of history and biography that I had not touched for many years: *The Prelude*, for instance, Byron's Letters and Journals, Fisher's *History of Europe*. It was a curious and exciting experience to read Arthur Koestler's masterpiece *Darkness at Noon*, which had just come out, at the same time as Wordsworth's story of his disillusionment with the French Revolution; the same story in each of idealists turning into despots more ruthless and bloodthirsty than the traditional despots they had dethroned; of what stood at the end of the road when, in the impatience of their fanaticism, good men persuaded themselves that ends justified means, and believed that the millennium, that dream of universal peace and brotherhood that Fisher revealed as an ever recurring dream of European man since the collapse of the Roman Empire, could be established tomorrow if enough throats were cut today.

As the Spring advanced, the raids grew more violent. The

bunks in the tube stations, to which a multitude of old people and women and children had fled, ignoring official objections, when the raids began in September, were packed every night: a phantasmagoric troglodyte population, never to be forgotten even if it had not been recorded, with profound imaginative insight and tragic power, by Henry Moore in his *Pink and Green Sleepers*.   One was conscious every now and then of a dangerous increase of strain, of one's reserve tank of strength falling precariously low.   One knew that the war at sea was intensifying, though rationing still functioned smoothly enough.   One was bleakly aware that the enormous resources of America, in spite of the active sympathy of the Roosevelt administration, were still not wholly committed to the British cause.   One put these thoughts away from one.

In order to have a more permanent pied-à-terre in London, I had, early in the year, taken an apartment in Athenaeum Court in Piccadilly, overlooking Green Park: it had many advantages, not the least of them being its solid modern structure of steel and concrete.   On the evening of Saturday, May 10th, I got home from Soho to my apartment about eleven o'clock.   Almost immediately the bombardment began; it did not stop until dawn.   Sleep was out of the question, with the continuous barking of the guns, the whistle and roar of the bombs, the deafening unheralded explosions of the parachute-mines, the whining zoom of dive-bombers.   The whole building swayed as if on a pivot, while the windows shook and the furniture trembled.   From time to time one heard incendiaries clatter down, and soon the air was filled with the smell of burning from behind the house: the lurid glow, as one peered between the black-out curtains, revealed that Park Lane and Shepherd Market were a raging fire.   In the early hours of the morning I went out to the fire-escape several times, to see the blazing fragments floating through the air over our roof.   There were too many calls on the N.F.S. that night, and it was not till long after daybreak that the fires were brought under control.   Athenaeum Court was, astonishingly, unscathed; and the best thing to do in the morning seemed, as usual, to change the water in the flower-vases.   But I felt as if I had had a very bad channel crossing.

A few days later, I had to find a small street in the City, and was taken by my taxi a long zig-zag drive through many of the worst bombed areas. The impression of devastation was stupendous; and yet it struck me as having a kind of fantastic beauty. If London had to be abandoned one day, and stillness descended on the wreckage, with green branches showing through the blank windows of church walls—walls still standing when roofs had fallen in—with the tangled girders of office blocks, the jumbled heaps of masonry, the broken statues, the bisected rooms, and weeds and flowers thickening through every crevice, it would, I thought, be a more extra-ordinary sight than eighteenth-century Rome as one sees it in the old prints of Piranesi and his followers.

If London had to be abandoned one day. . . . That thought was a little more real in those days than one likes to remember now. How many more raids like the one we had just experienced could the functioning of the city stand? And if they were stepped up, as seemed to be happening? What comfort was it if the German cities were also being smashed to bits? How much longer would the morale of the exhausted ants who still lived and worked in London hold?

But the raids, except for a rare and sudden retaliation for an attack of ours on Berlin, were over for a long time, though we could not know it then. That strange period in the life of war-time Londoners, the three-year breathing space, had begun, while Hitler's forces turned and massed themselves for the blow against Russia that even Stalin refused to believe was imminent.

III

THE OTHER DIMENSION

AT about this time I went through a severe emotional and spiritual crisis, about which I still find it difficult to speak coherently. I emerged from it, I believe, in many ways a different person; not different, perhaps, in what is called character—for the mixture of virtues and weaknesses in my nature remained much the same, and my will remained dominant, though only just, over my senses and emotions; but different in the way I interpreted our human existence in the world, and in my whole scale of values. Like someone who has hitherto been deaf to certain notes at the end of the scale, I began gradually to be aware of possibilities in experience that I would never have admitted before, and at the same time to find the universe immensely more mysterious. The change was not simply due to a sudden revelation, but was, I can now see, something towards which my thought had been tending for some time; the emotional crisis precipitated and completed it in rather a violent and frightening way. It is possible that if my upbringing had been different, and if some very persuasive and perceptive missionary had been at my side at the time, religion would thereafter have played a large part in my life.

The main record I have of this crisis is in a sequence of prose poems I wrote while I was experiencing the full force of it: I called them *Vigils*. I chose this form, partly because I had for years been interested in experimenting in prose poems, which I believed from my study of modern French and German literature to have possibilities that English poets had neglected; but more, at this moment, because I felt that the argument I was embarking upon was complex and difficult, that I would not know its outcome until I came to the end of writing the poems, and that it was absolutely essential not to falsify even the smallest detail in the interests of musical harmony, rhyme or metrical balance. It is in fact a measure of the limits of my strength as a poet, that I did not dare subject my thought, in

the midst of my spiritual upheaval, to the rigorous formal demands of any poetic stanza, even of the most accommodating
kind.

Three elements came together at the same time to make this
crisis acute: an unhappy love-affair, an entirely new sense of
death as nothingness in the midst of life and an almost unendurable anxiety about a younger friend who had gone to sea
in a state, I knew, of despair. These three elements interacted
to draw up the tidal wave which engulfed me for some months.
It was an experience of the deepest confusion and agony of
spirit; and yet when the waters ebbed and I gradually began
to lift myself, with the aid of friends and work, out of the submerged and glaucous state of being so unhappily in love, I felt,
paradoxically, that the ordinary dry-shore life to which I was
returning, with its smiling reassurances and solidity, the sun
shining on all the routine activities and daily preoccupations
of men, was almost ridiculously trivial and empty of meaning.
It was as if I were coming to from the effects of a drug, and
though the state of mind the drug had induced had been mostly
painful, and in a quite unprecedented way, the pain had nevertheless had some intense meaning which was all that mattered.

The partings of lovers during the war were especially hard
to bear, because of the danger which lurked everywhere and
the fear that every goodbye embrace would be the last; but
when suspicion and jealousy suddenly began to play their evil
role in the midst of these partings, the naked dependence of
one soul on another, which is the extreme of love, made the
suffering all but intolerable. Then the need for absolute
certainties became desperate, and the more desperate it became
the more impossible of satisfaction it revealed itself. One had
opened a trap-door to a shaft of blackness that stretched down
beyond knowing: everything seemed insecure and capable
without warning of turning into its opposite: and the result
was, of course, the total destruction of the relationship while
one floundered and twisted in the accelerating panic of insecurity. And yet probably the love was there all the time.

Now this terror began to mesh in a diabolical gyration with
the feeling I had of guilt and inadequacy in having let my
friend, who had joined up on a sudden impulse earlier than he

needed, go to sea in what appeared to me from what he had
said before leaving and what his subsequent letters revealed to
be a state of total unbelief and despair; with no conviction to
hold on to, and no ideal to live for. The sea itself became a
symbol of his despair; and I was filled with horror at the
thought of his possible death, in the dangerous convoy work
in which he was engaged, before this void of the spirit could be
filled. The desire to be destroyed seemed no better than the
desire to destroy; and as I had in the preceding years come to
see that the latter arose in our time from a vacancy of belief,
so I now saw the former as a direct result of the same despair.

In this double agony, it was as if I were holding a thinly
constructed door against a great tornado of nothingness. And
at the same time the continual facing of death, that had become almost as much the civilian's lot as the soldier's, at least if
he lived in any of the target cities of the warring nations, made
me realize that every one of the notions of survival or restitu-
tion with which men comforted themselves, was, if closely
examined, a deception or without certainty or proof. Not
merely the notions of after-life, but the notions also of surviving
as part of the thought of one's friends among scenes and objects
impregnated in some degree with one's personality. In the
war in which we were engaged, one had to envisage the total
destruction of a civilization, as it had not been since the
remote past:

> But if the pounding of the guns, the plunging of the massed bomb-
> racks rubs out, not just this house and that, but the whole monu-
> ment of love and history? Sands have covered cities, every stone
> lost and skulls forgotten. . . .

All of this long internal torment I tried to state, in its dialectical development, in *Vigils*; coming to the affirmation at
the end, almost without knowing that I was arriving there,
that even if the insistent presence of death was the trigger of
the whole crisis, one could not construct any worthwhile
philosophy without the experience of that presence. Demetrios was, very soon after, to put it exactly as I felt it, in words I
can never forget, at the end of his essay on Rimbaud: ' Nothingness might save or destroy those who face it, but those who

K

ignore it are condemned to unreality.   They cannot pretend to
a real life, which if it is full of real risks, is also full of real promises.'

I had learnt a great deal; and seen through a great deal.   I
knew now that existence was a mystery, which it was pre-
sumptuous ever to pretend fully to understand.   And that
even if we must try to understand it, and construct a working
system of values on that understanding, we have to realize that
our organs of perception are imperfect: there are forces in life
that defy our attempt to grasp them, and no construction was
so certain that we could be justified in forcing it on others.
Certainty, indeed, was a mirage;   the desire for the absolute
the most dangerous as well as the most useless of human
pursuits.

At the same time, I had come to a very curious conviction,
or rather, perhaps, intuition;   curious, that is, for one of my
sceptical and agnostic habit of mind.   In the midst of the
nightmares into which jealousy and the discovery of falsehoods
and infidelities in the loved one plunged me, I became haunted
by the feeling that these cruelties were, in a sense, involuntary.
I could not, I found, honestly say any longer that the person I
loved was callous, cold, evil or calculating in intent: in an
extraordinary way it seemed to me that this person was suffering as much as I was, was a *victim* as I was a victim of ex-
traneous forces that worked against love.   So it was that I
began, in my tortured confusion, to believe in demons, spirits
of evil that could capture and possess a human being, child of
love, an eternal soul exposed to the cross-fire of the battle of
life.

I am trying now only to put down, as faithfully as possible,
my mood and reasoning of the time.   But my future thinking,
my future action during the war years was conditioned by
these new discoveries and intimations.   In the poems I began
to write a little later, I was constantly trying to explore and
enlarge them, and to find adequate images for them.   They
gave me, above all, a new belief in poetry, in all art;   for only
in that supra-rational activity of the imagination did it seem to
me possible to express, and convey to the general mind, the complexity and paradox of the truth.   I wanted to bring that belief

to all those young people who, like my friend at sea, were looking for something deeper than a political faith, something more accessible than a religion hedged with dogmatic tenets; and at the same time to make their voices heard as they really were, in the authentic accents of their generation.

If I could do something towards this, I thought, I should not be wasting my time, in the midst of the destruction and the destroying creeds. As I struggled out of the unhappy love-affair, as I was lifted from the sucking mud of nihilistic doubt and confusion, it seemed that positive energies, inverse in strength to what had pulled me down, had been released in me to devote to these tasks that lay before me.

IV

YEARS OF THE AIRGRAPH

I

By the middle of 1942 my life had acquired a fairly regular, busy rhythm, very different from the kind of life I could possibly have envisaged for myself when the war broke out. We had lost Europe, we had been attacked with all the fury of modern aerial warfare, but we had survived the attack and kept our shores inviolate; and above all we had gained two gigantic allies in Russia and the United States. And now, after nearly three years of war, one was living in a not uncomfortable or uncivilized way, with minor deprivations and sacrifices but many compensations in stimulus for the mind and imagination; the chief one being the discovery that it was possible to go through ' all the dreaded cards foretold ' and still exist, still be sitting at one's desk and even booking a table at the Ivy for luncheon. There were dangerous moments when one was almost lulled into thinking that, as far as our own little islands were concerned, the Four Horsemen had ceased to ride; only one's constantly renewed anxiety for friends at sea, or in the African battles, and—in my own case— the awareness that my Austrian friends were bound to be involved in the sickening, never-ending slaughter on the Russo-German front, kept at bay the illusion that war could become a tolerable, settled way of life. Reason now as well as faith began to assure one that one's own side was not going to lose; one only pretended still to believe in invasion or a renewal of air-raids on the 1940–41 scale; Hitler's ' secret weapon ' had become little more than a joke, and my unscientific mind—like the minds of most of my friends—did not see as far as rockets and flying bombs.

After Michael Nelson was called up early in 1941, Sonia Brownell became my secretary, but left after some months to work in The Ministry of War Transport. I had a great fondness for the pretty, blonde-haired, vivacious Sonia, with her darting, gaily cynical intelligence and insatiable appetite for

everything that went on in the literary world: her revolt
against a convent upbringing seemed to provide her life in
those days with a kind of inexhaustible rocket fuel.   Later
still, she joined *Horizon*, in which she played an increasingly
vital role as Cyril's assistant, and provided yet another intimate link between the two supposedly hostile camps; and at
the end of his life, after the war, married George Orwell.   Her
place on *New Writing* was taken by Barbara Cooper: by a
lucky chance Leonard Strong, for whom she had been doing
some part-time work, heard that she was answering my adver-
tisement, and sent her along with a strong recommendation.
Thus began a partnership which, through many literary vicissi-
tudes, has lasted until today.   She quickly became devoted to
New Writing, which she had not known before, and began to
display three qualities which from the point of view of a literary
editor were almost—in combination—too good to be true:
a near-fanatical loyalty, an infallible memory and an unquenchable zest for reading manuscripts, no matter how dreary,
pompous, silly, ill-written or ill-typed.

Meanwhile, at the end of 1941, I had moved from Athenaeum Court to a flat high up in Carrington House, just behind
it in Shepherd Market.   With the end of the raids, it seemed
not unreasonable to take a three-year lease on a flat; and the
gain, with my increasing work and the opportunity it gave me
to entertain as well as to spread my books and papers around
me, treating it partly as an office, was immense.   It became so
useful, and I became so attached to it, that when the raids did
start again three years later, I stayed on.   It seemed as good
a place as any in which to face mutilation—or death—though
definitely not in the official shelter, which was in the deep basement, amid a formidable tangle of huge hot water pipes next
to the oil-fired boiler.   Instead, I used to drag a mattress out
into the passage, which was protected at least from flying glass.

My work as unpaid literary critic and adviser, and then, for
a few months, literary editor on *Tribune*, a job I took on out of
enthusiasm and sympathy for its antinomial left-wing views,
and interest in the personalities who ran it, came to an end
in the Spring of 1942: I do not think either Nye Bevan or
George Strauss was entirely happy about the evolution of my

political thought, which must have been implicit in what I wrote, and I was discouraged by the very small success I had had in persuading either of them that a really quite trifling expenditure in fees to contributors would pay off in the end. After all the work I had put into it I was not particularly pleased at the manner of my chucking out; but I had become very happily engrossed in work for *The Geographical Magazine*, with which I had kept up a close and friendly connection ever since my days in Central Europe. When Michael Huxley left for war-work, Harold Raymond asked me if I would join Ivy Davison, who had taken over from Michael, as advisory editor. The intention was that I should help her in thinking up ideas for individual articles and series, and introducing new authors. It did not involve more than visiting the office one day a week for discussions and drafting of letters and interviews; and from November of 1940 to 1945 I thoroughly enjoyed this association. Ivy was one of the most intelligent women I have ever met, well-read, perceptive, witty and energetic; I liked her dog, too, which was important, and we had the fun of persuading many poets and novelists to write for a magazine they would not naturally have thought was ' for them ', and the readers to enjoy a new kind of article not strictly ' geographical '.

As far as the war itself went, the tribute I paid still consisted in part of week-end service with the Home Guard at Bourne End. The local allegiance appealed to me, and the early volunteers began to feel the warm bonds of being old soldiers together as the lads from the valley factories were drafted in. As time went on, however, Sundays when work was too pressing for me to slip away to Fieldhead became rather more frequent, and to salve my conscience I arranged to do occasional fire-watching in London as well. It consisted mainly of being ' on tap ' for the night, with spells of patrolling on the roof of Carrington House and observing the stars.

In addition, I had my work for the B.B.C. and the Ministry of Information. Apart from occasional broadcasts on English literary subjects in the Overseas Service, I did some war-propaganda broadcasts in the German Service, and then, finding I suppose some measure of approval, was asked to start a

regular series of broadcasts in the Austrian Service. These
services were controlled at the top by Graham Greene's
brother, Hugh Carleton Greene, who had come from the
foreign staff of the *Daily Telegraph*, and beneath an appearance
of kindly, boyish simplicity concealed a keen, cool brain and a
shrewd grasp of political realities. Under him, Patrick Smith
was in charge of the broadcasts to Austria; but my actual
coaching was always done by German-speaking refugees, with
one of whom, Heinrich Fischer, I formed a lasting friendship.
The coaching, which generally included tearing to pieces the
script I had written with such anxious care and starting again
as soon as I had tried my voice on it, was pretty ruthless (as it
had to be, especially as there was never enough time), but,
however bruised and battered my ego, I never ceased to find it
a strange and rather thrilling experience to be launching my
voice into the ether, to be caught in the darkness (the trans-
missions were always at night) by an absolutely unknown,
secret audience, which perhaps included some of my own
special friends of the past. ' Lieber Pepi . . .' they began,
addressing an imaginary Austrian I might have known; but
the single person one knew for certain would be listening was
the monitor in Berlin. Anonymous, invisible, he became
almost a friend, as one imagined his technical appraisal night
after night. I learnt a lot about broadcasting in this hard
school, and I do not think that without the wartime training
in problems of pitch, pace of delivery, clarity of expression and
knowledge of my own voice, I should have come to literary
broadcasting after the war with a certain confidence and crafts-
man's pleasure.

My work for the Ministry of Information was all to do with
Russia, and started quite unexpectedly, a few months after the
Nazi attack on Russia, with a sudden barrage of telegrams from
my old pre-war acquaintance Timofei Rokotov, editor of
Internationalnaya Literatura in Moscow. He had decided to
TAKE OPPORTUNITY GREET LONGSTANDING FRIEND COMRADE IN
ARMS AGAINST NAZI TYRANNY; he wanted regular information
about the wartime activities of English writers, and regular
reviews of outstanding English books as they came out; and
he demanded that the latest issues of *New Writing* should be

sent to him, if possible by aeroplane. I did not at first see how I was to comply with all these urgent requests; but it was at least clear to me that a door had been opened through which one might be able to push some very useful propaganda for English literature and the war-effort with the minority but influential public that would be reading Rokotov's monthly. Soon after, however, something equally unexpected happened; the new British Ambassador at Moscow, Sir Archibald Clark-Kerr, who had made friends with Christopher and Wystan on their trip to China, and had long been a keen reader of *New Writing*, suggested in high quarters that I ought to be used in some way to further Anglo-Russian relations. Peter Smollett, head of the newly organized Russian department in the Ministry of Information, got in touch with me, and I took Rokotov's telegrams along with me to the meeting. The result was that he gave his enthusiastic backing to a scheme by which I sent an article each month to Moscow dealing with all the points that Rokotov had raised. I was to be allowed 5,000 words free cabling for every article, and could keep the fee the Russians promised to send. Rokotov appeared as pleased as I was.

At this distance of time, I do not know how I managed to add this work to all the other work I was doing; I can only fall back on the explanation which I have already mentioned and which many others have advanced for the extra energy they discovered they could tap during the war: that the presence of danger to one's country as well as oneself, caused some gland to pump a stimulating substance with the action of adrenalin into one's blood-stream. It was fun to do, but involved a great deal of gathering and sifting and reading, and snags of an awkward nature kept on cropping up, mainly due to the entirely different conceptions of the role of imaginative writers and artists in war-time which existed in Churchillian Britain and Stalinist Russia. Some idea of these snags will, perhaps, be conveyed if I quote the telegram I received from Moscow after I had sent off the fourth article in the series:

FOURTH ARTICLE RECEIVED SURPRISED ABSENCE FACTS ABOUT MOVEMENT AMONGST ENGLISH INTELLECTUALS FOR QUICKER OPENING SECOND FRONT PLEASE GIVE ITS RIGHTFUL SPACE TO

THIS IN YOUR NEXT ARTICLE KINDLY FORWARD INFORMATION
ABOUT ROBERT GREENWOOD AUTHOR BUNTING AWAITING
MATERIAL SENT

Of course there was scarcely such a thing as a ' movement '
amongst English intellectuals (apart from the small group of
Communists and fellow travellers) for a quicker opening of the
second front, and I had to put up the best show I could by
enlarging on the enthusiasm and admiration of the British for
the way the Russians were fighting in their desperate campaign,
and on the importance of the war at sea and the African campaign to us. The work was further complicated by the fact
that the Russians appeared to know practically nothing about
the literary scene in England, except for Jack Lindsay and the
PEN Club which they were puzzled to find I didn't devote a
great deal more space to: early on I was abruptly bidden to
send DETAILED CHARACTERIZATIONS WORK OF MANY WRITERS
MENTIONED UNFAMILIAR TO US HENRY GREEN NORMAN CAMERON
LAURIE LEE WALTER ALLEN EVELYN WAUGH ELIZABETH BOWEN
WILLIAM PLOMER. Coping with this kind of request began to
sap my morale; and at the same time, by a curious process of
empathy, something of the high fervour of Soviet propaganda
began to creep into my style and made me wonder whether I
had actually written the articles that were sent off under my
name.

If for nothing else, the experience was extremely valuable
to me because it brought me the friendship of Archie Clark-
Kerr. He was an unconventional figure among career am-
bassadors, the very opposite of the kind of stuffed-shirt diplo-
matist that the Left delighted to caricature before the war;
forthright in speech, shrewd in judgement, impatient of red-
tape and red-tape-minded people, a polished wit when he
liked but also of an extremely earthy humour when he knew
his company, he seemed to me at times to belong in temperament more to the eighteenth-century world of squire and laird
than the high diplomatic and social circles in which he moved.
His most valuable asset, at the moment in history which coin-
cided with the peak of his career, was, I believe, a certain restlessness of temperament, which might by some strict judges

have been thought to be a flaw in a public servant: it gave him at any rate a keen interest in the lives of people far outside his own class bounds, a freshness of response to new ideas and new attitudes and an intuitive awareness of changes in the spirit of the age. It was, I feel fairly certain, this quality that made him such a success as Ambassador in China in the late 'thirties.

He arrived in London on leave in December, 1942, and announced that he wanted to take back with him to Russia as big a collection as possible of the works of young English writers and books about new trends in modern literature. He asked me to help him in the choice, and we arranged to meet at my flat one morning to discuss the details. In a few minutes we were as if old friends, and it was with some difficulty that I dissuaded him from demanding of authority that I return with him to Moscow. He described to me vividly the tribulations of the situation he found himself in, with the Russians so hard pressed by the German armies and so little appreciative of our inability to launch an immediate attack in Europe to relieve the pressure. I am inclined to think that one of the chief reasons why our relations with our new ally were not worse than they were, was the forcible conviction with which Archie put our case across, and his determination to get into direct, man-to-man relations with Stalin. It seemed that he had succeeded—as far as it was possible to succeed with the suspicious Oriental despot that Josef Djugashvili had become— to judge from his account of long sessions at the Kremlin during air-raids, when they retired to the deep shelters and swapped (through interpreters) decidedly risqué stories. Molotov, I gathered, was sometimes present; and not particularly amused. ' They call him Stone-bottom Molotov in Moscow,' said Archie, ' but as far as I'm concerned he's stone from top to bottom.'

He flattered me gracefully by saying that the only book he had with him on the aeroplane, when he was rushed to Moscow, was my *New Writing in Europe*; and we made out the memorandum of books to be sent to him by adding to and subtracting from the list recommended at the end of that volume. I was impressed at once by his open mind and liberal

ideas, and also by the speed with which he was summing up
an England he hadn't seen for years. He felt that the old
political alignments were out of date; that new men, neither of
the old Tory nor the traditional Labour type, must come to
power if England was to ride high on the wave of the future;
he felt that such a ' silent revolution ' must be supported by
the intellectuals, and asked anxiously to what extent the poets
and novelists and critics of my generation were interested in
politics, cared enough and understood enough to support
unconventional moves in the future. What did he think of
Winston? I asked him in return. Full of admiration himself, he nevertheless spoke dubiously of the ' yes-men ' who
surrounded him. What of Cripps, Morrison and the top
men on the Labour side? He himself had been much impressed with Morrison, and the way his ideas were developing;
and believed that Cripps, if he had a proper ' general staff '
to assist him, was capable of great things. At first he spoke
warmly of Eden, but later in our conversation he let it be
seen that he thought him too narrowly enclosed within the
walls of his own career.

Archie was extremely anxious to meet the young poets in
person, and I managed to arrange a party in my flat which
was attended by Stephen Spender, Louis MacNeice, Cecil
Day Lewis and others. Most of us sat on the floor, while
Archie discoursed on Russian war problems and the Russian
attitude to writing in wartime, and questioned us about our
own views and the work we were doing within the war bureaucracy: I think he was particularly interested to hear Stephen's
account of the new technique of discussion groups that had been
started in the N.F.S. since the end of the raids. It was an unusual kind of gathering for a British Ambassador to ask to
attend; and as he left Archie closed it by an unusual remark,
going up to Louis MacNeice and saying to him, as one Celt to
another: ' You are descended from a seal! '

Meanwhile, a mysterious silence had fallen on *Internationalnaya Literatura*: my last article had not been acknowledged,
and copies of the magazine failed to turn up. It was not,
however, until March that Archie, back in Russia, sent me a
letter of explanation:

In case nobody has told you, I take it upon myself to report to you the demise of ' Internationalnaya Literatura '. Some say that it was euthanasia, others that it was a painful end. It cannot have been lack of readers, for it was the most sought after publication in the country. Nor can it really have been lack of paper, for new publications appear. It looks as if some of old Peter's windows on the West are being banged. I shall tell you if I can get at the truth. I am doing what I can to settle down after the terrific stimulus of those few weeks at home, to which you, by the way, made so handsome a contribution. They have left me restless and even rebellious. . . . As the years rattle by and I get nearer and nearer to the museum I find it harder and harder to feel grown up, and hardest of all to be tolerant of my own preposterous way of life . . .

Soon after, the Ministry of Information arranged for me to do much the same kind of work for *Britanski Soyuznik*, the British propaganda newspaper which the Russians allowed us to publish over there, and which had a phenomenal success: its circulation was severely restricted by a meagre paper ration, but copies changed hands on the black market at high prices.

At the end of his letter, Archie added: ' Alas! I see that your intelligent young Greek Minister for War has got the sack.' This referred to a meeting I had arranged between Archie and Panayotis Canellopoulos, politician, philosopher, close friend of Demetrios and his former teacher and inspirer at Athens University: one of the most remarkable men that modern Greece has produced. He came over to London from Cairo—for the second time—to have talks with Anthony Eden and our Chiefs of Staff at the turn of the year. We had made friends on his previous visit; and one afternoon in January he rang the bell of my Carrington House flat, settled into my room as though he had been there dozens of times (we had only met at the Ritz before), and said at once: ' *Je me trouve chez moi ici!* ' On that occasion, and others later, he talked with brilliance, a stimulating and inspiring flow: he discussed the flawed soul of Germany, and the contrasting way in which the British character seemed to him to be extraordinarily integrated— ' *Ce synthèse de marchand et de poète est vraiment un chef d'œuvre* ';

he held forth on the need for continuing Anglo-Russian understanding after the war, within a new internationalism established on a recovery of a passionate—though not chauvinist—
national consciousness on the part of each nation, including our
own. Above all he was fascinating to listen to on the subject of Greece, and his conception of the role of a contemporary
statesman as ' only the most self-effacing mouthpiece of a
great people in an hour that would be known in history as
glory '. I was able to tell him that my brother-in-law had just
reported to me, on his return from Cairo, that he had a close
friend whose one idea was to return to express in action what
he felt in admiration and gratitude towards the Greeks for
their stand against Mussolini and Hitler. Canellopoulos en-
larged on the theme of the importance for future Anglo-Greek
relations of that moment of common destiny. He described,
too, how he had been exiled before the war by the Metaxas
government, and how he had gone on working on his great
book on European philosophy in spite of all obstacles and discomforts. His pale and ardent face seemed suffused with a
sacred inspiration as he spoke.

Archie Clark-Kerr was immensely interested to meet him
when I told him of his present political role and his pre-war
legend as the great philosophy teacher, and I arranged a luncheon at my flat, to which I also asked Demetrios and my sister
Rosamond. Archie found himself chiefly in the role of listener, for Canellopoulos seemed more than normally eloquent
and intellectually far-ranging that afternoon; and Archie
told me afterwards that it was a most refreshingly unusual
occasion for him. They discussed the Russian situation at
length, and Archie was able to warn Canellopoulos against
sending a military envoy to Kuibishev; but what delighted
Archie most was to find himself arguing about modern literature in general and Gertrude Stein in particular with another
allied man of affairs, a Greek poet and an English novelist, at
such a moment in the war.

Rosamond wrote to me afterwards: ' I am haunted by
Canellopoulos. One has the feeling, when one sees such a
head lit by the sombre aureole of destiny, that anything so
bright must come to confusion. I pray not.' But come to

Virginia Woolf, 1939

Christopher Isherwood

*from a last photograph in England
by the author*

Demetrios Capetanakis

confusion he did; and very soon after, when he fell a victim to particularly sordid Greek intrigues in North Africa, and had to resign, and retire into the political shadows for a long time.

2

FOR most of the war, running The Hogarth Press was hardly more than a kind of holding operation. Our paper ration was extremely small, and when the calls on it for the reprints in most urgent demand had been satisfied, there was very little over. It was essential to keep the important volumes in Virginia's Uniform Library in print, as also Freud's works in the International Psycho-Analytical Library (in ever-increasing demand in America). Only occasional new novels or biographies or works of criticism could be published. Virginia's posthumous papers were, of course, the most important: after *Between the Acts* we went on to another miscellaneous collection of essays and critical studies, *Death of the Moth*, and then decided to do the volume of collected stories, including the earliest stories in her 'new manner' published in 1922 as *Monday or Tuesday*, which she had been on the point of preparing at the time of her death. After some debate, Leonard decided to call it *A Haunted House*. Next in importance, to my mind, were Henry Green's novels, a sequence which seemed to me to be excitingly exploring new territory as they came out of his workshop, beginning with *Caught* in 1943. For a long time I hoped that I should also be able to publish more of Christopher's books, and the possibility of a new novel from him was always at the back of my mind when I was making my jigsaw puzzle calculations about our paper ration. But as he became more deeply involved with the Yoga movement in Hollywood, that hope began to fade. Early in 1943, in response to my persistent questioning, he wrote: ' What am I writing, you ask? Well, before the sudden call to the movie-swamp stopped it, I was beginning a study of Berthold working at Gaumont British, which I intend to call *Prater Violets*.

L

And after that, I want to do the story of Heinz. And, after that, a somewhat modified version of *Paul is Alone* (remember?). Three novelettes, to make a volume. Is it just a dream? I don't know. I was as excited as hell when I got ready to start: the only trouble is that I'll have to find a new *tone of voice*: because the ventriloquist has changed somehow, and needs a new dummy. . . .' The war was over, and I had already left the Hogarth, when *Prater Violet* arrived; and neither of the other two stories was ever completed. As some kind of compensation and substitute, Christopher sent us an unique and beautiful novel by Lincoln Kirstein, *For My Brother*.

Within these very narrow bounds, it seemed to me that the best way to show that our interest in the work of the younger writers was as keen as ever, was by keeping going the New Hogarth Library of cheap poetry books which we had started in 1940, and by continuing to produce the hard cover editions of *New Writing* twice a year: they were at least a nursery for talent which we might be able to foster in times to come when paper-rationing was abolished. Between 1941 and 1942, however, these hard-cover volumes underwent yet another metamorphosis.

More and more, as the war went on, Leonard left the running of the Press to me. He remained for most of the time at Rodmell, but full reports went to him several times a week; and sometimes I went down to visit him there. My first visit after Virginia's death has left an indelible impression: I was haunted all the time by the feeling of her presence in the house, and it was difficult to believe she would not appear at any moment, and light one of her home-made cigarettes in her long holder, and say, ' And now, John, tell us a little scandal. . . .' It was on that visit that Leonard told me that he had discovered six different typescript copies of Virginia's last essay on *Mrs. Thrale*, and further variants of some passages. Another occasion I vividly remember was about eighteen months later. We had had the idea of preparing an anthology, selected from all the poetry the Press had ever published, to celebrate the twenty-fifth anniversary of its foundation. We were going to call it *The Silver Anthology*, and we

even announced it in our advance lists for 1944.   As Leonard
had a complete collection of the publications of the Press at
Rodmell, we decided to do the work down there.   When I
arrived, I found him at the back of the house, sawing wood in
his corduroys and what I used to call his ' French poacher's '
coat.   The house was cold and damp, but filled with a great
litter of books and apples and papers and jars of honey and
jam that gave it a friendly feeling.   We tackled our routine
Hogarth work directly after tea, and went on steadily with only
short breaks to dinner.   After dinner, we had already begun
our work on *The Silver Anthology*, when sirens sounded, followed
swiftly by a noise of gunfire on all sides and a droning of aeroplanes that scarcely stopped for several hours.   One or two
extremely violent bursts of firing shook the house.   It flashed
into my mind that perhaps the Nazis were raiding London as a
reprisal for our raid on Berlin; and sure enough this proved to
be so, for I rang up the B.B.C. and found all the Austrian section
down in their shelters.   The raid died down again before midnight, while Leonard and I conducted one of our long, tussling
arguments about the future of Germany and the organization
of Europe after the war.   In the middle of the night it began
again, with violent, house-shaking gunfire and the continuous,
mosquito-persistent droning of aeroplanes.   We learnt next
morning that there had been two attacks on London, not heavy
but an occasion at least for a gala warning display of the terrific
new London barrage that had been developed since the 1940–
41 blitz had come to an end.   Most of the morning we again
spent crouching over the fire in the sitting-room at the top of
the house, with all the Hogarth books of poetry spread out
around us.   From time to time Leonard exclaimed: ' No,
he's a hopeless poet ', or ' You know, we really *did* print rather
well ', or ' That was one of Dotty's * insane choices . . . '.
By lunchtime we had broken the back of the job, and I left
on the afternoon train for London.

I have already described how my interest in the refugees
from the Czech lands and from Slovakia brought me into

* Lady Dorothy Wellesley, later Duchess of Wellington. See *The
Whispering Gallery*, p. 165.

contact with a young Czech writer by the name of Jiři Mucha,
who had been in France at the time of the collapse and was a
close friend of Dr. Hodža's son Fedor. Jiři, because of his
passionate interest in contemporary literature and art in
France, as well as in his own country and the other Slav lands,
was just the person I felt I needed to have as a collaborator if
the ideas of the old *New Writing* were to be kept alive during
the war. His Bohemian charm, his lively mind, his family
roots in the old Czech–French artistic association—his father's
signature can be found in the corner of many a famous Parisian
theatrical poster of the early part of the century—made him
one of the most delightful of companions, and we soon became
firm friends, with ambitious plans for developing the cultural
side of the new exiled alliances. Jiři told me that there were
not only a number of interesting Czech writers, poets, critics
and dramatic experts in London, but also several distinguished
Poles who cared for the same things of the mind and who were
European in spirit rather than chauvinistic. Could we not
get together to produce a magazine which would provide a
place for the Czech, Slovak and Polish intellectuals to meet
their English colleagues, and also their French colleagues whenever possible? I told him that one of my best friends was a
young Greek poet who was in touch, in various roundabout
ways, with all the Greek intellectuals of his generation; and
after meeting Demetrios, Jiři was enthusiastic that the Greeks
should play an important part in the projected magazine.

There were technical problems, of course; we needed more
paper and more financial backing than The Hogarth Press
could provide; and I dreaded stepping into the quagmire of
inter-allied bureaucratic priorities. Jiři, however, managed
in the end to arrange a meeting with Jan Masaryk, witty,
imaginative and thoroughly westernized, who must (I remain
convinced) have been the nicest man ever to become a politician in our time. He saw the point of our plans at once, and
showed himself personally enthusiastic. Very soon after, I
received a telephone message that he was going to give me all
the support possible, and our problems for the launching
melted away in an instant. We decided to call the new magazine *Daylight*, and Jiři set about organizing contributions from

the Slavonic side with all his zest and persuasive powers, while I handled the Anglo-Saxons, the French—as far as we could get them—and the Greeks.

The first volume of *Daylight* came out in the New Year of 1942. As it turned out, the English and the Czechs were most prominent in the volume; so much so that we felt obliged in our foreword to say that we hoped in future to represent in juster proportion all the ' other European peoples who have a common cause with the Anglo-Saxon world '. It is true that the eager co-operation of Demetrios provided not only an admirable piece from his own pen, *The Greeks are Human Beings*, but also some translations from the poetic sequence *Myths of Our History*, one of the major works of his friend George Seferis, and two poems of a younger Greek poet, Pantelis Prevelakis; but from France we only had the translation of René Avord's study from *La France Libre* of the situation of the French writers in both the occupied and unoccupied parts of France, though in an effort to keep the balance I added some new translations of Rimbaud's poems which Norman Cameron was at work on at that time.

What is striking about this volume when I look back on it is, first, the quality of the poetry, which included, besides the poems of Seferis, Prevelakis and Rimbaud, a fragment of a verse drama on the Spanish Civil War by Stephen Spender, one of David Gascoyne's most beautiful and characteristic poems, *Noctambules*, and translations from the Czech poets Halas and Nezval; and second, the unity of feeling among the critical studies about the spiritual crisis through which Europe was passing, the recognition in all of them of the fantastic dangers inherent in modern power once the checks of the moral order were abandoned. ' A free nation is a living organism, because the lives of the people are rooted in the deepest sense of life,' wrote Stephen Spender analyzing the self-defeating weakness of the modern totalitarian dictatorship in his article *To Be Truly Free*, ' an enslaved nation is a maniac machine driven through the world '. And Rex Warner, in *The Cult of Power*, wrote: ' What in our present situation, would strike one as most remarkable, if one had not observed the same thing happening before us in history, is the rapidity with which generally

accepted ideals of the early twentieth century such as tolera-
tion, kindliness, objective truth, freedom, have been replaced
in many people's minds by their exact opposite. . . . Revolt
is the seed of progress. But revolt that is based solely on individual, anarchist self-assertion is against the nature of man
and society. The more successful the moral anarchists are,
the greater the feeling of insecurity in the minds of everyone,
including in the end, the moral anarchists themselves: for
in the end they have so sapped the general system of ideas that
they have nothing from which to revolt.' In my own article,
The Heart of the Problem (based on a talk I had given to an
Oxford undergraduate Society, in which Sidney Keyes had
been prominent), I was working towards the same conclusions.
I had been struck in three novels I had been reading, Hemingway's *For Whom the Bell Tolls*, Koestler's *Darkness at Noon*
and Hoellering's *The Defenders*, by a picture of European crisis
in the 'thirties which had the same features whether the
country was Hemingway's Spain or Koestler's Russia or
Hoellering's Austria: 'features which make it so terrifying,
which make it sometimes seem as if the whole machine of our
lives were running downhill without brakes, and with gathering momentum.' 'Here are the enormous possibilities of
power,' I wrote, 'offered by modern science and modern
methods of organization, and the reckless exploitation of these
possibilities in a moral void . . . and the all-embracing
phenomenon of men seeking desperate remedies for an unjust,
poisoned state of society, men who are tortured by the lack of
joy in their lives but only seem able to redress that lack through
violence or extremism of one sort or another.' This sense of
the need to insist on the value of the human being against the
machine out-of-control, was the conclusion of Demetrios's
article: 'What matters is not history as history, but human
beings. What matters is the Greeks of today and what will
become of them. What now matters is humanity and what
will become of it."

Daylight was well received, and sold well; but it soon became clear that to make it a regular publication was going to
be even more difficult than we had thought. The support
that the Czechs could give us over paper supplies was not un-

limited; and in any case I did not want to be constantly de-
pendent on the good-will of one only of our European allies.
The question of Czech predominance came up again over
contributions. Jiři managed to organize a big flow of Czech
material, some of it excellent but a great deal of it little more
than topical journalism; contributions from the other East
Europeans, however, were scarce. I began to see that if I insisted too much I should be asked by the Czechs why they
should give assistance to propaganda for the Poles—and so on.
Again, owing to supply difficulties, our original plan to make of
it a regular magazine, rather in the manner of André Labarthe's
La France Libre, had collapsed, and it looked as if *Daylight* could
only come out twice a year, as a book, just as *Folios of New
Writing* had been coming out. If that were to happen, both
I and the travellers for The Hogarth Press felt that the two
publications would be too similar to arouse much enthusiasm
from the booksellers or the public. I did not want to give
up *Folios*.

All these arguments increased in force the more I thought
about them. I talked the problem over with Demetrios on
several occasions; and finally came to the conclusion that the
sensible and bold thing to do was to amalgamate the two
ventures. I feared that Jiři might feel that all his efforts had
been in vain and I had walked out on him; but when I put it
to him he took it remarkably well, and very soon came round
to the view that the combined book-magazine would have
greater force and efficacy, and the taint of subsidized propaganda would be removed from it as far as he and his fellow
Czech contributors were concerned. So it was that *New
Writing and Daylight*—a title that always seemed curiously
clumsy to those who did not know the history, and was sometimes asked for in the shops under wildly garbled names, the
one I savoured most being *New Writing in Moonlight*—came into
being. It lasted until 1946. The new contacts I had made
with the exiled European writers in London, the new scope in
articles on the theatre, ballet and the plastic arts that the preparation of *Daylight* had suggested, restored to *New Writing*
something it had lost since the outbreak of the war. However
different the animating spirit, in scope and planning the first

number of *New Writing and Daylight* in 1942 has more in common with the last number of *New Writing* (*new series*) in 1939
than any of the volumes of *Folios*.

At the same time, some far-reaching changes were taking
place in *Penguin New Writing*. Allen Lane's enthusiasm about
its prospects as a monthly were soon clouded by rapidly increasing difficulties of production and paper supply. Some
printing works in England had been worse affected by the
blitz than others, but all had been slowed down by the drain
of their younger workers into the armed forces; and though
Penguin Books had started the war with good stocks of paper
and a ration just a little larger than their estimated needs, the
stocks had been used up by the middle of 1941 and the ration
had been cut again.* Allen Lane's suggestion was that we
should turn *Penguin New Writing* into a quarterly at once. The
struggle for its future went on for many months, but by Christmas it had been agreed between us that it should go on as a
monthly—though the name had already become a misnomer
and the interval between numbers was slowly stretching out—
until No. 12 had appeared in the early Spring of 1942. No. 13
was, then, to be the first of a new quarterly series.

The change-over to a quarterly seemed to me to be the opportunity to do something much more ambitious, parallel in
some ways to the development of *Folios of New Writing* into
New Writing and Daylight; something which would exploit the
extraordinary success we had found and meet some of the
suggestions I was getting from correspondents all over the world
to increase our scope in one way or another. To begin with,
so much outstandingly interesting material was coming in, of
the kind between short stories and reportage based on wartime
experiences, which we had previously used—one in each
number—in the series we had called *The Way We Live Now*,
that I decided to use at least three and sometimes four in each
number of the quarterly and rename the series *Report on Today*.
Again, the book articles which Stephen Spender had written
month by month (with Walter Allen taking over on one

* By December it was down to 37½ per cent of the pre-war standard
figure of annual consumption.

occasion) had been very popular, and though I felt very certain that a regular coverage of book reviews was inappropriate, I thought that we could have more articles dealing with general literary problems and specific literary personalities, and also a feature that could be used for reviews of books which were particularly important for our public, or any topic or topical event in the world of literature that it seemed worth setting people thinking about.   I finally decided to tackle this myself, under the pseudonym of Jack Marlowe, and called it *A Reader's Notebook*.   The time had come also, I thought, to bring Fanfarlo's famous *Shaving Through the Blitz* to an end— because the blitz had come to an end; but as I did not want to lose so precious a contributor, George Stonier obligingly went through another metamorphosis and emerged as Joseph Gurnard, author of a special kind of sketch, part topical reflection and comment, part invented comic story, that derived from the genre he had so cleverly developed in *Shaving Through the Blitz* (and had a not so distant ancestor, it occurred to me later, in the kind of sketch that was appearing thirty years before in *Punch* under the initials R.C.L.).

To make room for all these features, the number of pages in each issue was increased, and the page itself redesigned to accommodate a good many more words: clever work in the Penguin office made the page look much more elegant in spite of being more crowded.   But in some ways the most important to me of all the new developments was the addition of a section of photogravure illustrations.   It was the realization of an ambition that had been growing in me for some time: not just to have pictures in *Penguin New Writing* but to extend its range to cover contemporary theatre, ballet, music, cinema and painting, with illustrations from all these other arts.   It seemed to me—as it seemed to many others—that under the most unlikely conditions, in the middle of a total war, something like a renascence of the arts was taking place in Britain. I was excited by the revival of the romantic, visionary tradition in English painting, stemming from Blake, Palmer and Calvert, in which Graham Sutherland was undoubtedly the leading figure, and by the revival in stage-design which accompanied it.   I was excited by the extraordinary development that was

taking place in ballet, especially at the Sadlers Wells, where
the choreographic work of Fred Ashton, Ninette de Valois and
Robert Helpmann was creating a new intensity of imaginative
discovery, so that with the new stage designers and the new
composers assisting, one could for the first time envisage a
vigorous British style and school in that complex coming
together of many arts to make a whole greater than any one of
them.   Fred Ashton's *The Wanderer*, to the music of Schubert's
pianoforte fantasia in C major, with decor and costumes by
Sutherland, was one of the earliest pointers to what was to
come; but the ballet of *Hamlet* was perhaps the work in which
these new possibilities were most stimulatingly displayed.
Robert Helpmann, following up a suggestion by George
Rylands, had made the whole ballet take place in the dying
mind of Hamlet himself; so that all the great themes of the
play could be woven into the texture of dance and music
within the space of a short twenty-five minutes of vision or nightmare.   The sadness and the splendour, the insistent, tragic
questioning of fate that the music emphasized so effectively
were reflected again in the decor and costumes of Leslie Hurry,
where the style and bright colour of Pollock's ' penny theatre '
had suffered a sea-change that filled them with symbols of
pain and psychological disorder.   It was an entirely original
creation, not just a clever attempt to put *Hamlet* into terms of
the dance, and said something to us at that moment about war,
and youthful death, and the destiny of nations, that was
movingly topical and yet of no time or place.   By then, though
the call-up was making its inroads into the ranks of the younger
English dancers, they had found reserves among the Australian
and South African dancers, a large number of whom had
stayed in London after war broke out: Alexis Rassine, for
instance, with his natural grace and slavonic feeling for the
romantic ' classical ' roles, and Gordon Hamilton, character
dancer of great skill and vivacity.   I also believed that extremely interesting things were happening in the film world,
where a new kind of realism was being developed, that exploited for wartime purposes our pre-war skill in documentary
but without falling into crude propaganda or losing sight of
the individual and his human reactions.   And I had watched

with passionate approval a revival of interest in our dramatic classics, especially Shakespeare, on which new ideas on production were being brought to bear with, it seemed, almost limitless possibilities. All this I wanted to be pictorially illustrated and critically discussed and interpreted in the new quarterly, and having obtained Allen Lane's ready agreement to the photogravure section, I planned to get several experts to write for me under the cover name of ' Dance Critic ', ' Art Critic ', ' Theatre Critic ' and so on. . . . And all for a tanner, and in an edition of between 70,000 and 80,000, I kept on saying to myself, slightly disbelievingly.

As so often before in my life, as the war went on I began to be obscurely aware of forms I believed poetry, novels, art, should take to respond to the mood, the undefined spiritual impulses of the time; forms I imagined I could almost seize from the inchoate mists, but not quite, and so must find other poets and artists to create. I had for long felt that the mood expressed in the letters I was getting from young men in the Forces and in their talk when I met them, had no correlative in art; when a curious chance put me in touch with a new artist, who had only just begun to realize that he was an artist. Among the many descriptions of war experience that were now arriving in my office by every mail, one struck me as soon as I read its opening sentences: it was an account of the unloading of a Red Cross train full of wounded, among whom was a German. It was written by a young man who signed himself Keith Vaughan. What particularly interested me was the quietly expressed but deep human compassion that filled it, as well as the sense it showed of how to use words: ' The stretchers were held up level against the bunks and the men coaxed, like animals, to brave the crossing on to their steel meshes. Some moved suddenly and clumsily, hoping to make the journey before pain had observed their going. . . .' I wrote at once to find out more about the author, and learned to my surprise that he had done very little writing previously, that he had been a photographer before the war, and would like to let me see some drawings of life in the army camps that he had been at work on. When these drawings arrived, I was

immediately and deeply struck by them. Here at last, I
thought, was a pictorial expression of the mood of the new
army, with its young recruits from every level of civilian life;
a mood of resignation and sadness that, in the midst of alien
surroundings, regimentation and squalor, was illuminated
with a sense of spiritual adventure, with the chance of catching
sight of some great truth about human life, some great hope
for the future. Undeterred by the distinctly cool reception
they received when I showed them to a distinguished and influential art-critic, I determined to publish reproductions of
some of them in the photogravure section of the first *Penguin
New Writing* Quarterly.

The new Quarterly went down well: the three new writers
in the ' Report on Today ' section, William Chappell, Richard
Nugent (a pseudonym for Richard Rumbold) and Dan Davin,
attracted immediate attention, and the additional features
seemed, from the extraordinary number of letters of con-
gratulation and encouragement we received, to be exactly
what our readers had been wanting. Walter Allen wrote:
' It's good to see, in one collection, so much good poetry.
When I was in town the other week I went through all the
periodicals I could lay hands on, American mainly, and none
of them, *Partisan Review, Southern Review, Poetry* and the rest
had anything like as good in any one number as the poems by
Louis (MacNeice), Lee, Fuller, and Tiller that you have. . . .
The article on ballet seemed to me a good innovation; it
widens the scope; and it strikes me that you might follow it
with similar articles on music and contemporary painting—
I'm constantly being impressed by the enormous interest there
is on all sides and in all classes in music: a very recent development, I'm certain. I have an idea that people are much more
awake and receptive than they were before the war. I admired Vaughan's drawings very much. . . . What is so exciting is the quality of the work published for the first time.' A
young man I did not know at all, John Bate, who was organizing a periodical, *Oasis*, in the Middle East, thought that it was
' a vast improvement on the run of the others, and they were
good enough ', and asked: ' Is everyone on his best behaviour
for this beginning of a new phase of the *New Writing* enter-

prise?' In rather cool contrast to this, Alun Lewis, though he expressed admiration for the Keith Vaughan drawings, observed that ' on the whole it seemed to me a case of *plus ça change plus c'est la même chose.* To which I hasten to add "Thank God", for I have grown very attached to your Penguins.'

One immediate result for Keith Vaughan was that a large number of his drawings was bought for the War Artists collection. I think that after this he became convinced that his future was as an artist.

3

IN the long interim between the early blitz and the renewal of persistent raiding in the new year of 1944, the literary world of London became, paradoxically, something like a stable society. There were not a great number of us; most of those who were destined to spend at least part of the war in uniform had already gone; nearly all of us who remained knew one another (or very soon got to know one another) personally, and living more or less under siege conditions with very little opportunity of movement far afield, we were continually meeting to argue and discuss together, so that ideas were rapidly absorbed into the general bloodstream and hostile camps and intellectual schisms never lasted for long or remained very serious. We were united in a this-has-got-to-be-seen-through attitude towards the war which was taken for granted, and also in a determination to guard the free world of ideas from any misguided military encroachment. We *needed* one another, and for purposes larger than our own security or ambitions. This sense of cohesion was extraordinarily stimulating. In peacetime it might well have produced staleness and preciosity; but in the grand transformation scene of the war exactly the reverse, I think, was true, at least until nearly the end; and, as I have already described, our small and closely integrated society dissolved at the edges when our thoughts, day and night, reached out in longing and anxiety towards friends, lovers and relations involved in the fighting in distant countries and oceans.

The bonds that held us were not, however, an elastic that refused to stretch. Most of us, inevitably, because of our age group, had already established ourselves in the literary world; but from time to time a younger recruit joined us, a poet or novelist who had just begun to attract attention, and was living in London or within easy reach of it because he had been posted to the Fire Service, or the Censorship, or the Ministry of Information. Of these, there were three who seemed to me discoveries of especial interest; Laurie Lee, of whom I have already written; William Sansom; and Henry Reed.

Bill Sansom has described, in his *Coming to London* article, how in the advertising agency in which he worked just before the war, a ' comfortable rugger-bred middle-class youth ', who scribbled away but thought of the arts as ' something godly and distant, unintelligible and a bit dotty ', he found himself one day sharing a new room with a young man called Norman Cameron; how Norman transformed his vision of painting and literature; and how, having joined the Fire Brigade at the beginning of the war, he started to write in his Hampstead station, met William Makins, business manager of *Horizon*, who told him to send one of his stories in to the Editor; how the story—to his astonishment—was immediately accepted, and how, at Stephen Spender's instigation, he sent another one to me; which I promptly took for *New Writing*. After that first story, *Through the Quinquina Glass*, Bill continually sent me batches of the stories that now began to pour out of him; many of them I accepted straight away, but many others I sent back with critical letters trying to explain where I thought the weak spots were. Sometimes he re-wrote them, and I eventually printed these too; others he scrapped, others were printed elsewhere. It was extremely stimulating for me, whatever it may have been for him, because I had rarely before, if ever, had to do with an author so eager to learn from his experiments and to perfect them, and so little disposed to bite the hand that wanted to feed him—with the satisfaction of print. There were long periods of disappointment, when he seemed to be off the scent, but there was never a complaint about my sorrowfully posted return packets; then he would suddenly pick the scent up again, and another extraordinary, original, poetic story would arrive to delight me and the rapidly growing circle of his admirers. These pleasures were crowned when I persuaded Leonard Woolf to accept his first volume of stories, *Fireman Flower*, for publication by The Hogarth Press.

Of the stories in that volume, only one, *The Wall*, was a straight reportage of a fire-fighting experience. In the rest, if he used the setting and paraphernalia of the London fires it was to illustrate some subtle problem of psychology or to establish some symbolic truth. The pleasure his writing gave me came from the strange imaginative world he created, so that, in *The Peach House Potting Shed*, for instance, one was immediately drawn as into an intense dream; this world of fable and symbol owed something, inevitably, to Kafka, something perhaps also to the contemporary examples of Edward Upward and of Rex Warner; but Bill Sansom gave it a flavour and quality of his own, creating some of his most ominously compelling effects by, as it were, arresting the motion of life for a minutely described and timeless moment, as if a cinema operator had suddenly stopped a film at a point charged with transforming significance. Sometimes he attempted a more deliberate and elaborate fable, as with *In the Maze*, but even when his symbols as explicit fable did not entirely convince, this imaginative power remained. And his success, of course, came from the fact that he loved language; that he was inexhaustibly interested in what could be done with words, in renewing their force in experimental combinations and coinings.

I first became aware of the name of Henry Reed as the signature under an article about Auden's work in the Birmingham University magazine, *The Mermaid*. I was so struck by this article, that I immediately wrote off to the author and asked him if he would care to contribute to *New Writing*. Many weeks passed without an answer, and I had already given up hope of hearing, when, in the Summer of 1941, a letter arrived from 10557689 Pte. Reed, H., in Squad 48 'B' Coy. No. 3 Training Battn. R.A.O.C., whither my letter had followed him.

He promised poems as soon as he could get down to completing several he had drafted out, and articles, too, if later on I suggested themes to him, adding: ' If this seems a poor response to your charming note, you will blame the Army, where so much of my time is taken up with marching, drilling, bayonet-fighting, the Bren gun, heavy-charing and learning to be a clerk. If you write again, as I hope you will, perhaps you wouldn't mind addressing the letter in a plain envelope. I don't want anybody to notice me more than they must.'

It was a year, or more, before the poems began to arrive, but as those few which had already appeared in *The Listener* suggested, they were worth waiting for. A purity and exactitude of diction, a technical skill concealing itself under a perfect clarity and ease of statement, a cool, ironic intelligence keeping under faultless control a romantic imagination and an immense pressure of nostalgia: such gifts are rare in any young poet, rarer still in a young poet's first poems. The long poems, most of which were published in *New Writing and Daylight*, dramatic meditations or monologues by figures of classical or Arthurian myth, were, I thought, in spite of an echo of Eliot-esque music now and then, an imaginative and technical triumph, though the wit and fierce ironic tension of the shorter pieces on Army life, *Naming of Parts*, *Judging Distances* and *Unarmed Combat*, have made them the obvious favourites. As in Roy Fuller's poetry of this time, the sense of alienation and uprootedness is the dominant emotion in these ' Lessons of War ': they are rejection-of-war poems more emphatically even than Roy's. But the two long poems on classical themes, *Chrysothemis* and *Philoctetes*, are dominated by a similar emotion, a sense of exile and separation, desolate or bitter, and while the protagonist in each is an entirely valid dramatic creation they would not have made their extraordinary impact if one had not been aware of overtones arising out of the poet's personal emotion; if one had not felt that at a deeper level they were also parables of the artist's predicament in a world given over to violence. Both *Chrysothemis* and *Philoctetes*, I soon found out, read aloud remarkably well, as do the ' Lessons of War ' poems: a quality which one can now see foreshadowed Henry's later interest in the theatre and radio drama.

Erecting a Marquee at Night   by Keith Vaughan

acket design by William Chappell   Design by John Minton

pour John Lehmann
et New Writing
André Gide.

André Gide

The Editor at work in Carrington House

When the poems began to arrive, Henry, released at last from the Army, indicated that he could now find time for some critical work. We discussed themes, and a shrewd and caustic article on the state of poetry in general and of the poets of the 'thirties in particular, *The End of an Impulse*, was the first result. Henry showed that he was an ungullible critic and no respecter of reputations: too forceful to be called feline, it was the kind of article that a young poet or critic writes who is preparing to lead a literary revolution. No vigorous pursuit of the enemy, however, took place: instead, very soon after the war and the publication of his first book, Henry Reed abdicated from poetry. I have always deeply regretted it; though to refuse to go on churning it out when the inspiration has dried up is, I think, a kind of scrupulousness—even a kind of heroism—of which few writers have shown themselves capable.*

During these years, in spite of the difficulty of obtaining drink in adequate quantities, some of us managed to keep up the pre-war tradition of gatherings for cocktails or wine before or after dinner, sometimes inviting only a handful of friends, sometimes a couple of dozen, but never great throngs or routs; and because they could not be huge or miscellaneous, these parties, in which the central, most permanent circle was enlivened by visitors from the country, together with soldiers, sailors or airmen on leave or in transit to a new posting, have left a very happy and intimate memory. At my own gatherings, in my new abode on the sixth floor of Carrington House, I endeavoured to bring together old and more recently discovered contributors to *New Writing* and Hogarth Press authors, and other friends in the publishing and literary worlds. If I had an exact record of these parties, I could give a composite picture that would illuminate the anatomy of our wartime society in the most truthful detail. As I have not, let me describe an imaginary but nevertheless imaginable party attended by some of those who at one time or another, though not necessarily the same time, did in fact accept my invitations. . . .

* There are hopeful signs, as I write, that the long exile may be over.

M

First of all, I see friends from the various swollen departments of the bureaucracy, especially (and inevitably) from the Ministry of Information. Graham Greene is there—if the party takes place before he leaves for West Africa—full of sardonic stories about muddle and maze-like confusion of action, wheels that refused to revolve in the press of logs being assiduously rolled and axes furiously ground (one delicious glimpse of this he was to contribute to *Penguin New Writing* under the title of *Men at Work*). Cecil Day Lewis is regaling us with similar stories, finding more entertainment than bitterness, reliving the dottiness, the Alice Through the Looking Glass atmosphere that sometimes seemed to close in on him, roomful after roomful on all sides of his office, floors and floors of it above him, floors and more floors below. Laurie Lee, who now works with him in the publications department, is standing by the window, endeavouring to evade, with a grin of sly charm—which somehow suggests a shrewd young Cotswold farmer who's not to be had for a mug when he brings his cattle to market—my demands that he not only write more poems for *New Writing* but also sketches of his Cotswold village childhood for *The Geographical Magazine*. From the bomb-proof depths of the Admiralty, where he is engaged on secret work with Ian Fleming, William Plomer has arrived with a crazy story of a general who never recovered from learning one day that human beings consisted 95 per cent of water, and had to be retired; he has a new comic ballad in his pocket, thin folded sheets of paper handed to me when no one is looking; and from the Ministry of War Transport my former secretary Sonia Brownell, full of dark intimations about the future of our supplies of spam and pilchards from overseas as she shakes her head of pageboy gold. George Orwell himself is present: the keen eyes suggest more melancholy than humour and the deeply etched lines round his mouth only rarely stretch to a smile. He is working now in the Indian section of the B.B.C., and, planning a series of talks on the English poetry of our century, urges me to do the one on the poets of the 'thirties; with him is his assistant, Zulfa Bokhari, an amusing and intelligent Indian Moslem in a fur cap. Later, I overhear Orwell speaking, in rather different tones from those employed by Mr. Churchill, about Stalin as war-leader and about Soviet diplomacy to Demetrios Capetanakis, who has come over a little late from a long day at the Greek Ministry of Information. Louis MacNeice, also from the B.B.C., is there, looking more seal-like than ever and talking about problems of the recitation of poetry over the radio to his fellow poet Henry Reed.

There is a big contingent from the Fire Service: Henry Yorke, accompanied by his gentle and sweet-natured wife, Dig, telling extraordinary stories of his fellow firemen, at present bored and restless and getting on one another's nerves in the 'lull' (about which he has just written a sketch for *N.W.D.* to publish), and forbidding me to use a photograph of him in the Penguin, for fear a fellow-fireman should recognize him and give the game away—' I should never hear the last of it,' he says; Stephen Spender, looking taller than ever and quite improbable in his uniform, full of eager information about the organization of discussion groups in the N.F.S., which he claims as a great discovery in democratic education; and William Sansom, not saying very much and reserved even in his responses to flattery of his work, not (one suspects) from hauteur but rather from stiffly controlled shyness.

Some of my fellow-publishers and literary editors have also joined us. Cyril Connolly, who still ingeniously succeeds in giving literary dinner parties of a quality astonishing for wartime, discusses the problems of *Horizon*'s and *New Writing*'s paper ration with me; Roger Senhouse, oldest of friends and a director of the publishing house of Secker and Warburg, whom all the severities of the blitz at that end of London failed to dislodge from Great Ormond Street, where his living-room still houses the resplendent library Lytton Strachey bequeathed him, is talking with unquenchable twinkle in the eye to my sister Rosamond and to Raymond Mortimer, at this time literary editor and *eminence grise* of the *New Statesman*. I am in Raymond's good books, because I have managed, by a mixture of wheedling, reproach and bullying to force him to collect the best of his weekly book articles of many years into *Channel Packet*. ' V.S.P. sold 2,000 of his book; I shall think well of you if you sell 4,000 of mine,' he says rather sharply to me. The three of of them form a group under the painting of Charleston by

Duncan Grant, which hangs at the end of the room; and they are joined by Nancy Mitford, mistress during all these years of Heywood Hill's book-shop in Curzon Street, where she performs her skilled office of marrying the exactly desirable book to each questing customer and purveying the gossip of the town with her unique Mitford wit.

On the sofa my mother, who has come up for the occasion, is conversing with Veronica Wedgwood. She has an exceptional fondness and admiration for Veronica, in whose brilliant success as an historian she sees, I think, a kind of fulfilment by proxy of an ambition she might herself have entertained in her college days: Barbara Cooper overhears her urge Veronica to write a history of Europe to supersede Fisher's.

At the other end of the room Elizabeth Bowen, smartly turned out as ever in spite of wartime restrictions, is discussing novels with Philip Toynbee, lately released from the Army. Elizabeth is as usual in high spirits, radiating charm and vitality, the slight impediment in her speech giving an attractive touch of diffidence to the eager flow of her wide-ranging conversation: her stories of London in wartime—she was an air-raid warden all through the blitz—are just beginning to come out. Near them, Victor Pritchett, brilliant raconteur and wit, has enticed George Stonier out of his shyness: they are capping one another's stories about the Editor's room at the *New Statesman*, and their hilarity has affected a tall, burly figure whose name I have suddenly, distressingly forgotten (I am subject to such moments of total amnesia). My sister Rosamond informs me, with raised eyebrows, in response to a whispered question as she passes, that I ought to be ashamed of myself for not recognizing the distinguished author of *The Aerodrome*, especially as I have recently given a talk to the sixth form at the school in Wimbledon where he teaches. Rose Macaulay, symbol of some dauntless, indomitable quality of moral and intellectual integrity in the pre-1914 generation— you would never guess she has recently lost her most precious heirlooms and working manuscripts in a fire-raid—breaks in upon my confusion, asking why I don't get the authorities to allow the war prisoners to write for *Penguin New Writing*; but Derek Hill, up for the day from the Wiltshire farm where he works, suggests that it would be far better if she were to come down and interview some of the Italian prisoners who provide the labour there—and then write their stories up herself. Derek is not the only artist present: Laurence Gowing, who has recently received high praise for his still life canvases of green apples (that set the teeth on edge) and shadowy, exquisitely poetic landscapes, is in a group with Julia Strachey, who asks me to be patient about her short stories, describing creative struggles of a harrowing intensity; and Keith Vaughan, on leave from his pioneers, smiling and quiet.

Jiři Mucha has just turned up, a little late, and has brought another war correspondent in uniform with him, American or Canadian; and there is a sprinkling of younger men in uniform, one or two with their wives or girl-friends, all contributors or would-be contributors to *New Writing*. Later on, picking a party from these, and having seen my mother to her taxi, I go off to The White Tower in Percy Street where I find that Cyril Connolly, with Lys Lubbock and one or two other guests, has preceded us; and glimpsing out of the corner of an eye the vast patriarchal head of Augustus John that seems to float over the room as in a drawing by Blake, and at another table the bowed, reverie-sunken head of Norman Douglas with Nancy Cunard beside him, I climb upstairs to find a corner table behind a huge, hilarious party mainly consisting of G.I.s celebrating the wedding of one of their number to an Anglo-Cypriot bride.

All during these years, Cyril and I used to meet from time to time, not only at such parties but sometimes at my club, sometimes at his home, to exchange gossip and compare notes. I think the characters of our two magazines were very different; and yet there was a broad area of agreement between us, and an unplanned common policy; particularly about the need to defend the independence of the world of literature, and to provide young writers in uniform with a place where they could let off steam about their grievances, experiment exactly as they wished, and be gloomy about the way the war was being waged and its probable outcome, if that was how it took them. *Horizon*, it always seemed to me, had a chancy brilliance: chancy because there seemed to be long periods when Cyril lost interest in it as an editing job, but made up for this by the wit and flavour of his own contributions. *Horizon* also had less interest in theatre, theatre design and ballet than *New Writing*, and pursued a very different course about art. The art articles were, in fact, in Peter Watson's charge, and Cyril, over the port or the brandy in the blacked-out drawing room of the Athenaeum, was wont to complain about his inability to keep them under his control and the shudders the prose style of art critics and art enthusiasts gave him. I think there was bitterness sometimes between us, but much of it could be put down to the malicious gossip-mongering of mutual acquaintances, who liked to invent a rivalry more remorseless than ever could have existed between two heirs of Bloomsbury with their backs to the wall. And sometimes an author who had started in *Horizon*, came on to *New Writing* and thence to The Hogarth Press, for the further scope and opportunities with which we could provide him. William Sansom was an outstanding example. There was certainly plenty of room for both of us; and when I said one day to Michael Nelson that if ever *Horizon* was in serious straits I would subscribe £100 at once, I was in dead earnest.

To complete the picture, I must also mention those luminaries of our literary world, who, though established by choice or direction in regions of our islands fairly distant from London, seemed to be very much with us even if their visits were rare. John Betjeman had taken on a cultural liaison job in neutral Dublin at the U.K. Representative's office, and fulfilled his duties with immense aplomb and zest, charming the most suspicious among the local intelligentsia into at least keen interest if not wholehearted engagement with what writers and artists were thinking and doing in war-shattered Britain, and keeping an easy lead over his Axis opposite numbers all through the course; thus proving, not for the first or last time, that in such a job a dram of personality is worth a hogshead of bureaucracy. He acted, in fact, as a two-way channel between the countries, providing at the same time Irish intellectuals with a much-needed outlet into the wider Anglo-Saxon world of letters, the normal passages of which censorship, shipping dangers and every other kind of war-time restriction had all but dammed up. He managed to arrange a mutual exchange of *New Writing* and *The Bell*, and elicited stories or poems from some of the more interesting Irish writers which he sent over to me, with accompanying letters that would suddenly break mysteriously into Gaelic and were sometimes signed *Seán ó betjemán*. I tried in vain to get him to send new poems of his own: ' only Tennysonian blank verse pours out of me ', he wrote in the Spring of 1942; but a few months later: ' I feel as though I shall never be able to write again '.

Early in 1942 we had published, in The New Hogarth Library (as I have already mentioned) poems by Robert Graves, Norman Cameron and Alan Hodge in one small volume called *Work in Hand*. This brought me into correspondence with Robert Graves, who was living down at Galmpton in Devon; and having read and much admired his famous *1805* in *The Listener* I asked him for a poem for *New Writing*. He replied that he didn't mind contributing several poems, but didn't want to contribute one, as a single short poem was apt to lose its taste and smell if surrounded by other people's work. To explain the single appearance of *1805*, he said: ' This was shown to Ackerley by someone else, and he asked for it, and I used to be a neighbour of his so I said all right. I have also contributed a poem to the next number of the *Eugenics Review* beginning " Come, human dogs, interfertilitate " because the editor is my tame physician. . . .' Tantalized by this hint of what the next number of the fortunate *Eugenics Review* would contain, and hoping that the same vigorous spirit would inform all his work of the moment, I readily agreed to publish a batch of his poems. By return of post I received his *Satires and Grotesques*, six satires which contained that mordant comment on contemporary war communiqués *The Persian Version* and the miraculously free-and-easy song *The Oldest Soldier*, and his ' Grotesques ', the oddest of which contained a reference to a certain Dr. Newman (who was unknown to me) and his ' black imp, a sooterkin ' which he drew out of his pocket at a concert. I was puzzled; but Robert Graves anticipated me: ' In reply to unasked questions,' he wrote, ' Dr. Newman's " Sooterkin " is, or was, a

Dutch imp caused by the impregnation of women by the fumes
of charcoal when they stood over a brazier in their wide hooped
skirts. He is mentioned by Sam Butler in *Hudibras* and has
the characteristics of a gremlin: probably now in service with
the Free Dutch Air Force. . . .'

One of the most remarkable articles I ever published—in
fact, I believe, one of the most important published anywhere
during the war—was the first article of all in the first number
of the combined *New Writing and Daylight*: Edwin Muir's
The Natural Man and the Political Man. Edwin was in Scotland
during these years, in St. Andrew's and then in Edinburgh,
where he worked for The British Council in a job that brought
him into close contact with the Czech, Polish and French forces
in Britain. He was therefore particularly interested in the
experiment of *Daylight*. ' I think that it is splendid that you
have managed to start it just now,' he wrote to me, ' that is at
the right time for it—and the most difficult time for it.' And
very soon after he sent me the article, saying that he thought it
' an inadequate treatment of a real question, which would
need a volume to do justice to it '. *The Natural Man and the
Political Man* was an analysis, in philosophical depth, of precisely that problem which had loomed so large for the writers
of my generation as disillusion with the political developments
of the 'thirties grew; it showed, more clearly than any of us
had ever succeeded in showing, why Fascism and Communism had come about through a change in the traditional
Western attitude towards man during the nineteenth century—
a change from the idea that an individual's life was a conflict
to the idea that it was a development—and why Fascism and
Communism, beneath their violent surface opposition, were
really so alike; and how this way of thinking had permeated a
large area of modern literature, the novels of Lawrence, Montherlant, Hemingway most evidently. ' What has gradually
been brought into prominence by the religion of development
is the primacy of *things*. Control things and you control mankind. In this conception the moral struggle which possessed
the imagination of other ages, and was strong even a century
ago, recedes into irrelevance, and becomes like one of those
vestigial organs in the body which no longer perform any use-

ful function, but exist merely to plague us: a vermiform appendix. . . . Human life thus became a thing completely contained in an environment, and therefore a thing to which the imagination of the writer could give no ultimate significance, since there was not in it even the pretence of choice, even the day-dream of freedom. If this life of the individual is a development, then that development is simple and inevitable. If the life of the individual is a conflict, then that conflict implies a choice, and the choice, complexity, and complexity, the existence of more in human life than can be compressed into a formula. What has taken place in literature is a simplification of the idea of man, connected with this notion of natural process and development. The simplification is a general tendency; literature has not initiated, but merely reflected it; and only those writers who are deeply rooted in tradition, and possessed with the idea of time, have been able to make headway against it; such writers as Proust, James Joyce and Virginia Woolf, to confine ourselves to the novelists: there are similar figures in poetry. The obsession of such writers with tradition was called out by this human crisis.'

From time to time Edith and Osbert Sitwell came down from Renishaw, and entertained on an unwontedly lavish scale. It was Demetrios who brought Edith and me together: he had conceived a profound admiration for her wartime poetry, and, when mutual friends introduced them, an equal admiration for the bold renaissance outline of her personality. I myself had been deeply moved by many of the poems collected in *Street Songs* and *Green Song*, but I rather doubted whether the meeting would be a success, feeling that Edith saw in me one of the more political of the ' gang ' of the 'thirties, whose Left Book Club radicalism, I knew, had been unsympathetic to her and whose excursions into revolutionary agitator's verse she despised. Demetrios, however, overruled my doubts, and took me along with him one day to tea at the Sesame Club. His instinct was right (or had he prepared the ground very carefully without telling me?): Edith and I took to one another very quickly, and from that afternoon she became one of the elder literary generation I saw most of and felt most sympathy with. I was struck at once by the sculptural beauty

of her oval face, her fine intellectual profile and her aristocratic dignity of bearing and manner. A first, hasty glance
might lead one to suppose her haughty and cold—and indeed
Edith can be freezing to bores, enemies of the arts and all in-
considerate vulgarians; but I recognized at that earliest tea-
party, what was in fact perfectly clear from her poetry, and
could not be concealed even by the shower of shafts of satiric
wit that sometimes filled the air around her, that her response
to any genuine emotion was immediate and that she was extremely sensitive, especially to all forms of suffering, human or
animal.

Osbert Sitwell I came to know more gradually, but was impressed early on by the contrasting sides of his personality.
It was impossible not to be charmed by him if he set himself
to win your friendship; impossible not to appreciate the
warmth and generosity of heart and the passionate caring for
art and artists, whether they were poets, musicians, painters
or dancers; but the first impression he made, as he came into
a room, was of princely apartness, of soldierly authority; and
the quick hawklike glance he directed over the company seemed
to bode ill not only for foolish importances and gushing climbers
who presumed on his impeccable manners, but also for the shy
and simple. Their early struggle for recognition, their re-
bellion against both their upbringing and the accepted fatuities
of the time in the arts, had marked both Edith and Osbert.
Like all revolutionaries who win their way against great odds,
they were, it sometimes seemed, too ready to suspect conspiracy
and even treachery, a reaction that often baffled and dismayed
younger critics whose cracks were fundamentally inspired by
a form of the same need to defy one's successful elders that the
Sitwells themselves had felt. And yet the hand that seemed,
at one moment, to hover threateningly over the proscription
list, the next moment was extended in unreserved support and
friendship to some struggling poet or painter, or other fellow-
artist who found himself persecuted by bone-headed authority.
The Sitwells' out-and-out partisanship of free experiment in
the arts, the battle they never ceased to wage against philistinism and bureaucratic insolence, was of priceless importance
during the war. Osbert's *Letter to My Son*, which first appeared

in *Horizon* and then was reprinted as a little booklet, was a courageously witty defence of the artist's need for leisure and independence—particularly from bureaucratic bossing about —at a time when the pressure was all towards conformity. It was good, in a world of total directed labour and national service, to hear someone of Osbert's stature say out loud: ' We would always oppose the ants in their awful paradise '; it was shocking (but the shock was of pleasure) to be reminded, in the hour of the Great Captains, that ' Shakespeare out-distances Waterloo as an English triumph '; and it was de-licious to find that these provocative remarks lured an arch-philistine, in the person of James Agate, out into the open, where Osbert was able, in the most dignified way, to make mincemeat of him.

Morgan Forster, too, in quite a different manner, with an appearance of retiring diffidence, of a desire only to be gentle, and charming, and amusing, while in fact taking deadly aim, continued to wage his long-standing battle against the pre-tentious, the insensitive and the intolerant. He used to come up from Abinger Hammer briefly, but quite often, to broad-cast on the overseas services of the B.B.C., mainly to India, and from time to time he would come for tea, or a drink, or supper after the ballet with me. I remember one occasion, in the Athenaeum, when he was at the top of his form, making fun of everything. We talked of *War and Peace*, and he remarked how brilliantly Tolstoi understood what went on in the world of public affairs, the sort of things that were happening again today; for instance, all the little men rushing about, talking and writing about the importance of *problems* that have to be mastered. ' As soon as you've mastered one problem, there's always another! ' he exclaimed with an astonishing chuckle. The fact that he was appalled by the Dictators and their cruel-ties, that he thought the war had to be fought, did not mean that he gave an uncritical assent to everything our side did as necessary or right. In his pamphlet *What I Believe*, which the Hogarth published just before the war, he had written: ' Hero-worship is a dangerous vice, and one of the minor merits of a democracy is that it does not encourage it, or produce that un-manageable type of citizen known as the Great Man. It produces instead different kinds of small men—a much finer achievement.' I think he was well aware that war conditions were the enemy of that ' minor merit '. There was too much power concentrated in too few hands, and, as he wrote shrewdly in the explosive little pamphlet, ' as soon as people have power they go crooked and sometimes dotty as well, because the possession of power lifts them into a region where normal honesty never pays.'

Morgan Forster was always anxious to hear the latest news I had had from Christopher, to whom he had remained unswervingly loyal through all the public outbreaks of hostility. We were both conscious of the distance between us and Christopher slowly increasing: with the most sensitive sympathy in the world it was as difficult for Christopher to follow the changes that the war was gradually making in our attitudes as it was for us fully to understand Christopher's new leanings towards pacifist mysticism.   I showed Morgan a letter I had had from Christopher early in 1943, about the piece I had published in *Penguin New Writing* No. 14, describing his work in the Friends' Service Committee Seminar in California:

> I was very embarrassed by my La Verne thing: it reads like the parish magazine; but I'm sure you did right to print it.   It administers a kind of sour sip of quinine flavoured with prigdom. I wouldn't feel I had to do so much apologizing, now; or be so gloomy.   I sound as though I were being exiled to the salt mines, instead of starting a new life of the most absorbing interest and adventure, which this has actually been and is being. . . . I'm now temporarily free from the U.S. draft, because I'm over 38: they recently lowered the age-limit, so I'm going to live at the Vedanta ' monastery ' here in Hollywood, as from next month: more about this in another letter.

None of us were particularly enthusiastic about the news of the move to the Vedanta ' monastery '; fearing that it would increase the gulf between us, perhaps even to a point of total non-comprehension.

These social exchanges lightened the strenuousness of hard-working days and short nights, and gave relief from the speculations that never ceased to gnaw at the back of our minds;

even though it was just beginning to be possible to believe seriously in the turn of the tide. One day I was in the middle of preparing one of my scripts for the Austrian service of the B.B.C., when Patrick Smith, in charge of the programme, rang up to tell me: 'In a few hours you're going to hear terrific news, the biggest and best news to break for a long time. You can scrap your script; there won't be room for anything else except the news.' The Battle of El Alamein was on, and the news of the victory came through, as he promised, the next day.

4

THE literary and artistic life of London in the middle of the war had also its grand salons, where skilful hostesses brought writers, actors and painters together with politicians, soldiers and other men and women in public life they might otherwise never have had a chance of meeting. These salons flourished in spite of the hazards of bombing, the scarcity of good food and drink and all the absences and removals.

The chief of them, the most famous and the best frequented, were undoubtedly those conducted by Lady Colefax and Lady Cunard. Sybil Colefax's had survived since pre-war days, and all through the war Sybil not only managed to keep her smart interior decorating business going, but also to pursue her social mission with an indefatigable showering of indecipherable invitations on novelists, poets, theatrical stars, cabinet ministers, influential civil servants, visiting American celebrities and distinguished survivors of the European debacle. It was an heroic, scarcely credible phenomenon. I had had the privilege of being on Sybil's invitation list from before the war; but it was Archie Clark-Kerr who introduced me to Emerald Cunard's salon. She had only returned from America towards the end of 1941, and had established herself on a high floor in the Dorchester, in a suite which she adorned with her famous Marie Laurencins and Berthe Morisots and some of the most precious and beautiful of her bound books: the great house in Grosvenor

Square, setting of the parties of her heyday, had become a
melancholy, deserted casualty of the blitz.   In her Dorchester
suite she began again to entertain, sometimes to tea and cock-
tail parties, but mainly to dinner parties, keeping up the spirit
and tone of an already vanished epoch with astonishing courage,
attack and verve, although in her late sixties and giving the
impression of great physical fragility.

She was of slight build, with exquisite figure and legs,
advantages which were set off by the always impeccable elegance of her dress and the ropes of pearls and the diamonds
which even at that time of almost ostentatious austerity she
showed no intention of foreswearing.   Her eyes were her most
extraordinary feature: in the shaded lights of my first evening
they seemed to me more like semi-precious stones than human
eyes, *trouvailles* applied to the face in whose glaze none of the
transitory emotions of the soul could be seen to stir, an effect no
doubt produced by the severe face-lifting she had undergone.
Her neatness of body, her incisive profile and high, lilting voice,
and a certain way she had of holding her head, produced an
often remarked birdlike effect: of an exotic bird from a tropical
jungle.   An aristocratic (but also American) audacity, intelligence, wit and, beneath it all, an almost tragic sense of disillusionment were the keynotes of her character.   She gave a
superficial impression of being cold and hard, where Sybil
Colefax was so obviously warm-hearted and vulnerable.   If she
disliked or was displeased by something, she said so at once and
without concealment; even in wartime, the staff of the Dorchester trembled before her complaints about service and
cooking.   I could not break myself of the habit of arriving at
her parties punctually at the hour proposed, with the result
that I often found myself alone in the suite, and then alone with
her, for a considerable space of time.   It was a testing time for
the shy newcomer, for Emerald always seemed to be in a state
of nervous tension before a party began, complaining of windows being open or not open, curtains drawn or not drawn, or
the table for dinner not being properly laid.   As the party
progressed her tension relaxed and her gaiety and charm
increased: her capacity for putting her guests at ease, but at
the same time for communicating a certain glittering vivacity,

for challenging one to be at one's best, was extremely stimulating. Her values, one felt at first, were worldly, even snobbish, buttressed by the brazen assumptions of money and power that survived in England from Edwardian days of imperial supremacy; conversation at her table was often ruthless, sometimes coarse, but never dull; reputations were mercilessly investigated, wealth probed and shrewdly assessed; nevertheless, if the arts rather than people were under discussion, she showed a quite different side of her nature. I sometimes thought what a shock her talk would have given to the left-wing propagandists of Unity Theatre or of *Left Review*, for her understanding of literature, and especially of nineteenth-century novelists of many nationalities, was deep, and her judgement acute. I often found myself easily outdistanced by her detailed knowledge of the works of Dostoevsky, Tolstoi or Balzac; I listened to her with growing respect when she talked of *The Brothers Karamazov* or *La Cousine Bette*. It was only when the subject of poetry was broached, that she seemed deliberately to defer to me; and I can remember evenings when she persuaded me, after all the other guests had gone, to read Shelley or some more modern poet to her, and unburden myself of my own enthusiasms about poetry. It was at those midnight moments that her mask of diamond heartlessness slipped: one had glimpses of a pathetic and suffering creature below, a woman to whose heart wounds had been dealt that refused to heal. She dreaded being left alone with the night: she slept scarcely at all (as she ate scarcely at all), and spent long hours reading in bed after the last dinner guest had departed. She once exclaimed to me, when we were by ourselves: ' No man, John, has ever said to me " I love you! " But I have had letters—I have had *letters*! ' It was natural to assume that by this enigmatic and tantalizing remark she was referring to the letters she had received from George Moore, and of which she was sometimes ready to talk: but perhaps not only to those. I did not dare to ask.

She accepted me at once, because Archie Clark-Kerr had brought me to her; but unlike Sybil, she did not go out of her way to cultivate young poets, or any of the more bohemian denizens of Bloomsbury, of whom she was slightly suspicious. She never referred to her daughter Nancy, from whom she had been irrevocably parted many years before, nor did any of her friends, at least in public. If she was aware how well I had known Nancy in my pre-war Bloomsbury days, she never betrayed it. I was glad of this, for as I watched and listened to Emerald, I was constantly struck by the likeness between mother and daughter, in manner and voice and many small traits of behaviour: fascinating memories were evoked from the past of my association with Nancy, memories of absurdly different surroundings and a way of life of which Emerald could never have approved. They presented themselves in grotesque montage against the luxurious hotel suite; but, luckily, unknown to my hostess.

Emerald's salon had an unqualified right-wing bias. The politicians one met there were, with rare exceptions, Conservative, the outlook entirely Conservative, the prejudices almost at times a caricature of the conventional aristocratic class-consciousness, though sustained with a wit and vigour of mind that were delightful to anyone with an ear for dialogue. That Winter and Spring I remember as frequent guests Duff Cooper and the beautiful Diana. I had not met Duff before, and wondered whether, as powerful head of a ' Hush-hush ' committee on internal security, he had been told by Archie to discover for himself that I was not the dangerous agitator I still appeared, it seemed, to those who controlled appointments in the war bureaucracy. My first impression of Duff was of a small man, puffed up with his own importance, extremely choleric, self-indulgent and narrow in outlook; but it was not long before I saw that I was misjudging him, and that under the all too easily provoked outbursts of temper lay a complex personality, caring deeply for the things of the mind, extremely well read, especially in French literature, and capable of displaying quite extraordinary charm in intimate conversation when once his distrust was dissolved. By Diana I was completely captivated, once and for all. Even with her great and genuine enthusiasm for music, the theatre and the ballet, Emerald showed a conventional reserve towards artists who did not come out of the same social drawer as herself, or who had not at least enriched themselves into it; Diana, I saw very soon, had no such prejudices, liked bohemians, and helped by

the fact that she had been an actress herself, could get on at
once with every sort of person who lived by and for the arts.
This absolute indifference of Diana's to class and political
allegiance in the world of the creative imagination, was to be
the cause of fervent admiration, dismay and amusement at a
later date, when she became Ambassadress and dazzling hostess
of the British Embassy at Paris. I was struck by the penetrating sense of her observations on people and events; but above
all by her beauty, which exercised, and still exercises, an
hypnotic power upon me.

Among other notable figures of the Conservative political
world I met for the first time at Emerald's parties were Lord
Margesson, at the house parties of whose clever and attractive
American wife, Frances, I had been a guest before the war;
Oliver Stanley, who commanded respect for his intellectual
powers and his open mind; James Stuart, the Chief Whip, who
touched me by his unvarying mournful demeanour, his intense
gloom about many aspects of the war, especially the future of
Anglo-Russian relations, and his sincere and kindly attempts
not to be profoundly depressed by the writers of my generation;
and a dashing young peer and naval officer, my younger contemporary at Eton, Lord Stanley of Alderley, a favourite of
Emerald's, who teasingly referred to him as Lord Stanley
Disorderly. This was a new world for me, as almost the only
politicians I had met before were Liberal or Labour: I found
it extremely invigorating, though I was too uncertain of myself
to join battle about political issues. About literary issues, however, I could not remain silent. Literary ' scamps ' of the past,
Dostoevsky, for instance, and Rimbaud, and of course Lord
Byron, were favourite themes at these dinner parties, and discussed with keenly perceptive knowledge and respect, if not
always with love; but the attitude towards the modern masters,
T. S. Eliot, D. H. Lawrence and Virginia Woolf, was grudging
and perplexed; towards my own contemporaries, with few
exceptions, one of revulsion and rejection. I remember an
occasion when I had to defend the reputations of Wystan and
Christopher—the old charges of betrayal had raised their
heads once more—against an onslaught that was pressed from
all sides with a passionate energy that startled me: I felt

N

suddenly like a soldier alone in a pill-box, ringed by enemies with grenades in their hands.

One of the most curious phenomena in social London at this time was the emotion and enthusiasm with which certain members of the American forces stationed in England were taken up. These young soldiers and sailors came from good families, had great charm and excellent manners, and obscure assignments which seemed to leave them almost unlimited time to cultivate everyone who was anyone. One evening, during dinner at Emerald's, she suddenly exclaimed: ' I'm expecting the *Sergeant* after dinner, isn't that delightful? ' A murmur of pleasure greeted this, to me mysterious, announcement. A little later, when coffee had been served, she trilled up: ' I wonder where the *Sergeant* is? He promised faithfully to come in if he could.' All at once everyone was talking about ' the Sergeant ' with the utmost animation. I was baffled. It was so unlike Emerald to know a sergeant at all. Perhaps he was the son of a peer, who was working his way up from the ranks? All the other guests assumed that I knew who the Sergeant was, and I began to feel rather embarrassed. It was clear that I was living too much out of the world. I was about to summon up desperate courage to ask for information, when the Sergeant appeared in person, to cries of delight reminiscent of the clamour of sea-gulls when you throw them a biscuit. His name was Stuart Preston, he was American, and with his boyish charm, his detailed knowledge of the world of social and other celebrities that seemed to stretch a good deal further than Who's Who, and his well-stocked mind and excellent taste in the arts, he was more unlike the conventional image that the word sergeant still called up, than I could have believed. Not very long afterwards I learnt, in Sybil Colefax's house, that he had had to go to hospital. A noise of lamentation arose from the assembled guests. Harold Nicolson, an important minister at that time, reassured us all by announcing that he had hurried to hold his hand by his bedside, and that he was on the mend. . . . I became very good friends with Stuart Preston, and wonder sometimes what he really thought of the *tourbillon* his London presence caused: he is too discreet to speak himself. A year or two after this another, even more extraordinary case of 'Yankee Fever' broke out; but the story of the 'Lonely Loot'nant' does not belong here.

A great hostess and creator of a salon needs an unflagging curiosity about other people, a flair for making them feel at home, or at least stimulated in her circle, almost unlimited time to organize her entertainments and to devote herself to the pursuit and domestication of those rising celebrities her shrewdly selective eye has marked down; and plenty of money. It was in the matter of money that Sybil Colefax was at a disadvantage compared with Emerald Cunard. Her furnishing business was a success, her social contacts increased the number of her customers, but as she entertained continuously and well, to luncheon, to tea, sherry, dinner and the theatre, she sometimes had to rely on the discreet assistance of friends who not only held her in deep affection, but believed that she filled an essential mediating function in London life. It was a great honour to be invited by her to become one of the regular, or rather semi-regular guests at her Wednesday dinner parties at the Dorchester, where I used to meet not only authors and artists from my own world, but people from the world of politics and power, the Jebbs, the Kirkpatricks, the Jowitts, and many others, and have the opportunity of talking with them at ease, in a kind of Colefaxian republic; and neither the honour nor the pleasure was diminished by the fact that a few days later one received a little bill for one's share of the entertainment. It had never been mentioned; but it was assumed that one knew. She pursued lions, I think, more assiduously and more single-mindedly than Emerald. About this time she noted that Victor Pritchett's star was rising. She had read his short stories, she admired his regular literary ' middles ' in the *New Statesman*, which were then at their most sparkling. As she knew he was a contributor of long standing to *New Writing*, she persuaded me to engage him to accompany me one evening to sherry at the exquisite little house in Lord North Street, where the guests sat round in an arrangement that was continually being shuffled by Sybil, who dashed about, perching on a footstool at one's feet for a few moments' conversation, inevitable prelude to a removal of oneself to another part of the room and a fresh conversation. She pounced on Victor with lion-worshipping ardour, and he very soon became one of her most frequent and most doted-on guests. She spared no pains about the really big prizes, and would, even in wartime when travel was difficult and uncomfortable, speed down to the quay-side, however far, to meet the boat that brought American celebrities of whose arrival she had been warned by mutual friends across the Atlantic. Nor did she do this simply in safari rage: she was full of kindness and consideration, and would shower touching little attentions on any member of her circle who was ill or in difficulties (though she had, of course, her favourites).

In September, 1941, the famous London conference of the PEN Club took place, a demonstration against the Axis not merely because it was held in battered London and attended by so many distinguished writers from the free world, but also because the refugee writers from occupied Europe who were settled in England used it to send out their challenge to the military masters of their homelands. John Dos Passos, Thornton Wilder and Robert Sherwood headed an impressive American delegation; and Sybil set herself to arrange a dinner party for them at the Dorchester, in which they would meet and talk with some English literary figures outside the conference. She enrolled Elizabeth Bowen and Roger Senhouse to help her in the organization, and I, with Cyril Connolly and several other writers, figured among the guests invited to Victor Cazalet's rooms. Sybil was at her most energetic, pressing the conversation whenever it seemed for a moment to flag and pitting English and Americans against one another in debate, and at the same time finding the opportunity to elicit from each guest the particular *pabulum* she knew he could provide her with: encouraging me to describe to her the last weeks in the life of Virginia Woolf, and the Americans to tell all the stories they knew about Roosevelt. The occasion was only a little spoilt by the fact that Robert Sherwood, the dramatist, who was said to be one of the very few men in America who knew what was going on inside the White House, kept a poker face and sealed lips almost the entire evening.

I only saw Sybil and Emerald together on one occasion, and that was in the Spring of 1943 when the first of the famous Poetry Readings took place, in aid of some wartime charity. These Readings were patronized by Royalty, packed with celebrities from both the literary and social worlds, and the scene of *contretemps* and scandal that provided stories to dine out on for weeks after. To this first Reading the Queen had agreed to come, and bring the two young Princesses with her. Edith Sitwell had been appointed one of the organizers, and a few days before wrote to me, on the brink of despair: ' The shades of—less the prison house than the lunatic asylum—are drawing ever nearer to me. The Reading—the Reading! The letters to poets about their collars, the threats to faint on the part of one female poet, the attempt to (*a*) read for 20 minutes instead of 6, (*b*) change the time of rehearsal, (*c*) be rehearsed all by herself *by me just* before the Reading, (*d*) read a funeral eulogy of Yeats—on the part of another female poet. And other troubles of this sort! Life is very difficult.' Her fears were justified on the day. Lady Dorothy Wellesley was one of the poets invited to read, but in spite of a momentary, distraught appearance on the platform about ten minutes before the Queen arrived, failed to take her place. The poets performed in alphabetical order, and as the end of the alphabet approached Vita Sackville-West slipped into the wings, only to return a few minutes later with a look of great shock on her face—but without the missing poetess.

The poets were ranged on either side of D. L. Murray, at that time editor of *The Times Literary Supplement*. No greater contrast could be imagined than between Tom Eliot, looking wearily benign and noble, Edith in her black robes and green hat shaped like a laurel wreath, as dominating as a Roman Emperor, and Walter de la Mare, a wizened gnome king. Nearly all of them, with the notable exceptions of Tom, the Sitwells, and Vita, gave very bad performances, and reduced the professional verse-readers, of whom there were a number in the audience, to a state of squirming misery. And yet I found it impossible to agree with Eddie Sackville-West, who, at the back of the hall, was suffering more acutely than anyone else, that it would have been far better to have had only

I Am My Brother

professionals. The gathering of so many notable poets on one
platform was exciting in itself, and even when they were difficult to hear and showed little or no understanding of an
audience's natural expectations, there was a fascinating juxta-
position of personalities and styles, and every now and then,
even in the bad performances, moments that shed a new illumination, precious as coming from the creator himself, on poems
one had always loved. This was not, I fear, true in the case of
W. J. Turner, who went on monotonously reciting inaudible
verse long beyond his strictly apportioned ration of time, and
seemed quite incapable of taking the hint implied in the
continual bursts of applause that interrupted him ever more
violently as the recitation proceeded. The Princesses appeared
delighted by this atmosphere of near-riot that developed so
spontaneously, and so unexpectedly enlivened their poetry
lesson. Gordon Bottomley, Grand Old Man of the occasion,
was also all but inaudible as he murmured through half a
dozen poemlets, but the rapturous applause that greeted the
little smile that broke between moustache and beard as he
reached the end, was genuine appreciation of a personality
that had captivated us all. But the Reading would have been
worthwhile, apart from its comedy aspect, if only for the opportunity it gave us to hear Tom reciting ' What the Thunder
Said ' from *The Waste Land*, starting on a deep, incantatory note
and working up to a climax of superb passion and drama.

Emerald had invited me to join her party, which included
Duff Cooper and Leslie Hore-Belisha; it was as we left the hall,
passing the distressed figure of the future Duchess of Wellington
at the head of the stairs, that I saw Emerald and Sybil come
together and talk animatedly for a few moments. But Emerald
was in one of her most ebullient moods, and as we emerged
into Bond Street she pranced away from Sybil and up to Hore-
Belisha, crying: ' Leslie! Recite me some Ronsard!—You do
it so beautifully! ' The former War Minister, however, did
not oblige.

5

SOMETIMES, after these excursions into the salons at the top, where still, through its disintegration, one could catch glimpses of what an older *beau monde* had been like, the need came over me to plunge to the other end of the social scale.

So I would sally forth into the black-out, to visit the pubs of Soho and the Fitzregnum, the French pub, the Swiss pub, the Fitzroy Tavern, the Wheatsheaf and others in remoter districts; or if it was after hours, the cafés and late-night snack-bars into which the stragglers emptied themselves. There a floating population of bohemians, actors, firemen, soldiers, sailors and airmen on leave or of the London garrison, and of many nationalities, poets and artists sometimes in uniform and sometimes in civvies, drifted together in chance and ever-changing groups: never have the London pubs been more stimulating, never has one been able to hear more extraordinary revelations, never witness more unlikely encounters. And one could keep one's ear to the ground.

There was certainly little to hear that could have given the enemy's most hopeful propagandists of demoralization in Britain much encouragement. One evening I had on one side of me a tall, fair-haired soldier who turned out to be on special leave from Tunisia, and complained bitterly of missing real soldiering at home—' people are just chocolate soldiers round here '—and of missing British beer in Africa—' nothing but vinn reuge, frightful stuff, red vinegar that's all it is, none of us would drink it if there was anything else to get pissed on '. On the other side of me was a fat, red-faced, cheery-looking sailor, who confessed that before the war he had been ' on the boards ' in the suburban music-halls, and had once seen *Desire Under the Elms* at Golders Green and had greatly admired Beatrix's performance. When war broke out, he had volunteered, and had been in minesweepers for three years and ' bloody well liked the life '.

Views on danger and on being under fire varied. The

fair-haired soldier remarked, about the fighting round Medjez
which he vividly described to me, that he 'just forgot to be
frightened' though he'd always expected he would be.
Another night, a young sailor who had joined the Navy as a
boy, and had earned his D.S.M. as a gunner in the second
battle of Narvik after he had been wounded by shell splinters,
told me that he hadn't cared at all until he had been hit the
first time, but after that it 'made him think'. The same night,
in another pub, an older sailor, very merry and lit up, talked
exuberantly about being under fire during convoy work. He
had been in the Far East, Madagascar, and before that at Alex.
and in many Malta convoys. He was a stoker, and admitted
that it wasn't particularly nice down below during an air or
submarine attack, you felt 'all cooped up'; but he'd found that
when the pompoms started to go off—and that meant it could
only be a matter of seconds before the bombs or torpedoes
arrived—the best thing to do was to concentrate on some small,
particular job, cleaning a piece of machinery with a rag, for
instance. Afterwards there was all the business of picking up
survivors from merchant ships that had been set on fire or sent
to the bottom: it wasn't so bad if they were men—'you just
picked 'em up and shook the water out of 'em, and then if they
was dead you just tossed 'em back '—but if they were women,
and wounded into the bargain—and these Norwegians and
Greeks took their women folk with them—well, then it really
'made you think'.

There was an 'old soldier', a decorated young veteran
already of many battlefields, who was a fairly regular visitor
to one of these pubs, and used to come up and talk (unless his
W.A.A.C. girl-friend was on leave) when he saw me arrive. A
tall, good-looking, gentle-voiced Scot from the Glasgow slums,
he had interesting views on this as on every other aspect of
soldier lore. 'The highly-strung, intellectual chaps are very
often the best in danger '—that was the considered opinion of
one neither highly-strung nor an intellectual himself; and
that some of his pals preferred the front line and the reality of
comradeship, and begged to be sent back to it if they were
taken out—that was his repeated experience. As a sergeant,
he had to watch his men very carefully, and he maintained that

he could tell at a glance if a man had anything in him—' even
if he *looks* tough he may betray himself by the way he walks '.
At the end of these discussions, his constant refrain was: ' Take
my word for it, John, this is the finest country in the world.'

The conversation was not always, however, on that note.
One night in Spring, when the lightless streets seemed to be
bathed in a pure milk of moonlight, I met a young soldier
whom I had known in the early days of the war, three years
before: a boy with strange trap-doors in his nature, a capacity
for imaginative suffering that had grown shockingly since I
had last seen him. His tongue was loosened over the beer, and
he talked and talked. He poured out his story of the Norway
campaign—it was a groove in his mind the needle couldn't get
out of—and spoke first of the bravery and fine military qualities
of the Bavarian soldiers who had been his opponents; but then,
switching round, told me of his horror at seeing women and
children fleeing from their ruined homes, and his burning
fury at what the Germans had done to a peaceable country.
He had an inseparable friend, a sharer in everything he had
done, enjoyed, endured; but the army machine had taken this
friend away from him. He could hardly express the misery
this separation had caused him, and as he dwelt on it, he began
to work up to a torrent of outrage and hatred against war: I
had never seen a soul in torment so nakedly before me.

The Fitzroy Tavern has changed now: gone are the dusty
rows of naval cap badges pinned up above the bottles near the
ceiling, famous names enough to conjure up a mighty fleet,
the military caps and strange barbaric weapons beside them
even more deeply dust-encrusted, too sacred and no doubt too
fragile for a broom to touch; gone the cartoons of the proprietor
and the recruiting posters of the first world war with their
period pathos; gone all the famous old soaks, male and female,
the groups of battledressed guardsmen like plants that had got
more than their fair share of fertilizer and shot up above the
rest, the Canadian and American sailors honeying with the
painted girls of the town, the stray, argumentative intellectuals,
the quiet couples, the squeaking hard-as-nails pansies who
would only have made a facetious ' camp ' joke if a bomb had
fallen next door, the tinkling piano and the jingling box

handed round for the pianists' collection, all that came to mean a kind of invincible London spirit in those years.   And yet in the middle of the general warmth, the tough high spirits, the thought of something very different was never far absent.   One night, alone with my own ruminations there, I pulled out of my pocket and re-read a letter that had arrived that morning from my ex-secretary John Lepper in the Middle East:

> While out in our truck the other day we were caught in a hell of a sandstorm which blew up without any warning.   It almost seems at times that Nature gets irritated by the death-like silence which hangs over these wastelands and sends a sudden wind to disturb the stillness.   It was about three hours before we could see sufficiently far ahead through the dust haze to risk a move— knowing that there was a minefield somewhere in the vicinity, we were not disposed to take any chances.   It continued to blow very strongly all that night;   towards two o'clock our tent collapsed and we had to fight devilish hard to prevent the whole issue from being blown all over the maidan.

> Contemplation of an old battlefield inspired the following fragment:

> > Litter of paper
> > Burned tanks and smashed sky-tilted guns
> > Discarded weapons split shell cases
> > Dead men sprawled with twisted faces
> > Flies swarming on the bloody places
> > And everything so still
> > Throughout the tawny waste of rock and sand
> > Nothing had life and nothing moved until
> > A rebel wind disturbed the silence and
> > Sent an empty tin clattering over stones.

I began to wonder whether John, and all the other soldiers and sailors who had known these pubs in the earlier phases of the war, thought of them nostalgically sometimes in the middle of the desert or in the wastes of the Arctic Sea.   Somehow to be arguing, laughing, singing there was a vote of confidence in them; and the printed sign that hung up above the counter, WE ARE NOT INTERESTED IN THE POSSIBILITY OF DEFEAT, was not just a piece of bravado or a warning to spreaders of ' alarm and despondency ', but the statement, nine-tenths of the time, of a simple truth.

6

IN a letter to Christopher at the end of 1942, I told him that the ranks of the regular *New Writing* contributors and the new young authors in uniform who were apt to turn up in London on leave, or passing through from one posting to another, were gradually growing thinner: ' airgraphs to Africa take the place of invitations to pilchards and cheese '. It was in fact a time when the lines of communication between *New Writing* and its contributors and would-be contributing enthusiasts were stretched to their most tenuous, across all the oceans and continents where theatres of war were to be found. Letters came in every day by airmail letter card or by that ingenious, handy invention of the war years, the airgraph, from Kenya, Persia, Egypt, Palestine, Cyprus, India, Burma and every other country of the Middle and Far East that was still in allied hands, reporting the at-long-last arrival of copies of the Penguins that had been sent off months before, or complaining of their failure to arrive, anxiously enquiring after manuscripts entrusted to the precarious surface mail, and disputing or agreeing with points of criticism I had made of manuscripts that had arrived safely and made their slow way through the increasingly congested editorial machine. My contributors could not see the bulging files (additions to which were so difficult to obtain), the heroic attempts by Barbara Cooper and her occasional assistants to find room for newly arrived manuscripts in inadequate chests of drawers already stuffed beyond capacity, or the struggle to correct proofs by airgraph texts, for some of the poets at least had begun sending their poems in this way to save time and danger. Punctuation in these minute photographic reproductions was sometimes extremely difficult to decipher; and occasionally, when the poem was long, or one of a series typed out over a whole sequence of airgraphs, the middle version would mysteriously fail to appear until a few weeks later, causing meanwhile odd misapprehensions in Carrington House about the jumps of thought, the pregnant sense-gaps that modern poets appeared increasingly to indulge in.

One of the chief contributors with whom I kept up a long-distance conversation in this way for many months, and even years, was Roy Fuller in the Fleet Air Arm unit at Kilindini. The editor–contributor relationship with Roy was in some ways the most satisfying of the war for me. He had been an interesting ' second generation ' poet of the 'thirties who, in spite of obviously strong intellectual equipment and deep feeling for poetry, had never quite emerged with an individual voice to catch and keep one's attention. Then, early in the war, he was drafted into the Navy and began to write a new kind of lyric about his training and the mood of his fellow-recruits, behind the straight simplicity of which extremely sharp observation, irony and deep emotion were closely packed in:

> Once as we were sitting by
> The falling sun, the thickening air,
> The chaplain came against the sky
> And quietly took a vacant chair.
>
> And under the tobacco smoke:
> ' Freedom,' he said, and ' Good ' and ' Duty '.
> We stared as though a savage spoke.
> The scene took on a singular beauty.
>
> And we made no reply to that
> Obscure, remote communication,
> But only stared at where the flat
> Meadow dissolved in vegetation.
>
> And thought: O sick, insatiable
> And constant lust; O death, our future;
> O revolution in the whole
> Of human use of man and nature.

When I read this poem, and the others he sent me which were written at the same time, I felt at once that they were the answer to the disgruntled old buffers and impatient well-wishers who were still complaining that there were no war-poets, though the disillusioned, anti-heroic note might well not be to their taste; a more promising answer than the still rather soft, nostalgic poetry that Alun Lewis and Sidney Keyes were writing at this period, and far more effective than the rather tediously inflated verse that some members of the so-called 'Apocalyptic' school and their fellow-travellers were producing at the same time. Several of Roy's new poems were published in *Penguin New Writing*, and were quickly noted by the connoisseurs. After he had finished his naval training, Roy was drafted eventually to his land-job in Kenya. He wrote at the time:

I feel more and more that I ought to develop in some way those simple things I was writing in England. The trouble is I seem to have escaped the war again—it must be fated that there shall be no war-poets. I just have the disadvantages of noise and gregariousness without the stimulant of action. I shall have to do some nature poems—there is certainly enough nature. For the rest, discipline is sensible and the Navy, as usual, in its rather bearish, clumsy way makes us as comfortable as it can. Sixpence a day colonial money, 50 cigarettes, 2 boxes of matches and a cake of soap free every week—it is like a kind but poor and vulgar aunt. I wouldn't be in any other service for 5s. a day more! And I still find my fellow-ratings witty, kind and simple. A man in the next bed to me, an airgunner, regular service, one long service badge, announced his intention of going to a concert in the town last night. They asked him what it was. 'A Bach concerto, Mozart, Brahms.' A howl of derision. But he howled too—'I've heard the bloke that plays the piano—and he's SHIT HOT.' 'Shit hot' is our catchword at the moment—it is the highest adjectival praise known to the F.A.A.

Out of Roy's feeling for East African nature, the sudden, fresh impact it made on him, came such beautiful poems as *The Giraffes*. But his mood of irresolution about the future direction of his poetry did not last long. He began to write poems of more elaborate organization and of even greater intensity of feeling, in which were mingled his vision of an African tribal life, horrible but satisfying to the primitive mind and spirit, now ruined by the corruption of white civilization which gives material benefits but has destroyed the meaning, and the meaninglessness of the lives of the soldiers involved in the war,

symbols of whose grotesque pathos and suffering he found in
the animals he watched—crabs on the beach or captive mon-
keys. All through these poems is a sense of almost terrifying
despair, an apprehension that something—which once existed
in the world and can somehow be put back in it—is absent,
drained out of life:

> . . . It says the human features
> Are mutilated, have a dreadful lack.
>
> It half convinces me that some great faculty,
> Like hands, has been eternally lost and all
> Our virtues now are the high and horrible
> Ones of a streaming wound which heals in evil.

It is the mood of the first book, but far more powerfully
expressed, without sentimentality or rhetoric and with a marvellous control of language and use of poetic shape and rhythm
to heighten his effects:

> For what is terrible is the obvious
> Organization of life: the oiled black gun,
> And what it cost, the destruction of Europe by
> Its councils; the unending justification
> Of that which cannot be justified, what is done.

Another contributor from the old days of *New Writing*,
novelist exiled into uniform, but at the same time old cam-
paigner from the Spanish War, was John Sommerfield. He
spent the early part of the war as an Aircraftsman on remote
airfields in the North—from one of which he sent me the letter,
in the Summer of 1940, from which I have already quoted.
Later he was drafted to India, where he wrote one of the most
remarkable wartime stories *New Writing* ever published, *Above
the Clouds*. But his *Worm's Eye View*, written while he was still
in England, had already attracted a great deal of attention,
especially among his younger contemporaries who found in it
an almost classic expression of the mood of their war in its
earlier phases. John's outstanding gifts, which he had already
demonstrated in his pre-war sea stories and the book about the
fighting in Spain, were, first, a power of creating atmosphere by
the elaborate manipulation of prose rhythms and a careful

building up from innumerable small touches, and, second, a very acute ear for dialogue and difference of speech and self-expression among his working-class characters. (Early on he became an enthusiastic collector of R.A.F. slang and claimed that he was actually in at the birth of more than one phrase that passed into general R.A.F. currency.) The nostalgia in *The Worm's Eye View*, for both the past under a haze of illusions and the future in a mist of impossible radiance, accentuated by the feeling that oppressed the aircraftsmen, of an unreality caused by their own inactivity while Europe was being drenched in blood, may seem today to impregnate the scene almost too heavily; but it did not then. John Sommerfield caught, with a craftsmanship beyond the range of most of my contributors, a reality about the inner world of experience of the young men in the Forces that was concealed by the journalists and the ' chins up ' humorous or heroic story writers. In the Spring of 1942 he wrote to me from his troopship en route for India, describing with extraordinary vividness a feeling about the great nineteenth-century novels that more and more people were coming to read or re-read:

Lying on deck in a sunblaze, dimly heaving and not noticing the seaswish and the undertones of the turning propellors, I enjoy *Jane Eyre* and feel in three different worlds at once. Because I keep thinking of the last time I read it, in University City. I remember the large bare room, with November wind and rain blowing through the shattered windows that were barricaded with books, behind which our machine guns stood. . . . There I was rolled up in a piece of old carpet reading away like mad, the war noises, intermittent gunfire, thin wail of bullets, distant crunching of bursting shells, were as remote as the sea noises of now. And both then and now, in such different worlds of different wars, I lived in that extraordinary, passionate, *stable* world of the book. . . .

It was, I think, exile—exile from intellectual companionship and the world of argument and discussion—that most writers in uniform minded more than any other aspect of the war. Norman Cameron, sending me three ' travel-sketch kind of poems ' from North Africa, wrote:

In a letter I got from you some time ago, you said something about living in mud and cold. I'm afraid I can't claim to be suffering any hardship, except lack of sheets. I live in comfort. I did do a trip recently to a comparatively forward area, and there I was more comfortable than ever, since soldiers in the field look after themselves as well as they can, when they can. In a Polish mess, for example, I had the best meal since 1940—all made out of ordinary British rations, but quite unrecognizable.

What else? I'm beginning, despite all this comfort, to feel the effects of exile. As Robert Graves remarked about his stay in Egypt, one can live on one's hump only for so long, and my hump is not large. I want to meet some friends again. . . .

Then there were the younger poets, like Roy Fuller, struggling to hold on to the literary world of England by the frail capricious threads of airgraph and air letter, poets to whom the connection was even more important, as they were at the beginning of their careers and in danger of having no career at all at the same time. Alan Ross, slim, dark-haired poet of twenty from Haileybury and Oxford, sent me a batch of poems one day from a destroyer which he had recently joined as a Sub-Lieutenant. He had already, I discovered, had a smash in the Fleet Air Arm that nearly cost him his eyesight, and had since taken part in the Arctic convoys, which were among the most dangerous operations of the war. A combination of freshness of lyrical feeling and sophistication of approach in the poems appealed to me, and I accepted one at once. On his next shore leave he came to see me, and I found him bursting, not with stories of the hair-raisingly horrible adventures he had been through (I found out about them afterwards) but with ideas about poetry and pictures and plays. Every time his ship came back to port, he threw off his naval disguise and put on corduroys and a brightly coloured shirt, and made for the first bookshop he could find, to emerge with his arms full of volumes of poetry, new novels and biographies. He informed me, to my amazement, that on board his destroyer as many as thirty people, officers and ratings, read *Penguin New Writing*; and though they had begun to read it casually and dubiously, persevered perhaps because one particular story appealed to them for a background they recognized or for a character who might have come out of their own lives; so that they had now reached the stage of holding highbrow discussions about Auden and Lorca. Alan was already the most heart-warming enthusiast for both the big and the little *New Writing*, and must, I felt, have done much to produce this highly satisfactory state of affairs by ceaseless propaganda himself. His letters conjured up pictures of devotion to literature and the idea of an *avant-garde* under the most impossible circumstances, that haunted me at my desk in Carrington House and stirred visions of a Kingdom of Art established in a post-war world, and England at last transformed. ' Now I am at sea again,' he wrote after one hurried week-end in London, ' and already the guns have fired. I am as tired as hell. I have with me *N.W. & Daylight, Caught, The Seed Beneath the Snow*, Montherlant's *Lepers*, so I am fairly happy. My fellow matelots are good, I like them. I am beginning a new, longish poem. . . . Now I am going to my bed of hard boards and a blanket, and my sweater for a pillow.'

In the fullness of time, after the war, Alan Ross was to be one of the poets I published under my own imprint; as was another young poet whose work began to interest me at this time, though he could scarcely have been more different from Alan in temperament and outlook on the world. Hamish Henderson never let me forget that he was a Highland Scotsman, and though as a concession to evil times he wrote in English, thought Gaelic superior to all other languages. A colourful character, he not only wrote poetry but was connoisseur and collector of Eighth Army slang, part-author of many army ballads (the less publicly printable of which he issued after the war to private subscribers from the ' Lili Marlene Club ' of Glasgow), and composer of two slow marches for pipes which were played on the Anzio beachhead. He belonged to the Cambridge generation of Nicholas Moore and Raymond Williams, and had begun to send me poems in 1941 before he was drafted to the Middle East. In spite of rejections, he persisted; this was fortunate, because he suddenly began to write some moving poems based on the desert war and his experiences at Alamein, in which he at last found his voice as a poet. The first I took was a short but effective poem which

o

I published in *Penguin New Writing*, but this was followed by the
very impressive *Fragment of an Elegy*, which appeared first in
New Writing and Daylight, in the Winter of 1943–44; by then
he had been with the famous 51st Highland Division through
all the fighting in North Africa and Sicily and Italy. It
struck a new note in the poetry that had come out of the fighting, not so much because of the compassion for the innocent
dead and the feeling *beneath the propaganda* for the enemy, but
because these emotions were allied with a fighting pride:

> There were our own, there were the others.
> Therefore, minding the great word of Glencoe's
> Son, that we should not disfigure ourselves
> With villainy of hatred; and seeing that all
> Have gone down like curs into anonymous silence,
> I will bear witness for I knew the others.
> Seeing that littoral and interior are alike indifferent
> And the birds are drawn again to our welcoming North
> Why should I not sing *them*, the dead, the innocent?

I used also to have a lively correspondence with Terence
Tiller, who was teaching at Cairo University and one of the
leading spirits responsible for *Personal Landscape*. This was, in
my opinion, by far the most interesting of the many briefly
flowering literary magazines that appeared in Egypt during
the war; indeed one of the rare ' little ' magazines that have
made literary history in our time. ' Environment and personal
friendship, and not a specific poetic practice was the bond,'
wrote Robin Fedden in introducing the *Personal Landscape*
anthology after the war, and described how he and Laurence
Durrell and Bernard Spencer had all got to know one another
previously in Greece. Robin and Bernard were, of course, of
my own generation; Larry, a little younger, had begun to make
his name in Paris just before the war; Terence, the youngest
of the original contributors, had attracted my attention a few
years earlier, as I have already described, and had appeared
in *Poets of Tomorrow* while still at Cambridge. ' His tensity of
style and piercing metaphysical eye,' wrote Robin, ' added
something that none of us had got and emphasized just that
variety of approach and absence of poetic *parti pris* that we felt

was desirable.' Beside the qualities Robin Fedden noted, Terence's poems had a remarkable verbal music and subtlety of rhythmic life; they particularly delighted me because, almost always carefully wrought, often arcane and yet never guilty of the confused grandiloquence that disfigured so much poetry of the time, they seemed to me the nearest thing to pure poetry to come out of those years. While I was printing his poems in occasional batches in *New Writing* and then collecting them into volumes for The New Hogarth Library, I also acted —as I did for Roy Fuller—as a distributing agent among the periodicals for those poems I could not use myself. In November, 1942, he wrote to me, telling me that the fourth number of *Personal Landscape* was ready and that he was having it sent to me, and added:

> Thank you for what seems a tremendous periodicals campaign; the list of publications you sent me was breath-taking, and divided me between astonishment and gratitude. Apart from the poems to *Horizon* and to Alexander Comfort, I have sent nothing to England independently. . . . I do not know if Comfort is mixed up with the Apocalyptics—probably not, as I see he is in *N.W. & Daylight*—but I hope I am not going to be, through sending stuff to him. At least, not unless the policy expressed in a letter to me by John Bayliss has considerably altered, and the manifesto in *The White Horseman* greatly modified.

Side by side with the young poets came the prose writers of the future: none more promising, more full of exciting possibilities in the context of the time, than Julian Maclaren-Ross. In 1940, he had sent me some stories which I had just not liked well enough to accept, because, for all the skill they showed, there seemed to me something a little *made up* about them (subsequently he sold several of them and made a success, especially with *A Bit of A Smash in Madras* which appeared in *Horizon*). Apparently harbouring no resentment about this, he suddenly wrote to me in July of 1942, from the Beach Café, Bognor Regis, in his extraordinary neat, marmoset's handwriting—he never then, and has never since used a typewriter— to say that he had started writing again:

> Having kept quiet for two years, since I've been in the Army, I have suddenly embarked on a series of Army stories and there are

twelve of them so far . . . I've read everything that's been written about the Army up to now and find that most of the stuff is either journalism, or deadly dull: I liked a story you printed called *They Kept Him on the Square*. The best actually are those written by Alun Lewis and not yet published, which I read in typescript when he was billeted in the house next door to me; and Gwynne-Brown's book *F.S.P.* . . .

I wrote back and told him that I too had enjoyed *F.S.P.*, that I already had one of Alun Lewis's stories in reserve, and that I very much wanted to see one of his new Army stories. This was the beginning of a long literary relationship with an eccentric, brilliantly gifted author who sometimes seemed as if possessed by a demon whose satanic mission it was to thwart and wither at the root all the uniquely valuable talents Julian had been born with. The first story he sent me was *Y List*, an account of his own experiences in an Army hospital, done with a wit, a story-telling flair, and a kind of dry pathos of characterization that marked it out at once as the work of a highly original writer; but not the masterpiece of humorous observation that I was lucky enough to publish for him a couple of years later, *The Swag, The Spy and The Soldier*. Julian's greatest gift, in these war stories, was, I thought, his intuitive sympathy for those who have fallen foul of The Machine; for those who are too simple in their eccentricity as well as for those who are too complex and sensitive, to fit into the conventional set-up; a passionate feeling for life, on the edge of despair, informed the best of them. He had, I reflected when reading these stories, the makings of a Dickens in him—a Dickens who had read Dashiell Hammett.

Julian's creative eye was focused on the unprivileged shadows, the stoker's hold of life: very different was another young writer who was introduced to *New Writing* by William Plomer, but no less authentic in his observation. Richard Rumbold had become a Pilot Officer in the R.A.F., very much in love with the St. Exupéry *mystique*, a dream of an élite in the air, the god-like pilot fraternity. The piece I published for him, under the pseudonym of Richard Nugent, *From a Pilot's Diary*, was, for the civilian, full of intensely interesting aperçus about the young men who were indeed at that time looked up to by the English public as almost sacred warrior-guardians, and it cast light on places the journalists deliberately avoided; but the *mystique* nevertheless aroused violent opposition from some of *New Writing*'s contributors and fans.   One intelligent soldier, in fact, wrote to me angrily denouncing ' this completely manufactured sense of other-worldliness—detachment—aloofness—superiority—demanding no personal inner effort, nothing but the efficient firing of a 1,000 h.p. Merlin and the ordinary ability to drive a car ', and maintaining that such pseudo-Promethean young men were a danger to the making of a better world after the war.   But in truth Richard Rumbold was a more complex character than that, a young man for whom the flying *mystique* was, I felt, a technique adopted in the hope of resolving contradictions in his own nature.   To the careful reader, the game was given away by such passages as the following: ' an escapist by nature, I have tried many things—lovely spots of the earth, art, violent action, inner seclusion, even, occasionally, danger—but I know of no escape world as satisfying as that of the world two or three miles above.' Not, in fact, the New Superman, but one of the prototypes of the *malaise* of our time: his autobiography, *My Father's Son*, published some years after the end of the war, made all this much clearer.

My main object, in the stories and sketches of wartime life that became a central feature of *New Writing* during these years, was always, I think, to find the writers who could reveal a truth more authentic, more intimate in detail than the propaganda to which we were (ever so gently) subjected could admit, something that slipped through the coarse nets of the journalists. Sometimes, however, it was the journalists themselves who provided it, breaking away in a moment of illumination from the uncommanded conventions of their calling.   F. J. Salfeld, born in 1905, was trained as a reporter from early youth, worked for the *Liverpool Daily Post* and eventually joined the *Daily Telegraph*, which was about to send him to Moscow in 1941 when he was called up.   He joined the Navy, and was in several of the Malta convoys about which he wrote for the *Daily Telegraph*.   One day he sent me a story, which we decided to call *Fear of Death*.   It appealed to me immediately for the vividness of its human details—the stoker caught in the showers when the call to action stations came—the sailor bidding his canary farewell before the dive-bombing started—the embarrassed kindliness deep down in the magazine towards the one who had lost his nerve—the boy sailor who had seen his ' winger ' killed in front of his eyes.   Another example was R. D. Marshall, twenty-one at the outbreak of war and on the reporting staff of the *Glasgow Herald.*   He became an officer in a Highland regiment, and in one of the North African actions lost his arm.   This experience produced *A Wristwatch and Some Ants*, one of the most vividly recollected descriptions of battle I was ever to publish, deeply moving and convincing.

Then there were the artists turned into soldiers, who seemed to be more cruelly victims of circumstance than the poets, Cinderella reversed, glittering coach turned into pumpkin upon the midnight-hour-for-the-duration.   Useless to say that all suffer alike: what you feel depends on your capacity for feeling, what you suffer depends on the Eden you are driven out of.   Keith Vaughan, changing from one camp to another, wrote:

> I am still without anchorage, rudderless, with a drunken crew, condemned it seems like Kafka's Graccus to endless voyaging. For the moment I am caught in a net of barbed wire, under canvas, in a barren orchard, in the central ordnance depot. All ballast was dropped on the voyage.   I have now but a pocket full of possessions, safe only until they strip me naked, and such shreds of memories as still cling to an unhinged mind and shaken heart.   This is the inner temple of Mars, here behind steel walls, guarded by sentries, it can spin its red tape like a demented fiend in unchecked riot.   The yells and stamping of the barbarians within the sun itself.   But take no notice, my dear John, I am overwrought and helpless. . . .

And Billy Chappell, ballet-dancer and stage-designer turned gunner, anatomizing his darkness, wrote in *The Sky Makes Me Hate It*:

> Before the war, and during my first months in the Army, my thoughts streamed from me in a jerky rhythm, outwards, into the

world. Now they turn inwards, probing: and I feel in my brain that an endless transformation scene is taking place. A panto-mime transformation in which curtains of membrane that are patterned with my life endlessly dissolve and part. My thoughts pick and knock at things which stir somewhere behind the farthest curtains. My mind knows that there is something more than it was aware of to be found behind itself. It claws and scratches gently at the walls of its dimly-lighted caves, sensing, more than seeing, a suggestion of forms it cannot picture, they are so distant, remote and unknown. Perhaps, lurking there, is the enormous comprehension that humanity needs; the lack of which makes so pitiful its efforts to manage itself. To tackle decently the handling of its relationships, its loves, lives and deaths.

This turning inward of my thoughts cannot be happening only to me. I look . . . into the faces of the men who fill the camps and barracks in this district; the faces that crowd my sight in the streets of the town, in the pubs and restaurants and cinemas and on the buses; faces oafish, brutal, cunning, noble, sensitive, and beautiful. . . . No one can be genuinely happy at this time. War, as it welds the people of a nation together, makes every life an isolated life. Everyone is lonely. We have all become strangers; and when the war is over we shall have to start learning once more to know each other. . . .

Later, in North Africa, like so many others of his sensibility, Billy Chappell found a way to make a treaty between his old, inner artistic self and the outward soldier on active service; he threw himself into Army show business, entertaining the troops while performing his duties as Assistant Adjutant at the School of Artillery of B.N.A.F. 'Having produced 9 revues since I came here,' he wrote, 'and played an average of 5 performances a week for the last 10 weeks, in and on every sort of thing except theatres, I feel I am in a fit position to shoot my mouth off. I have made the fullest and most complete spectacle of myself that has ever been seen, culminating last week in my somewhat startling appearance as Carmen Miranda's Aunty, with a quite funny song written by an intelligent Air O.P. officer. She's a fairly gay old soul and received with quite a lot of glee by the troops because she's very obviously revolting and very noisy. If some of the fans who liked me years back in *Gods Go a Begging* could see me now. . . .'

In the British Navy, the drafted or volunteer ratings who had joined up only for the duration, were known as H.O.—' Hostilities Only '—sailors. In the world of letters also there were ' Hostilities Only ' writers. Some of them, like Rollo Wooley and Gully Mason, might have taken up writing as a serious occupation after the war; one can never know, because they were killed so soon after having written their two or three stories or poems, evidence only of their intention of the moment and not of the unrevealed strength of talent and will-power. Rollo Wooley, whom I only met once for half an hour very shortly before his last flight, was a sensitive, good-looking boy of twenty-three from Rugby and Oxford, the dreamy look in whose eye was reflected in the slight but haunting story *The Search*, which I published in *New Writing and Daylight* in the Winter of 1942–43. A crew go out to search for an aeroplane reported missing. But is it really for this aeroplane they are looking? Loch, mountain and ocean take on a sad, timeless, symbolic aspect in the young airman's eye:

> What did they expect us to find? No we had seen nothing. All our lives we had been searching and had found nothing. Only the whitewashed cottages and some strands of seaweed. Only some fragments of cloud and the blueness of the sea. Only the thinness of the empty glittering waves. I felt too weary to remember the original object of our search. Certainly it had been quite clear a little while ago: a plane was missing: one of our pilots had not returned. But that was only the previous night, and surely we had been searching for longer than that? Ages and ages before we had begun the search . . .

Who can tell whether Rollo Wooley would have been able to develop the delicate poetic vein which these three pages revealed? Slight though they are, they have a curious perfection of expression in their time and place: an achievement which has nothing to do with bulk and complexity, and is rarely granted, even to those with far greater ambition, will-power and luck in survival. Very different was the case of Gully Mason, young airman of the same age as Rollo Wooley who invaded the lives of myself, Cyril Connolly and Stephen Spender in 1941, with his humour and charm, his longing to write, his extroverted zest for life, and his practical and public interests that made one think that imaginative literature might well not have been the sphere in which he would eventually have made his mark. Voicing the characteristic political anxieties of his generation, he wrote to me from the Sergeants' Mess of his airfield in Carmarthenshire in the Autumn of 1941, not very long before his death:

> I think I have found the ideal way of spending a war. The idea is to surrender yourself to it absolutely. Treat flying as a job for which you receive a fixed salary. Like being a coal miner or an insurance agent.
>
> You are then in the position of a normal working man, and have the gratification of knowing that nearly everybody else is similarly placed. So one has the unique opportunity to read and study and accumulate knowledge, that later, in days of action, will be invaluable. . . .
>
> But it seems to me that the future is very dark. I can see what will happen when we win the war. Our leaders will seize the opportunity to consolidate their position. At the khaki—or will it be sky-blue election—we shall hear all the old catch-words, disguising a policy that will lead us to another war when I shall be an old fogey on the ground staff and my son will be flying the 1,000 m.p.h. Spitfire Mark 7002 . . .
>
> Do you think that the armies will return to their bank desks and their cash counters when they can march in the People's Army? When their country calls them? So few of us who can see and check the beginning of disaster by the tremor of a needle and an inch-pressure on the stick, will be able to perceive the real issues that their propaganda will conceal. And we, the airmen, will be the first people they—who must recruit the youth —will seek to attract.
>
> On the other hand, if we stood together, we could smash them.

Gully Mason never produced anything for *New Writing*, though we had long discussions about it, and about the meaning of poetry, and what writers could do and ought to do in the middle of a war, in the pubs when we happened to meet and in the bar of Athenaeum Court; long, animated arguments interrupted by sudden explosions on Gully's part, adumbrations of fantasy campaigns to ensnare the girl he had lost his heart to.

But there were those, luckily a greater number, who survived, and yet were never able in peacetime—so it seemed—to recapture or exploit the moment of truth they had discovered in describing some wartime experience for *New Writing*. John Hillier, for instance, who had been Assistant Town Clerk in Tunbridge Wells before the war, and became a Pilot-Officer, then Flying-Officer in the R.A.F. Some urgent need to express, to record a quality in the new life in which he found himself suddenly grew in him, led him to send me a short story *Bad for Discipline*, the theme of which he described in his letter as ' the feeling men in remote air force camps get on seeing an attractive woman after perhaps months of solitary existence . . . which makes them incapable of ordinary social advances and drives them into a rough apparent misogynism '. He had been brought up without any knowledge of the literary world, had tried a course with one of the lamentable ' schools of writing ', and had been told that *Bad for Discipline* had everything possible wrong with it, before he sent it to me. A man of enormous charm, of sensitive feeling and sterling character, he wrote several other stories of his experience, some of which I published (after the most futile and ludicrous struggles with the official R.A.F. censorship), but nothing with the irony and tension of *Bad for Discipline*, which found the approbation of Desmond MacCarthy and several other critics when it appeared in *New Writing and Daylight*.

With Denis Glover, who began as Ordinary Seaman in the New Zealand Navy in H.M.S. *Onslaught*, I already had a connection, as he was Director of the Caxton Press in Christchurch, and as such printer and patron to the group of New Zealand writers, which included Frank Sargeson and Roderick Finlayson, whose work I had begun to publish in *New Writing* before the war. The New Zealanders continued to provide a far higher proportion of interesting young writers than the size of their population and the remoteness of their homeland from the great cultural centres might have led one to expect. Charles Brasch, a gifted poet struggling to define the soul of his country, was working in England; from the Middle East, two promising new writers, who were to settle amongst us after the war, sent me poems and sketches: Erik de Mauny's *In Transit* and Dan Davin's *Under the Bridge* both appeared in the ' Report on Today ' feature of *Penguin New Writing*. That

Summer, a long short story which Frank Sargeson sent me at the
end of 1942, and which I published in three instalments, was
one of the outstanding successes of these years. An English
officer, in command of a unit on the Burmese frontier, wrote to
me after the appearance of the second instalment demanding to
know when the third would appear, as his men were in a state
of extreme excitement and impatience to discover how the
story would end.

The chances of war brought Denis Glover to my flat one day
in 1941, looking rather like Mr. Punch in naval uniform, sturdy,
stocky, sanguine of complexion and temperament, a man in a
million, imperturbable and with a great sense of humour.
' The Navy is rather like going to school all over again,' he
wrote to me in 1942, ' the initial shyness and reserve, the viola-
tion, unwittingly, of a few sacred taboos, the strict supervision
by prefects and housemaster, the complete lack of privacy.
Everything, really, which I would have hated a few years ago,
but now find tolerable and even amusing.' In the same letter,
he produced an image that brought home more effectively than
pages of description the overcrowding of the Lower Deck:
' With five or six faces in front of a mirror it sometimes becomes
a problem just which one to shave.' I published Denis's
Convoy Conversation in *P.N.W.* No. 16: it was remarkable for its
unforced truth, for the nerve-tauteningly vivid description of
battle at sea, and the shrewd, dry humour of the story about his
wife that the ' Geordie ' gunner pursues through all the violence
of action. Denis remained all the war through perplexed but
fascinated by the nature of his British shipmates: ' They may
have travelled the world over,' he wrote home, ' and stepped
from one sinking ship into another, but their thoughts remain
obstinately rooted in Wigan, or Glasgow or Swansea with a
parochialism that is somehow not so ridiculous. England has
always been a puzzle to us outlanders.'

Later, Denis Glover, by then Lieutenant in charge of a
landing craft, wrote a brilliant piece about the invasion of
Normandy, called *It Was D-Day*, which we published in No. 23.
I have always regretted that, since his demobilization and
return to New Zealand, he has not exploited the considerable
gifts he showed that he possessed in these two pieces.

There were many other sailors whose letters came into our office. Fred Smewin, for instance, A.B. from the West Country, who wrote poems on his ship H.M.S. *Jeannie Deans*, always up against authority—' I find it hard to understand why Hitler is so famous, he walks in every street, swaggers in every ship, and makes life bloody everywhere '—yet always constant in his devotion to living poets and novelists, to a contemporary literature that might somehow, some day, cleanse the Augean Stables of life. And Jerry Lawson, another youthful A.B. from Lancashire with an extraordinary curly, rococo handwriting, who for months and months sent me in stories and descriptions of his Navy life, pleading with me to lift him from the anonymous mass to the election of print. He had no gift but his natural sincerity; and before he could learn any more, I heard from his mother that he had been killed.

And many, many others. From all the Services, from every front, manuscripts poured in. One day there would arrive a satirical ballad from a young man serving in the Royal Marines, who had already been in many of the most spectacular naval engagements of the war: it came in an envelope stamped *On Active Service*, and as I read it I was aware he might well be about to make a descent on some secretly chosen beach in enemy-occupied territory. Another day would arrive the story of a leave spent in Cairo from a Gunner in the Long Range Desert Group: long before the MS. had made its slow way to London he could have been captured or wounded in a furious sudden encounter with Rommel's tanks. A Monday morning's batch would include some reflective poems from a nurse in Malta, poems that had survived in a convoy that had had to fight off enemy attacks for days and nights without stop; an airgraph from a newly-gazetted Lieutenant in PAI-Force, which contained a neat epigram on the meeting of Russian and British soldiers; a rather battered-looking packet, with Indian stamps outside and an unknown Aircraftsman's diary inside, which had taken nearly four months on its way by the long sea-route; and a letter from a prisoner-of-war camp in Germany containing elegies and sonnets written in the endless tedium of that remote, flat landscape of Northern Europe.

There were times when, looking through all these works so precious to the young men and women who sent them off, I felt as if I were in a telephone exchange into which confused, half-audible messages were being sent pell-mell, in a never-ending stream. The human appeal of these manuscripts was nearly always immense, but how vastly their literary value varied, how rarely the authentic gift revealed itself! The more of them I read as the months went by, the more pity I thought it that these burning shrapnel fragments of experience and reflection-in-action, from places where the meaning of the war was most keenly felt, so many of them so much more real and significant than what normally got into our wartime newspapers, could so seldom be used. The messages were too confused, too incomplete, the thing that needed so urgently to be said lost before the end in a tangle of clichés.

From the window of the room where I worked in Carrington House, the eye was directed, by high flanking walls to right and to left, southwards through a gap between the top floors of steel and concrete buildings, over the trees of Green Park to a confused ridge of chimney-pots and domes, in the middle of which rose a slim tower of vaguely oriental aspect, the tower of Westminster Cathedral. Every now and then a white plume of smoke puffed up into the air somewhere along this ridge, indicating a train arriving or departing in the terminus concealed there. On a clear day a further line of wooded hills appeared behind the tower, the extreme limit of the view. To reach that line of hills, the eye had passed over the hidden chasm of Piccadilly at the foot of the steel and concrete buildings, the only evidence of which was the faint continual rumble and rustle of traffic, too faint for the ear to distinguish depth or distance; and the more remote chasm of the river, which only reminded the ear of its presence when the busier sounds of day had ebbed and the mournful hooting of a tug was heard to echo hollowly against the early morning or late evening sky.

The sofa table which I used as desk was always piled with manuscripts waiting to be read or re-read, and letters waiting to be answered. Often, trying to make up my mind whether a poem or a story was really worth accepting, or what to write to an author who seemed to me just not to have made the grade,

I let my gaze stray out into the landscape, losing the thread of thought for a moment, letting the changes of light stir strange irrelevant imaginings.   Sometimes the arrangement of trees and buildings, the haze of a fine day mounting towards noon, would begin to obliterate the vast city; as the sun illuminated a concrete wall to a certain tone of pale gold against the pale blue atmosphere, one could for a moment fancy that out there, only two or three hundred yards away, a curling line of foam was cooling a beach of sifted, white sand, and fishing boats of a shape and colour no English seaside knew were sliding across the sparkling satin of the water. . . . Even in London the Spring smells of the earth cannot be altogether effaced by smoke and petrol fumes; and straying on a light breeze through the open window they evoked disturbing mirages in the mind, sudden half-glimpsed memories of other, peacetime Springs in other places, chestnut leaves unfurling against baroque porches and balustrades.

After working in London for several years of war with scarcely a break, one's mind was particularly susceptible to these transformations.   Everything in the war seemed to be happening on a distant rim; and the two illusions underwent curious identifications in moments of extreme nostalgia, so that the fighting in Africa or the East, where so many of one's friends had been transported, appeared to the imagination not as the exile and ever-renewed danger of those friends, but as the fortunate experience of a younger self.

There was a great deal of weary work in the sifting and judging of these innumerable manuscripts, in spite of the keen pleasure of the occasional authentic finds; but it was constantly relieved by the eccentricities and unconscious humour of a certain proportion of the would-be contributors.   I always intended to make copies of the dottier poems and ' yarns ' for the amusement of myself and my friends in the darker days that might be coming, but neither I nor Barbara Cooper ever seemed to find the time.   Even if we had, I could not have quoted them here, for fear their authors might still be alive. In spite of the prevailing anti-heroic tone of wartime poetry, these eccentrics proved to me that the spirit of Sir Henry Newbolt was still alive, and when I read the clarion-call of a first line ' Day Lewis, arise! ', I realized that the mood of defending ' the bad against the worse ' was chagrin and disappointment to at least one patriotic songster.

When number 16 of the Penguin series came out, in the Spring of 1943, I felt that I had at last come as close as I could get to realizing the ideal that had been at the back of my mind all this time. Everything in it was new, except one outstanding story (Jean Paul Sartre's *The Room*); the ' Report on Today ' feature contained Laurie Lee's *Good Morning* as well as Denis Glover's *Convoy Conversation*, John Hillier's *Daylight on Berlin* and Anthony Verney's *The Cat and the Soldier*; in a batch of poems by Louis MacNeice there were perhaps two of the best half dozen ' war ' poems written during those years, *Springboard* and *Brother Fire*, as well as Demetrios Capetanakis's famous *Abel* and Roy Fuller's *The Giraffes* and *The Green Hills of Africa*; there were two excellent literary articles, *Sensuousness in Modern Poetry* by Stephen Spender and *An Introduction to Melville* by William Plomer; and an article by Keith Vaughan (writing under the pseudonym of ' Art Critic ') not only gave an illuminating critique and interpretation of the war painting of the time but was also illustrated by photogravure plates of the most wonderful pictures by Leslie Hurry, John Piper, Edward Burra, Keith Vaughan and Leonard Rosoman, the visionary quality in which seemed perfectly attuned to the poetry beside them.

One day, a clipping came in from the *New York Herald Tribune*, in which the reviewer, Babette Deutsch, wrote of a batch of *Penguin New Writings* which had just arrived from Britain: ' These small books, thin, unbound, printed on shabby paper. Yet one handles them respectfully; they have come through. There is a challenge in the determination that got these pamphlets printed and distributed and shipped across the Atlantic.' And I thought of a line in a poem I had published by Norman Hampson, written while serving in a corvette, on convoy duty, on the high seas:

> '. . . We keep
> The truest course by the best light we know.'

7

IT was clear, as soon as the first number of *New Writing and Daylight* had been published, that it was liked, and was going to be able to maintain itself: and I could therefore indulge in some long-term planning for its future. For the rest of the war, I suppose that scarcely a day passed without my two *New Writing* offspring being in my thoughts: and at week-ends when I could get away to Fieldhead, I used to take long walks by the river, evolving schemes for a special feature or a symposium for the next number, deciding whom I would invite to write for it, or how I would arrange the authors I had already accepted.

There were obvious similarities between *New Writing and Daylight* and the Penguin, and these increased when the former, like an elder brother at school passing on blazer or bat to a younger brother, gave some of its most successful contributions a second life at a year or so's interval in the Penguin. Nevertheless, I always saw the chief function of *New Writing and Daylight* as providing an international meeting place of the arts, as the original, pre-war *New Writing* had, and I was constantly trying to find new foreign contributors among the exiled writers in London, or to extract from those in privileged places copies of new poems or stories that had been written abroad. So it was that I managed to publish some of Aragon's most beautiful *Crêve-Coeur* poems in a skilful translation by Louis MacNeice; a short story by Nikolai Tikhonov, whom I had met in Russia before the war; poems by Czech poets still in the Protectorate which Jiři Mucha obtained for me, Polish and Portuguese contributions, and many from occupied Greece through Demetrios and his Greek friends in many parts of the world.

But I also intended to devote more space in *New Writing and Daylight* to critical studies, with all the arts within their range. My most cherished aim was to find, and give encouragement and scope to the kind of critic who has always interested me most, and has always seemed to me most capable of acting as a creative agent on the making of literature: the poet or poet-novelist whose intelligence is constantly exploring the philosophical raison d'être of his art, testing his conclusions by examining them in relation to the great artists of the past or his more formidable contemporaries, the writer with a bent for constructing systems out of the ideas which have filled his own mind for the time being; who is miles apart from the pedantic critic awarding marks and arranging schools, or the clever talker-critic with nothing new to say, who treats a book as a sort of tennis-court in which to play a brilliant game. Good—that is, stimulating and persuasive—philosopher-poets of this kind are unfortunately rare; and many hopes I entertained (though not all) were disappointed. In spite of this, and though I was well aware of the dangers of trying to ' impose a line ' on my contributors, a tone, a direction of thought did, I believe, emerge from *New Writing and Daylight*, and more recognizably as it went on; largely because the writers I went to for critical articles were generally friends with whose thought I was intimate through many a discussion, but also, perhaps, because there was a ' spirit of the time ', a sense of the need to emphasize the human, and, to put it at its simplest, the over-riding importance of human-kind-ness, which all of us to some extent shared.

In these critical studies, I was also anxious to provide some kind of commentary on contemporary literature; and, as it seemed to me that there were hints of some very interesting, indeed exciting developments, and my head was teeming with them, I undertook this job myself, in a series of articles which I called *The Armoured Writer*. I spent a great deal of the war years in reading, not only manuscripts for The Hogarth Press or *New Writing*, but also the newly published books that stood in any relation to imaginative literature, perhaps more than ever before or since; at the same time I read and re-read the great classics, looking always for some new relevance to the times we were living through. I should give a false picture of my life and mind at this time if I were to leave out all this reading and the restless experimental reflections it gave rise to: the continuous, rather undisciplined laboratory-researcher's testing and speculating.

In writing my article *The Heart of the Problem* for the first

P

number of *Daylight*, I had complained of the fragmentariness,
the imaginative inadequacy of the prose fiction of the period to
deal with the crisis of civilization in which we found ourselves.
In those early days I was thinking mainly of the novels that had
come out of the experience of the 'thirties, each illuminating a
small area of experience powerfully enough, but failing to provide the complete X-ray of the *sickness in the bone* of our time.
But the first years of the war had, it seemed to me, given us
even less than this; and in poetry, too, there was as yet nothing
to compare with Auden's *Look Stranger* and what it had done
for the English left-wing fermentation of the 'thirties.

This was still the central theme of my *Armoured Writer* articles.
I realized, of course, that I was asking rather a lot in expecting
a Tolstoi to appear at once: *War and Peace* was written years
after the end of the Napoleonic wars, though the fighting scenes
were based on Tolstoi's far more recent experiences in the
Crimean war.   Nevertheless, Malraux and Silone had written
in the full tide of events, and written well, and Yeats's superb
poems on the Irish Civil War had not had to go through more
than a few months of incubation.   What was beginning to
disturb me was that the impulse of writers to wrestle with the
real under-the-surface material of their time seemed to be
flagging.   The relationship of literature and life is complex and
obscure, and the experiences of the 'thirties had warned me of
the dangers of thinking that it should, or could be immediate
and realistic; but I still believed profoundly that if literature is
to exert all its potential power as hidden healer in our lives, it
must speak about the problems of the day in the language of
the day, even if indirectly or by allegory and symbol.   I did
not think there could be any going back to purely esoteric
literature after what had happened in the 'thirties, and while
we were still in the middle of the revolution that the 'thirties
had begun and the war was accelerating.   I wrote in my first
article: ' What one has a right to anticipate is a work of art,
whether it is written in prose or dramatic verse or some new
mixture of both, which will cover all the ground that the Marx-
ists and the Freudians opened up, but much more as well, a
novel (to use a term which already embraces works as different
as *To the Lighthouse*, *The Castle*, *The Counterfeiters* and *The Plumed*

Serpent) that will have profited from the deeper insight that dis-appointment or disillusionment brought to those who pinned their faith to the formulas of the 'thirties.' There was little enough to bolster this confidence when I wrote that article; nevertheless there were a few signs and portents, and in the course of the next two or three years they gathered strength and frequency.

Novels which had the conditions of wartime life as their setting were already beginning to appear. By far the most interesting to me was Henry Green's *Caught*, which describes the life of an Auxiliary Fireman, Richard Roe, in a London sub-station, from the period of his pre-war training down to the time when he is recuperating for a few days in the country after the great air-raids of the Autumn of 1940. *Caught* contains two unforgettable characters: Pye, the unlucky, unhappy officer in charge of the sub-station, and Mary Howells, the cook who goes ' adrift ' and so, by chance, sets in motion the machinery of the trap in which Pye finds himself caught indeed in the end. It also contains two brilliant character sketches on a smaller scale, Piper, the toadying old soldier, and the ex-seaman Shiner Wright who, in the superbly described dock-land fire at the end, sheds a light of almost superhuman courage on a resolutely anti-heroic book. What impressed me so much about Henry Green's developing art in this novel was the way the characters are defined and exposed by their dialogue. Again and again I found myself re-reading passages to savour this rare and marvellous gift: no one in his generation, even when one remembers that it includes Christopher Isherwood and V. S. Pritchett, has so accurate an ear for the way people talk, for the peculiar conversation patterns and word choice of every type of person, and above all for the element of the absurd and the irrational that is always cropping up in uninhibited English talk.

Caught mirrored, with something like genius, the compound of tragedy and comedy that was the truth of the war, the heroism that showed itself in spite of an extreme distaste for and distrust of heroics; and because as a work of art it was more satisfying to the spirit than any amount of simpler literature, whose consciously morale-building authors would not have dared to show the Auxiliary Firemen, the ' heroes ' of the blitz, as selfish, mean, coarse, absorbed in petty intrigues and petty anxieties about their careers, when they were not chasing girls in the black-out.   This was a distinction that was impossible for our state-controlled Russian allies to appreciate; but of that more later.

It seems to me that the novels which appeared during these middle years of the war were all important in the degree they got away from the propagandist-heroic.   For all the skill and expertise brought to bear on them, books like C. S. Forester's *The Ship* were, I thought, radio-actively dead, and did far less to support the will-to-victory and heal the breach in our culture than books like *Caught* which had no propagandist design on their readers at all.   Even when writers were laudably determined not to write *for* the war, it often managed to worm itself into their work in some concealed way.   The stress of wartime life, the continual sense of danger and effort were still there even when they had become too habitual to be remembered; and they introduced twists to one's judgement and one's emotions, streaks of hysteria and sentimentality, without one being entirely aware of it.   It was just because the element of hysteria was so notably absent, that I thought Anthony Thorne's *I'm a Stranger Here Myself* so good: a work of real imaginative penetration into wartime lower deck life done with an abundance of sympathy and humour, though I would not be prepared to say that a touch of sentimentality did not appear towards the end.   In *I'm a Stranger Here Myself*, as in *Caught*, the imaginative leap across class boundaries that baffled the 'thirties was achieved with what seemed an almost effortless ease.

One of the few authors, apart from Henry Green, who attempted to do something new with words and style, was Arthur Gwynn-Browne, a former hotel manager who joined up in 1939 and went to France with the B.E.F.   An avowed pupil of Gertrude Stein, he adapted her method to give a picture of the first year of the war as seen through the eyes of the slightly mysterious section of the Army to which he belonged—Field Security Personnel.   I thought *F.S.P.* was a brave attempt to explore away from the conventional ways of writing about the war; it was perhaps a little too mannered, too idio-syncratic to have much issue, and Gwynn-Browne did not entirely succeed in making his characters three-dimensional; but there were moments when the deliberate flatness, the dead-pan way in which ludicrous or fantastic events were suddenly brought into the flow without any change of note or speed, pro-duced an effect of truth about the war and the stoic, humorous fatalism of the average soldier taking part in it, that could hardly have been achieved in any other way.

Gwynn-Browne, incidentally, was convinced that the publi-cation of *F.S.P.* was the cause of his sudden removal from it—cause and effect, he said, followed one· another too closely. But as his removal was immediately followed by a commission in the Army Catering Corps, this punishment seemed to me more like the ' kicking upstairs ' of a politician guilty of an indiscretion about Cabinet secrets. A minor triumph, at any rate, of an author in uniform against the war bureaucracy.

For the third volume of *New Writing and Daylight* (Summer 1943), Gwynn-Browne produced a characteristic, subtle and amusing piece called *Thirteen Aims—What is Yours?* It ended with a curious prophecy of the Angry Young Men, who took another ten years to materialize:

The thirteenth feels the necessity for fundamental change: his aim is vague. He is restless and disturbed. His aspirations are clarified as the thin red end of the wedge and he is beguiled or liquidated according to expediency or power. The thirteenth makes notes of promises pledged in his name and dismisses them: they are superimposed. They are emanations of society already soiled and blamed whose language is inoperative; their words mean not what they say. The thirteenth has been misled too long to hear or to care for the interpretation of views and the maintenance of pious vows. He is shaping images like concrete piers sunk in the bed of his mind, deeper than words. The cement is setting. He will not easily give way, for the thirteenth is forming a white hard core of contempt and anger supported by rising pride. He bides his time. Do we, do you, will they?

Perhaps it is wrong to call this a prophecy: for the ' thir-teenth aim ' produced the Welfare State and voted the Labour

Government into power in 1945, and it was his younger brother who turned in disgust from the realized Utopia he grew up into, and, with even vaguer aim, became the A.Y.M. of the 'fifties.

Of course I realized that the experimentation of *F.S.P.* and the artistic detachment of *Caught* were not what the public as a whole was looking for. Books like *The Ship* were much more to their liking; and, even more, those personal narrations of war experience written by young men in uniform, that served to communicate the mood of the generation in the front line and to define images of tragic and heroic destiny for their elders at the same time. They were, up to a point, at book length what the *New Writing* sketches aimed to be in brief; but more factual perhaps, less concerned with literary effect—and in most cases less capable of it. This may sound ungenerous towards, for instance, Paul Rickey's immensely successful *Fighter Pilot* (published anonymously in 1941), and even more to the most famous of all, Richard Hillary's *The Last Enemy*; but the *mystique* that surrounded Hillary, and the doom that seemed to pursue that brave and tortured young man like a lover, cast a glamour over the prose expression that was not, I believe, inherent in it. *The Last Enemy* is, nevertheless, a classic description of the discovery by an apparently disaffected young English cynic that, when it came to the point, he was neither disaffected nor cynical, but braver and with a deeper feeling for what his country stood for, than most of the patriotic tub-thumpers. I shall never forget the sight of his smiling, mask-like, re-made face at a party of Sybil Colefax's not long before his death.

A far greater chance of doing something for the literature of the war was offered the war correspondents, and I read their books as they began to come out with hopeful avidity. They could see everything for themselves, they could meet and talk to those taking part in the fighting, and those who were directing the battle behind, and all the technical means, the priority calls on the international telephone lines, the seats on the V.I.P. aeroplanes, the recording vans and the expense accounts were put at their disposal to be history's witnesses. If there had been major artists among them, with a sense for the epic, what marvellous material, what marvellous opportunities! Stendhal had the experience of the Moscow campaign at least to inspire him in his description of Fabrice del Dongo at Waterloo. But the very fact of having to work at furious tempo, to bash away at their typewriters pouring out their stories for immediate consumption, and beyond that of having to meet the importunate, insatiable demand of the public at home for books pieced together from all their on-the-spot records, in nine cases out of ten prevented the journalists from making the most of their opportunities.

From all this I found to single out, to preserve, to re-read, to ruminate over, occasional marvellous passages in many books— such as G. L. Steer's description of the Emperor Haile Selassie's triumphal return to his capital in *Sealed and Delivered*; and, exceptionally, Alexander Clifford's books on the Desert War almost entire, and Alan Moorehead's *African Trilogy*, the work of a writer less humanly sensitive than Clifford, perhaps, but more interested in the vision of war within the shaping hand of politics. These two in their different ways, seemed to me to get as far as it was possible to go within the limitations imposed on them by their job as war correspondents. How far that best was, I kept on reflecting, from what their opportunities seemed to the civilian, confined within his war-time cage, to invite.

While these books were being published, far away in a prisoners' camp in Italy, and unknown to any of their countrymen, Dan Billany and David Dowie were at work on what I am now inclined to think was the most original, the most moving and the most promising of all war books written *at the time* by actual participants: *The Cage*. How much one regrets their fate, that remains so obscure: when Italy surrendered in 1943 they were released, were seen in Mantua in late December, and then—vanished. (There are grounds for believing that they were done to death by the Germans, but they are not conclusive.) An Italian farmer who befriended them kept the manuscript of *The Cage* until the end of the war, when he sent it to Dan Billany's parents. It was only published in 1949. Perhaps the post-war drought in the novel and the theatre would never have occurred if these two young men had been with us to stimulate and lead a vital avant-garde.

As in warfare, the direct assault, the direct approach was yielding little enough, but there was also the indirect approach. By the middle of the war, a handful of novels had appeared which, though not immediately concerned with the war, had been written or finished at least under its influence, and had a deep symbolic or allegorical relation to it. The two most important were undoubtedly Virginia Woolf's *Between the Acts* and Rex Warner's *The Aerodrome*. About Virginia's posthumous novel I have written at some length elsewhere. Though the time—the late Summer of 1939—and the place—the countryside of southern England—are precise, I find it difficult to believe that its poetic overtones, its intensely charged and haunting imagery will not be as full of significance twenty or thirty years hence as they were to the wartime generation. Like all works of genius, it is timeless. Nevertheless, there is, I think, an unmistakable sense all through the book of being on the brink of catastrophe, and of the themes that run below the surface being all the more acutely urgent because of the particular predicament of that time.

Rex Warner began *The Aerodrome* before the war broke out, but evidently at a time when the collapse of the Republican cause in Spain had started the process of re-appraisal in disillusionment which had affected all the writers of the 'thirties. If one compares *The Aerodrome* with Rex Warner's first ' novel ', *The Wild Goose Chase*, one sees at once the distance he had travelled in thought and feeling; the difference between the two books can stand for the journey taken by so many of his more sensitive contemporaries. *The Wild Goose Chase* is a success story, an anti-fascist fairy tale of the simplest basic pattern, subtle and imaginative and dramatic with the intensity of nightmare though many of the details are. In *The Aerodrome*, in contrast, there is a deep sense of inescapable imperfection, of good and evil fatally intertwined in life, which is the essence of tragedy and the very opposite of the fairy tale. The Air Vice-Marshal is obsessed with the possibilities of power that the science of our age puts into the hands of men who are daring and intelligent and ruthless enough to grasp it; he is an idealist, dreaming of the perfect organization for controlling the lives of human beings for their own good; but even when it collapses, because it demands an inhumanity from man that his moral nature cannot in the end acquiesce in—because the ends do not justify the means—even then, when a future order is envisaged arising out of a fusion of the old order with what was good in the Air Vice-Marshal's dream, there is still no certainty, life is still ' most intricate, fiercer than tigers '. *The Aerodrome* seemed intensely relevant to what was happening in the early years of the war; but the battle between the Air Vice-Marshal and the Village is still going on, is in fact the central conflict of our century. It was not surprising that the book caused such a stir in foreign countries when it was translated after the war.

In both these remarkable books, poetic symbolism was used in various ways *against* surface realism. There never could have been a village pageant like the one that took place at Pointz Hall; nor could there ever have been a village inn like the one near the aerodrome, where the rat-catcher bites off the rat's head to amuse the company. Another author, writing at very much the same time, was using poetic symbolism in much the same way for similar ends; but he came from the other side of the war lines, and his book had come by devious routes into the hands of a friend who lent it to me. It was a most curious and exciting experience to read Ernst Jünger's *Auf den Marmorklippen* in the middle of the war, in an edition openly published by a famous German firm, with Jünger's note opposite the title page that it had been finished in 1939 ' beim Heer '; for it could be read as a scorching condemnation of the Nazi state, and, though one could deduce from it that the author approved of fighting and war under certain circumstances, as a kind of recantation of much that he had stood for in the eyes of the German people.

Personally, I find the story of *Auf den Marmorklippen* a little too heavily loaded with symbolism, a little too abstruse, too elaborately woven, but nevertheless in the main remarkably compelling, especially in the long, dramatic climax in which the tension is so cleverly built up. The style has what is to me a slightly repellent, luscious quality, but every time I read it I gradually succumb to its spell. As it was generally unobtainable, I wrote about it at length in one of my *Armoured Writer*

articles: the interest this description aroused made me eager to
make it available in English translation, and some years later,
after the war had ended, when I had my own publishing firm, I
succeeded in obtaining the rights and added it to my *Modern
European Library.*

A hundred touches in the development of the story suggested
to us then that the Nazis were being described: Wotan riding
again from the ever unquiet depths of the German soul, as the
great philosopher Jung later imagined it. And yet, I would
not be so sure today; obviously Jünger could not have written
Auf den Marmorklippen without the story of Hitler's rise to power
in mind; but some of the symbols in this extraordinary book
may well refer to other levels beside that of the political and
social order; and now, twenty years later, one sees that it can
almost equally well allegorize other manifestations of our Grand
Guignol century; an imaginative criticism of all those anti-
moral upsurges of the lust for power in which one country
after another seems forced to take the victim part. The Air
Vice-Marshal of *The Aerodrome* is a distant relation of the Head
Forester of *Auf den Marmorklippen;* and both had been nurtured
on what Edwin Muir, in his article *The Natural Man and the
Political Man,* had called ' the religion of development ', on the
idea that if you control *things* you control mankind.

I was already becoming convinced that the great theme of
our time was this problem of power running amok, power without moral sanction or restraint; and that there was something
in the claim that the real image of the world we lived in was to
be found in a certain class of detective and spy stories. A
ceaseless murderous struggle for power, in which the protagonists are always, in peace or war, retreating behind more and
more elaborate barriers of concealment and camouflage; a
struggle which uses the individual with utter ruthlessness, and in
which, if he is luckless or foolish enough to become too closely
involved, he has no more chance than a sparrow hitting a
high-tension cable; the world of industrial secrets and espion-
age networks and war—this, the world of the modern thrillers,
seemed to me the truest picture of our own inescapable environment. And for this reason, I was particularly drawn to
Graham Greene's *The Ministry of Fear,* which appeared in 1943.

Graham called it ' an entertainment '; but the basic difference between his ' entertainments ' and his novels has always been a little difficult to discover. The ' entertainments ' can, perhaps, be classed more easily as thrillers, though there is a ' thriller ' element in many of the best novels; but *The Ministry of Fear* is certainly as serious as *Brighton Rock* or *The Power and The Glory* as a criticism of the world we live in and the life we lead, and has moments of astonishing, poetic illumination about the pursuit of power in an unstable civilization. The passage that has always haunted me is where Arthur Rowe, sheltering in an Underground station during an air-raid, has a half-waking dream in which he imagines himself talking to his dead mother:

' This isn't real life anymore,' he said. ' Tea on the lawn, evensong, croquet, the old ladies calling, the gentle, unmalicious gossip, the gardener trundling the wheelbarrow full of leaves and grass. People write about it as if it still went on: lady novelists describe it over and over again in books of the month, but it's not there any more.' His Mother smiled at him in a scared way but let him talk: he was the master of the dream now. He said: ' I'm wanted for a murder I didn't do. People want to kill me because I know too much. I'm hiding underground, and up above the Germans are methodically smashing London to bits all around me. . . . It sounds like a thriller, doesn't it, but the thrillers are like life—more like life than you are, this lawn, your sandwiches, that pine. You used to laugh at the books Miss Savage read— about spies, and murders, and violence, and wild motor-car chases, but dear, that's real life: it's what we've all made of the world since you died. I'm your little Arthur who wouldn't hurt a beetle, and I'm a murderer too. The world has been remade by William le Queux.'

This idea of a world ' remade by William le Queux ' had obviously bitten deep into Graham Greene's mind: it was interesting to find it again as a dominant undertone in another of Graham's ' entertainments ' fifteen years later—*Our Man in Havana*. . . . When he read what I had written about thrillers and spy stories in *The Armoured Writer*, Julian Maclaren-Ross wrote me an enthusiastic letter, telling me how completely he shared my opinion and that he was actually engaged on a novel of that sort himself, and proposed to call it *The Fields of Night* from the phrase of Virginia Woolf's I had quoted in the article. (What a pity the war prevented him from finishing it!) 'The thrillers are like life,' said Graham Greene; *The Ministry of Fear* was more like life, to at least one reader, than the Catholic miracle tales that invaded his work after the war.

The contribution that the poets were making to the understanding—the cathartic interpretation—of this world 'remade by William le Queux' was beginning, by the middle of the war, to show itself far greater and far more significant than one could possibly have expected in the first twelve months. In retrospect, in fact, it seems to me that in the whole field of what was written during the war, English poetry comes out on top.

8

At this point, however, I begin to feel bellicose and polemical impulses stirring in me. I am in sight of a terrain over which, while I have been writing this book, trenches have suddenly been dug and manned by invading commandos, and most of the genuine features of the landscape camouflaged to look like something else. I feel an urge to don battledress myself, and fire a few bursts at these trenches, if only to warn those who come after me.

Not long ago, I was asked to address a School society on ' something to do with poetry ', and though I could not at the time make the journey, the following letter, addressed to one of the young members who (as I happened to know) wrote poetry himself, formed itself in my mind. . . .

' Dear Poet of Tomorrow,' I began, ' the secretary of your Literary Society (as I'm sure you know, as you put him up to it) has asked me to come down to your school and talk to you about poetry. I receive quite a large number of such requests, and do my best, in the midst of a fairly busy life, to say yes as often as possible. On this occasion, however, I just can't make myself free, being surrounded by what my great-grandfather Robert Chambers called " a botheration of articles to be finished and proofs to be corrected "; but as I fancy I detect from the tone of the Secretary's letter that he is kind and even genuinely interested (unlike those secretaries of youthful societies who only invite their speakers down in order to send them up), and as I know *you* are, I propose to try and put down in a letter the gist of what I should have liked to say. The subject I was going to choose was the poetry of the 'forties, or rather of the early 'forties, and my idea was to talk about it from my own point of view; that is, not from a historian's point of view, but rather following what particularly interested me as a literary editor working in London at that time, what seemed to me promising or significant, and what disappointing, boring or meretricious.

' To begin with, I feel fairly certain I shall need to dispel an illusion, or myth, about the poetry that was being written during the war, which has, in one form or another, been assiduously spread about in recent years, even by intelligent and gifted young critics who ought to know better. Of course you may have an extremely sensitive and well-read English master, who doesn't encourage you to put too much trust in the fashionable slogans of the day; he may have given you all the books, and told you to make up your own mind; if so, you will be exceptionally lucky. It would be unwise of me to proceed on that assumption.

' Like all myths—as you will know from your classical studies or at least from Mr. Robert Graves—this particular myth has a number of forms which vary from locality to locality, or rather from critic to critic. The main features, however, seem to be fairly constant. The first is, I think, that the poets of the 'thirties were entirely absorbed in social–political problems and wrote only when inspired by what they read about in the newspapers. This is assumed to be one hundred per cent reprehensible, though it would appear to condemn a large number of sonnets by Milton and Wordsworth and such famous poems as Yeats's *Meditations in Time of Civil War*. I won't go into that at the moment, because it is the rest of the myth which I am interested to demolish for you. For what is alleged is that the most remarkable poet of the 'thirties, Mr. W. H. Auden, saw through all this before the end of the fighting in Spain, washed his hands of it and left for America. Auden's departure and the outbreak of international war, which followed a few months later, were, according to the myth, crushing blows for the whole generation of the 'thirties (which was, as you know, my generation), and stunned it into silence. They never, it seems, recovered sufficiently to utter a single squeak again. Instead, they abandoned the field of English poetry to Dylan Thomas, his followers and his feeble imitators. Thus, apparently, the poetry of the 'forties became sententiously vatic, hysterically apocalyptic and pretentiously emotional overnight, in fact turned into the most recklessly undisciplined pseudo-poetical raving.

' Now it is perfectly true that, as the war went on, and everyone began to read more and more, as if hoping to find in literature an explanation of the mess that the modern world had got itself into, almost any young poet of the most moderate promise could get a volume of his verse published; and in this way a great deal of quite horribly feeble stuff appeared. A school of young poets calling themselves " Apocalyptics " were, in my opinion, among the worst offenders, and can justly be arraigned for debasing the intellectual standards of poetry; while more than one magazine appeared to me to be acting as a waste-paper basket for the sloppy jottings and rantings of innumerable immature and incoherent pseudo-poets. In fact, all this thoroughly dismayed me at the time, and on several occasions, in my articles in *New Writing* and elsewhere, I went in to the attack against the fluent and windy wordstringing of these poets, and, giving examples, complained that a cliché-ridden, sentimental style " like a sickly fungoid growth on decaying jam ", had spread to so many of these poets to such an extent that one could hardly distinguish one from another. Some critics at the time, I remember, had rather disgustedly picked on their prevalent mood of defeatism, of " Petainism "—a mood impossible for any of the poets whose sympathies had been engaged on the anti-fascist side in the 'thirties—but what seemed to me to matter was that they conveyed little or no impression of truly deep feeling, that they only succeeded in being plaintive when they attempted to be passionate, and when they tackled larger themes their sentiments sounded inflated and insincere.

' A decade, however, has a right to be judged by its best poetry and not by its worst, for—as any literary editor knows only too well—there is always an enormous amount of bad poetry being written in any decade or (as I would rather put it, since this division into decades is a slightly absurd modern mania) at any time. And the first thing that my experience with *New Writing* made clear to me was that, so far from the poets of the 'thirties having fallen silent, dispersed like a routed army when their general has fled to exile and safety, several of them were writing better than ever. Some of the most beautiful and intellectually vigorous work of Louis MacNeice, Cecil Day Lewis and Stephen Spender appeared at this time. I did not find in it any violent break with what they had written before the war, but rather a not illogical maturing from it. They had certainly shed some political illusions—that, as I am sure you know, had begun before the war broke out—but these political ideas had never dominated their poetry to the exclusion of everything else; and if one was conscious of a fairly thorough-going revaluation of values, the fundamentally human pre-occupations of their wartime poetry had in fact been there from the beginning. The poems in *Word Over All* (1943)—I will chance my arm over this—still seem to me far and away the most striking, taken together, that Cecil Day Lewis ever wrote, more remarkable technically and more profoundly felt than what went before or what came after. Stephen Spender's *Ruins and Visions* (1942) and the wartime poems later collected in *Poems of Dedication*, had moments of illumination more extraordinary than anything since his earliest work, the period of " I think continually " and " O young men O young comrades ". Louis MacNeice, too, attained a greater depth and power in the poems he wrote between 1941 and 1944, after his return from America—and they include the dazzling *Brother Fire* and *Springboard*.

' At this point, you will, of course, be impatient to ask me how Dylan Thomas fits into the picture. Was he, in fact, with the

" Apocalyptics " and in opposition to the older poets of the 'thirties? Must he take a large part of the blame for the more disastrous manifestations of poetry during the war? Now the truth is that Dylan had no wish that I could ever discover to put himself forward as the leader of any school, and he did not write (or at any rate publish) a great many poems between *The Map of Love* in 1939 and the end of the war; but some of them, in particular his wonderful *A Refusal to Mourn*, are among his most complex and brilliantly controlled achievements. These poems certainly had nothing to do with " poetical raving " or the " fluent and windy word-stringing " that I deplored myself in the bad verse-making of those years. Nor had the poems which David Gascoyne presented in his romantic, Sutherland-decorated volume of 1943 (if Tambimuttu's Poetry London Editions had produced nothing else, one would be in their debt for that book). I suspect that it's difficult for you to realize how great an impression these poems created, appearing as they did at a time when other poets of David's generation were trying, in one way or another, to take up an attitude to public events: their intense and almost exclusive concentration on problems of the inner life, their almost complete technical insulation from what his contemporaries were experimenting with, were as totally unexpected as Hamlet might be if he walked into the second act of *The River Line*. In these poems I felt that David was trying to embody a new philosophical, or if you like religious conception, far more significant than the marxist or surrealist implications in the poetry he was producing previously.

' Inspired by your Society's invitation, I have been looking back through the pages of *New Writing*, of Cyril Connolly's *Horizon*, and of *Personal Landscape*, and I see that the dozen or so names of poets in their twenties which stand out are not those of wordy ranters, but of fastidious artists: for instance, Roy Fuller, Lawrence Durrell, Keith Douglas, Terence Tiller, Alun Lewis, Henry Reed, Norman Nicholson, Laurie Lee. All these young men have a perfectly sound claim to be considered poets of the decade, even though Roy Fuller and Lawrence Durrell had begun to publish before the war. And I also see that it was precisely their respect for form and tradition—so sweepingly denied by those who were boosting the wares of the young poets of a later date—that I was at pains to emphasize in my critical discussion of their work. " What is interesting in them," I wrote on one occasion, " is the way they have created lyrics, taking the basic verse shapes of the past as their vehicle, which show no signs of enervation, of the jaded end of a tradition about to be discarded, but are fresh in their harmonies and novel in their juxtapositions of ideas and symbols." Nothing had struck me more in the wartime work of the poets I admired than their effort towards a new integration—their attempt to map some system of thought and feeling wide enough and deep enough for our culture to exist in. The crowded and terrifying events of only a few years had not only shaken a great many cosy settled beliefs and assumptions, but they had also done something more exciting. It was as if some hills that had always blocked the view had subsided in an earthquake, and given one a sudden glimpse of great mountains behind, whose existence had been forgotten—if ever known. The imagined and the fantastical seemed on the verge of becoming true. It was these new conceptions that I saw the poets endeavouring to assimilate and to embody in their poetry.

' In his Preface to the anthology *Lyra*, which had been edited in 1942 by Alex Comfort and Robert Greacen, protagonists of the neo-romantic and " pacifist " movement, Herbert Read had written: " This anthology appears in the third year of a war which every day reveals more clearly its apocalyptic character: it is not war in the ordinary sense which we are enduring, but a world revolution in which all conventions, whether of thought or action, break down and are replaced—not by new conventions, for conventions are of slow growth—but by provisional formulas which are immediately tested under fire." This seemed to me to describe very well the situation in which we found ourselves; but the trouble was that the word " apocalyptic " had, as I have just described, already been appropriated as banner and slogan by a group of poets from which most of the good poets appeared anxious to dissociate themselves. And yet this apocalyptic sense was everywhere in the poetry that was being written at this time. In Stephen Spender's lines, for instance:

Q

Yesterday you built those towers
Of your money making
In the city of bought doom,
With workers barked at by the hours,
And in the safe of heart-breaking
The rich locked with their boredom.

Break locks! Burn fire! It
Penetrates interstices
Of a skeleton of stones:
The concrete lid over the spirit
Laid by a century of successes
Is stripped bare from the bones.
How new you are! And real!

'It was really extraordinary how widespread it became. I remember how struck I was by the sense of old certainties dissolving under the pressure of some deep upheaval of the spirit, when I first picked out of its envelope the long poem, *The Jungle*, which Alun Lewis sent me from India shortly before his death, with its—to me unforgettable—last lines:

A trackless wilderness divides
Joy from its cause, the motive from the act.
The killing arm uncurls, strokes the soft moss;
The distant world is an obituary,
We do not hear the tappings of its dread.
The act sustains; there is no consequence.
Only aloneness, swinging slowly
Down the cold orbit of an older world
Than any they predicted in the schools,
Stirs the cold forest with a starry wind,
And sudden as the flashing of a sword
The dream exalts the bowed and golden head
And time is swept with a great turbulence,
The old temptation, to remould the world. . . .

'I think you ought to remember that Alun Lewis had started off as a convinced, proselytizing socialist, in order to understand the distance he had journeyed to *The Jungle*.

'The younger poets were not alone. Before his death in 1943, Laurence Binyon was also at work on a small group of

poems, in which he suddenly seemed to free himself from whatever had kept his work so polished technically and yet in fact
so empty of any real content.   What was so deeply moving
about the whole sequence of *The Burning of the Leaves* was its
combination of passionate vision and intellectual honesty.
Binyon didn't try to find any easy, sentimental way to escape
the shapes of death and destruction in whose shadow they were
written; but recorded, with a dignified simplicity, how they
made some things in life appear suddenly quite tawdry and
shallow, and how other things, suggesting hope and renewal,
seemed to endure against them.   And in the fragments at the
end, the sense of approaching revelation and of darkness is
sketched with an extraordinary intensity:

> Horizon opening into unguessed horizons
> And I with the earth am moving into the light
> > The earth is moving, the earth is rolling over
> > into the light. . . .

'The more I think about it, as a matter of fact, the more
convinced I am that the early years of the 'forties were—the
pundits of the 'fifties notwithstanding—exceptionally rich in
poetry.   Don't forget that T. S. Eliot completed his great
sequence of meditations on the meaning of time, art and God,
the *Four Quartets*, during those years. *East Coker*, *The Dry
Salvages* and *Little Gidding* were as exciting to me, as they came
out, as news of great military victories.   (I was all the more
staggered, therefore, when, in answer to a request for a poem
for *New Writing* in the Summer of 1944, Tom wrote to me: " I
am pleased by your request for a poem, but I literally have
written no verses at all since *Little Gidding*, and I cannot say with
any confidence that I shall ever again write anything worth
printing.")
'T. S. Eliot was not the only poet of an older generation who
seemed to be stirred to new vigour and beauty of achievement
in those years.   To most of us in London it seemed, when
Street Songs was published early in 1942, that another great
event had taken place in English poetry.   I had been delighted as a young man with Edith Sitwell's *Façade* and *Troy*

Town poems; I had been moved by the brilliant violence of her
satiric *Gold Coast Customs*, remote though it was in technique
from what particularly interested me in the 'thirties; but I had
not, I must admit, expected that she would make such a big
leap forward.   In her new poems all the gaiety of the early
work was gone, but so was all the extravagance and unreality,
and all the romantic private-world dreaminess of the poems
that came after that; the poems in *Street Songs*, and *Green Song*
that followed very soon, were tragic, and often bitter with a
kind of savagery of bitterness, and they were written with an
astonishingly easy-seeming mastery of her medium and an
assurance of voice that was deeply impressive.   I still think
that *Still Falls the Rain* and *Lullaby* are two of the most original
poems *about the war* that were written during the war; but I was
even more struck by the series of great odes, or elegies, wrought
with an infinitely subtle and sensitive technical virtuosity.   In
my opinion they were in the truest sense war poems, though the
war itself was only alluded to indirectly, through symbol and
myth, because they were inconceivable without the background
of the war—without the impact of the world-wide tragedy on a
poet capable at the same time of passionate grieving and sublime praising.   I have heard some young people of about your
age complain that there is a kind of wearying excess in these
odes, that there are too many of them, on the same note, using
variations of the same symbolism.   But that is a criticism made
in the light of Edith Sitwell's *Collected Poems* many years later,
and I am not concerned here to rebut or admit its truth or
partial truth; what I want you to understand is how exciting
these poems were when they first began to appear during the
war.   It was a great moment for me, when for the Winter
number of *New Writing and Daylight* in 1943 she offered me
Invocation, with its marvellous opening diapason:

I who was once a golden woman like those who walk
In the dark heavens—but am now grown old
And sit by the fire, and see the fire grow cold,
Watch the dark fields for a rebirth of faith and of wonder.
The turning of Ixion's wheel the day
Ceased not, yet sounds no more the beat of the heart

But only the sound of ultimate Darkness falling
And of the Blind Samson at the Fair, shaking the pillars of the
    world and emptily calling
For the gardeners cried for rain, but the high priests howled
For a darker rain. . . .

    ' This, like Tom Eliot's *Four Quartets*, was poetry, I thought, equal to the spiritual demands of an apocalyptic age.

    ' My Greek friend, Demetrios Capetanakis, used to say to me sometimes that, in some unexpected way, the war *physically* was not frightening enough; but that, *metaphysically*, for anyone who cared to think, what was happening was so disturbing that poetry of a high order must come out of it. To have death standing constantly next to one is certainly no situation to breed conventional thoughts, but rather such lines as Demetrios wrote in his best-known, most extraordinary poem *Abel*:

    And then he chose the final pain for me.
    I do not blame his nature: he's my brother,
    Nor what you call the times: our love was free,
    Would be the same at any time; but rather

    The ageless ambiguity of things
    Which makes our life mean death, our love be hate.
    My blood that streams across the bedroom sings:
    ' I am my brother opening the gate.'

    ' Certainly death sat uncomfortably close to Alun Lewis when he wrote *The Jungle*; and to Keith Douglas when he wrote the poems by which I believe he will be chiefly remembered, *Vergissmeinnicht* and *How to Kill*:

            This sorcery
    I do. Being damned, I am amused
    To see the centre of love diffused
    And the waves of love travel into vacancy.
    How easy it is to make a ghost.

    The weightless mosquito touches
    her tiny shadow on the stone,
    and with how like, how infinite
    a likeness, man and shadow meet.
    They fuse. A shadow is a man
    when the mosquito death approaches.

' And the chilly, imagined proximity of death inspired the best lines that Sidney Keyes ever wrote:

> I am the man who looked for peace and found
> My own eyes barbed.
> I am the man who groped for words and found
> An arrow in my hand.
> I am the builder whose firm walls surround
> A slipping land. . . .

' There were war poets in the end, all right. The nostalgic elderly schoolmasters and the vulgarians of what is now called The Establishment, whose cry in 1939 had been " Where are the war poets? ", were answered; but the answers were not the answers the young Rupert Brooke had given or the young Laurence Binyon; and I can only say that I deeply regret that some of the more reckless, simplifying critics who gained the ear of the public in the early 'fifties, seem to have become allies of these tone-deaf gentlemen.

' I make no apology, as you see, for the poetry of the war years, in which I was fairly intimately involved myself. That poetry, in fact, was one of the things that made that time tolerable. I am not talking of the dross; but of the authentic vein of precious metal. And if you would like me to try and sum it up, and define what I find impressive about this poetry, I would say that it is not only its technical vitality, but above all its deep seriousness. The poets took a good look at death without hiding their faces: they saw how easy it was to kill without thought, how cheap the individual's life had become. They were aware that they were living in an age in which human affairs were getting increasingly out of control. They saw that civilization was reaching a point where monsters could be born more terrible than had ever been imagined possible in the modern world, but that this danger also evoked the possibility of the rediscovery of great spiritual affirmations to counter it. They saw that what was needed was a restatement of faith: faith, if you like, in imaginative creation, but above all in the value of the individual and the reality of moral choice against man-made machines of organization and the crudity of material "Progress": against a world based on values of power only. . . .'

If I had gone down to the school I would, I think, have counselled my audience to balance my case for the defence with a view of the poetic scene through the eyes of a contemporary satirist: Joseph Gurnard's *Poets' Excursion* (which appeared in *P.N.W.* No. 18). Among connoisseurs, this has reached almost classic status: though the foibles and pretensions it so gaily mocks, on the long bumpy train journey from Paddington Goods Station to St. Audyn's on the Height, are rather of the late 'thirties than the 'forties, they still had an uncomfortable relevance to the wartime scene: ' Stephen Spendlove, Don Layman, Dick Chapel, Walter Turntap, Herbert E. Pilgrim, Louis (' Borzoi ') MacNoose, old Kate Cuspidor and new Kitty Rainy, Schreechpen, Fuddlepuss and Gurk: all of us, with a coach to ourselves and bound for—who knows where? '

9

AN irony that every literary editor knows is that, just when one believes that the time is ripe for, say, a Tolstoi, a Firbank writes his first book. Byron, one feels, could never quite forgive Keats for not writing like Crabbe. In a closed society, of course, such mutations and eccentricities are kept well out of sight or throttled at birth—if recognized in time. Woe betide the author in a totalitarian marxist country at war (as I was about to find out) who dares not to write on the approved pattern of patriotic heroism; but in an open society there should be no *ought* and *must* in the realm of the arts. What one hopes to preserve—or to develop—is sufficient suppleness of imagination to recognize what is good when it is quite different from what one had been looking for so expectantly and so long, with one's field glasses trained on the distant passes.

One day, early in 1943, a young man who signed himself Denton Welch sent me a story called *The Barn*. His name was

not new to me, for some months earlier I had read a quite
extraordinarily vivid and irreverent description of a visit to
Walter Sickert in *Horizon*; and only a few weeks before the
MS. reached me, his first book, *Maiden Voyage*, had been published, with an introduction by Edith Sitwell. As so often
happened during the war with books that were not expected
by their publishers to have more than a limited sale, but were
nevertheless enthusiastically received by the critics, it had
become unobtainable almost at once. I had not yet been able
to read it: but this story struck me immediately, by an altogether unusual quality in the writing and in the observation it
recorded. With a mediaeval miniaturist's clarity and pre-
cision, the author described a slight episode in the life of a
young boy at home; he is bored and lonely, and overhearing his
father give a tramp permission to sleep in their disused barn,
decides to join the tramp secretly during the night and set off
with him in the morning. The tramp allows him to sleep in
the hay beside him, but sends him back contemptuously when
he leaves. Nothing very much; but the sensuous impact of
everything was so minutely and freshly described, and the
author seemed to be able to see himself from the outside (for
obviously the story was autobiographical) with such extraordinary detachment and truth, that it was clear to me that the
admirers of *Maiden Voyage* had been right when they said he was
a born writer. It was a rare and exciting experience to come
across a passage like this:

> I was in darkness, which smelt of dust and mist and hay.
> Chinks and cracks in the walls shot beams of light into the black-
> ness.
>   I climbed on to some boxes, then caught hold of a beam and
> swung there, like a monkey. I gnashed my teeth and contorted
> my face. I gibbered and hung on with one hand as I scratched
> under my arm with the other.
>   I grew hot, swinging in the darkness, and my arms began to
> feel the strain. I broke my last imaginary peanut between my
> teeth and spat as disgustingly and coarsely as I could on to the
> invisible floor; then I sank down on to the boxes and thought
> that I was miserable and lonely indeed.
>   And as I lay there, I decided to be a slave who had to sweat and
> labour in the barn all day. . . .

I wrote to Denton Welch accepting the story, but suggesting that it could do with a little re-writing and pulling together. He replied with a letter that was shrewd, sympathetic and revealing; telling me that he had already re-written it twice, but that he'd go over it again if I really thought it necessary. ' Do you think its lack of very perceptible shape is due to its being, almost completely, a plain statement of fact?   Whether this is a good thing to attempt or not, I tried very hard to keep it only to this; and consequently I may be a little more inept in some passages than I would otherwise have been.   I do hope you will use it, for although I too thought it was clumsy, I still liked it for some reason; that is why I sent it to you.'

I wrote back and told him I certainly didn't want him to change it unless he was convinced himself that it could be improved.   A fortnight later he did, in fact, send me a slightly revised—and certainly improved—version.   ' I did not like one or two sentences and adjectives, they did not really express my true feeling,' he wrote, and added: ' I could, of course, have changed it a great deal more, but I resisted this temptation, as I knew that I would make it into something quite different and perhaps worse if I persisted.'

The truth was that practically everything Denton Welch wrote was autobiographical.   He had a passion for exact accuracy about thoughts and feelings, and therefore he was always up against the problem of accommodating the artistically feasible to this strict conscience about his own experience. Even when writing in the third person, he admitted to me, it made little or no difference; and it is for this reason that I have sometimes wondered whether, if he had lived, he would have gone on writing fiction.   I see him, rather, developing into the most disconcerting diarist of our day: an English Gide, but a more delicate and exotic bird than the (sometimes a little self-important) *cher maître* of the rue Vaneau.

His fantasy, curiously enough, seemed to go almost entirely into his exquisite little drawings and decorations, and the rare paintings of his mature style, so full of strange, poetic symbols; of which one of the most beautiful and mysterious, the cat with the arrow, hangs beside me as I write.

At the time when he sent me *The Barn*, Denton Welch was

only twenty-six, but had already been for eight years a cripple, slowly wasting from the disease which had followed the accident when he was knocked off his bicycle by a passing car. Many years after the war, and after his death, I was destined to publish his own story of that time of almost intolerable spiritual and physical suffering, in his third ' novel ', *A Voice Through a Cloud*. Perhaps it was the conviction, which must have come to him sometimes, that his life was going to be short, that made him want to record every detail so exactly. And perhaps it was the pain, from which he was seldom free, that was the cause of the streak of slightly cruel malice which sometimes appears in his portraits of people: as in *The Judas Tree*, a story which I printed very soon after in *Penguin New Writing*, where he so brilliantly and so mercilessly exposes the old schoolmaster. On the other hand, it is possible that this appearance of cruelty came from a tension in his spirit between the need to be loved and to lavish affection and his hatred of all pretension and sentimentality, including sentimentality in himself; as if he had to over-compensate a little for the quick warmth of response that was natural to him. It was revealing, I thought, that he was afraid (as he told me in a letter) that the critics might sneer at *Maiden Voyage* as the story of just one more rather sissified boy who couldn't fit into school life and was bad at games; and believed that Edith Sitwell's Foreword had prevented such a reaction. Edith certainly did him a good turn, just as she had done Dylan Thomas a similar good turn a decade before; but I think that only the most crudely philistine critics could have failed to spot, in *Maiden Voyage*, the sharp critical intelligence at work and the expert appraisal of beautiful things. And even if it was not what he felt *ought* to be written in the heroic post-Dunkirk epoch of his dreams, I think Hugh Walpole would have fallen for it had he been alive. Even if it was not exactly what I was looking for, I fell for it.

10

ONE thing is quite certain: the Russians would never have understood the case of Denton Welch. This was brought home to me by the tremendous hot water I suddenly found I had got into with our Red allies.

My work for *Internationalnaya Literatura* and *Britanski Soyuznik* had, I suppose, directed Russian attention to my own writings and to the progress of *Penguin New Writing*. They did not fail, therefore, to read in one of the numbers an article called *State Art and Scepticism*, in which I discussed the difference between the Soviet and the British attitudes to imaginative literature during the war.

I had told Archie Clark-Kerr how keen I was to be kept posted about developments among the Russian writers, and from time to time he had digests of articles and controversies of particular interest to me sent through the Bag to London. In one of these I found a summary of a long article by my old friend Nikolai Tikhonov, from the magazine *Bolshevik*, on *The War and Soviet Literature*.

To explain how I reacted to this article, it is perhaps necessary to repeat that, though British writers managed successfully to keep regimentation and censorship at bay all through the war, the battle was never finally concluded in their favour: sentries had to be posted in continual vigilance. And as the perfectly reasonable and justified boosting of Russian achievements proceeded, some of us began to feel a little nervous lest our own bureaucracy grow jealous of the firm control under which the Soviets appeared to keep their writers. There were straws in the wind. I can remember being invited to dine at the Ministry of Information with two officials of their Russian department, in order to meet the new Tass correspondent and discuss how to improve Anglo-Russian cultural relations. It was an infuriating and entertaining occasion: infuriating, because the British officials launched into an attack on Freddie Voigt, who as Editor of *The Twentieth Century* had refused to

I Am My Brother

soften his mordant anti-Soviet articles in the slightest, and showed clearly enough that they thought a good deal more control should be exercised over our writers; entertaining, because it was the Tass correspondent fresh from Russia who firmly proclaimed an absolute view of art and literature, and to my total enchantment explained that the reason why Moscow radio produced, for instance, no historical feature-drama about the rise of Hitler, and so on, was that the Russians simply wouldn't stand for propaganda.

It seemed time to fire a few warning shots from my own small corner of the redoubt. It struck me that this article of Tikhonov's provided an excellent opportunity.

Tikhonov, who had contributed to the very first number of *New Writing* in 1936, and whose wartime sketch, *The Apple Tree*, had been sent me for *Daylight*, had become Chairman of the Union of Soviet Writers: he was, thus, Headmaster of a school with very rigid rules and intolerant Governors, and he had to keep the boys in order. His article in *Bolshevik* was obviously of considerable internal significance. A grand summary and analysis of Soviet Literature since Hitler's invasion, it reminded me of nothing so much as the children's *Krampusfest* I had often witnessed in Austria on the eve of St. Nicholas's Day: presents for the good boys and birch-rods for the bad ones. Only it was in earnest; and the unfortunate humorous writer Mikhail Zoschenko, one of the few who was known and appreciated in the West, was one of those who had clearly had it . . . for ' serious ideological mistakes '. ' The voice of the writer,' Tikhonov announced in ringing tones, ' is a power in our country. It accompanies the soldier to battle, and helps towards victory in the front and in the rear.' With this inspiration illuminating his countenance, the Soviet writer was evidently expected to square his shoulders, seize his ideological rifle and thank Stalin for the glorious opportunities vouchsafed him. Most of them, however, I could not help feeling, must have experienced a slight shudder, devoted patriots though they may well have been. Poor Selvinsky happened to write in one of his poems—obviously doing his best—that Russia was ' a land with serene smile '. Down came the thunder at once: it was a bad poem, a slander on the Russian people, riddled with ideological faults. Dovzhenko, admired author and film-director, was also sent straight to the Headmaster's study for ' serious mistakes of a fundamental character ' in his story to which he had so hopefully given the name *Victory*: neither eminence (and world fame) nor good intentions saved him from being told that his story was ' in essence a slanderous estimate of the struggle of the Soviet peoples '. Even the luckier authors who got past without castigation, had the cane rattled warningly on the desk at them; Vera Inber, for instance, who had written a long poem commemorating the terrible siege of Leningrad, was reminded, after brief words of praise, that in the past she had ' sinned on the side of aestheticism '. The Headmaster's talk ended up with a terrifying bellow of authoritarian menace: ' It is the writer's responsibility to mould the coming generations. Soviet literature *must* deal with moral problems, *must* strengthen the ideas of the state, the great ideas of socialism, it *must* build up the moral health of the people.' Remembering the fate of such people as Prince Mirsky in the past, many a poet and novelist must have felt that only the most flatulent praise of Stalin or the corniest kind of black-and-white propaganda writing about the war could save his skin.

Comically enough, the Governors of the school did not appear to see where all this would lead them—or why it had led them where they found themselves. ' The young poets,' observed Tikhonov, ' still show faults of triteness, wordiness, insufficient care.' And even more wistfully: ' The style of our authors rarely gives that impression of freshness and easy clarity, which so captivates one in the classics.' That there might be a connection between the brutal and narrow State imperatives and this result, did not seem to occur to him; or at least he could not admit it.

In my article, *State Art and Scepticism*, I tried, without indulging in polemics, and without in any way suggesting that heroic exploits were not an excellent theme for writers in wartime, to point out the absurdity of the Soviet attitude, the extreme unlikelihood that such imperatives would produce any masterpieces, and their total incompatibility with the sceptical British temperament. ' The Russian writer,' I said, ' has been expected to " take his part " in the national war effort in a very emphatic way. We—if we think about it at all—are apt to conclude that the writer is most successfully " taking his part " if he pursues his researches into the truth about human life and fate according to his own inner light; and if our leaders bade us " take our part " in the way the Russian writers are bidden, would feel that the words had been given a most shallow and philistine interpretation. For the Russian writer is expected to write exclusively about what is happening in the war, and his story is expected to conform to a pattern in which the Soviet citizen triumphs by unparalleled endurance, devotion and heroism on whatever front he is fighting, in which the enemy is always a brute and the lesson learned is flaming hatred against him and fanatically reinforced love of the Soviet Fatherland, Stalin, and the local Commissar (who always does prodigiously better than anyone else). Such rigid rules of creation are unknown and indeed unthinkable in our country. . . .'

If I had left it at that, perhaps my sin might have been overlooked; unfortunately, I indulged in a little fun directly afterwards. I ought to have remembered that joking is the worst of all crimes when one is criticizing a dictatorship or totalitarian set-up. ' Let us imagine for a moment,' I continued, ' what it would be like if such standards were applied here. I'm afraid very few of our more distinguished writers would escape censure for weakness of " ideological–political approach ", in Tikhonov's phrase, or for absence of the " proper high patriotic note " which the Moscow correspondent of the *New Statesman* tells us the official mentors insist on. Soviet authors are, in addition, apparently expected to travel everywhere and produce like rabbits. Suspicion falls on E. M. Forster for having transgressed these rules quite flagrantly. The case of the Sitwells is worse. " Some of our writers," says Tikhonov, " imagine they can sit in their burrows and watch events go by. If the writer takes no part in life, in its stormy and heroic doing, then he condemns himself to barrenness. He begins to write beside the point." Renishaw Hall is no doubt a large burrow, but neither Sir Osbert nor Miss Edith can expect mercy for that reason. Tikhonov goes on: " Many writers have lived for long periods far in the rear, but have written nothing, or next to nothing, about the hard work of people in the rear." Where are Sir Osbert's Odes to the Gallant Miners in the Derbyshire pits? Where are Miss Edith's Songs for the Sheffield A.R.P. workers? The more one thinks of it, the worse it becomes. Robert Graves, too, is wasting his time writing facetiae and prose epics about the Argonauts way down in Devon. There is no connection with the present struggle at all, as far as one can see. His proper study should be the British Land Girl through the ages, or a rollicking tale of Sir Walter Raleigh's boyhood. As for the charge of " aestheticism " or " formalism ", which rouses the peculiar rage of the Soviet pundit of today, I'm afraid British authors have a record that could hardly be worse. T. S. Eliot, with his *Four Quartets*, is hopelessly lost before his case opens; and is followed into ignominy by Walter de la Mare (for his poems in *Orion*), Laurence Binyon (for the title poem of *The Burning of the Leaves*), Dylan Thomas (most emphatically, for his recent poems in *Horizon*), George Barker, Stephen Spender and Terence Tiller for their love poems (" erotic in the worst sense " as *Komsomolskaya Pravda* furiously complained about some verses by the unfortunate Joseph Utkin), and a whole cohort of the young. Prose writers are in no securer position. Elizabeth Bowen, in particular, beware! Subtle descriptions of atmosphere in the Irish countryside are no substitute for a healthy pugnacious note against the foe. William Sansom, again, what is he up to with his distempered fantasies of potting-sheds and phallic lighthouses? And that " high patriotic note "? How does it happen that Day Lewis has been allowed to talk about defending " the bad against the worse "? To write a poem about an album? And MacNeice one about alcohol? What frivolity towards the great issues of the day! What was J. B. Priestley doing to pretend, in *Black-Out in Gretley*, that England was riddled with fifth-columnists? And Henry Green, in *Caught*, to suggest that the N.F.S. was addicted to the foul oath, the french letter and the whiskey bottle? As for Julian Maclaren-Ross: the less said the better. His work can only stink in the nostrils of anyone who recognizes, as Tikhonov says the Soviet author must recognize, that the only permissible task of the author in wartime is to describe more and more of " the splendid people around " and " depict the heroes of our time in full stature ".'

Of course this article was not really aimed at the Russians, but, as I have explained, nearer home; partly to expose the uncritical nonsense that was being written in some quarters about heroic Russian war literature, partly to ridicule in advance any attempt in the last phases of the war (or first phase of the peace, for that matter) to tighten bureaucratic control of writing. In an effort to make my standpoint quite clear, I said at the end of the article that I had heard (which was quite true) that in top Kremlin circles the absurdity of some of the results of the official line had begun to be recognized, that it seemed possible that a much greater freedom would be restored after the war, and that I believed ' the genius of the Russian people, now so magnificently displayed in feats of organization, endurance and military élan, is bound to reassert itself in the creative arts as well '.

All in vain. Some months later I was shocked to discover, from the press service which was sent me, that the article had been read, marked and totally misunderstood in Moscow (or Kuibishev); and in spite of the fact that not a single Russian intellectual (other than the privileged Party high-ups) was in the least likely to read the copy of *Penguin New Writing* in which the article appeared, a ludicrously wrathful offensive had been launched against me. I had become overnight a decadent, a reactionary, an ally of the Brown Beast, a calumniator of the heroic Red Army: all the clichés of communist rage were trotted out, all the dented old cannon balls came hurtling over in my direction. It went on for years—was still going on long after the end of the war.

My first reaction was the indignation of someone who has been grossly slandered; and I made some attempts to get a hearing and explain the misunderstanding. They proved fruitless, of course, because the attack had passed rapidly beyond reason into hysteria, as the following quotation from an article by a gentleman called Alexei Surkov in the *Literaturnaya Gazeta* will, I think, make clear: ' to the Soviet public, who were not separated by dozens of miles of salt water during the grim years of their lonely struggle against German fascism, and who were never for a moment aware of any war aims muddle, Lehmann's idle chatter about the "sacred freedom of the artist" and about the right to stand apart from the fray seems the blasphemous twaddle of a self-satisfied literary philistine, passing off vice for virtue. . . . If we wrote about a rose, we stated that instead of dew, it was nourished with human blood; if we described a bird, we remarked that the war had deprived it of its nest; if we dealt with lovers, it was from the point of view of the soldier who in the midst of the cold draughts of war was warming his heart with reminiscences of his beloved. . . .'

Of course I had not meant to assert that in Britain no good books or poems had been written on the great themes of the war, or might not be written in the near future; but that sufficiently important point passed unnoticed amid all the rage and rhetoric. I had touched them on the raw, and it was clearly no use trying to make amends. With some melancholy I marked in the margin a passage I was reading at that time in Jakob Burkhardt's great *Reflections on History*: 'What methods were applied by the state in Assyria, Babylon, Persia, to check the development of the individual, which at that time was, most probably, simply synonymous with evil? There is every likelihood that individuality sought to raise its head wherever it could, and succumbed to civil and religious restrictions, caste institutions, and so on, leaving not a trace behind. The greatest technical and artistic geniuses were powerless to make any change in the utterly uncouth royal fortresses of Nineveh. The meanness of their ground plans and the slavishness of their sculptures were law for centuries.' And I wondered whether, in the libraries of Russia, anyone ever came across, and pondered these other noble words of Burkhardt: 'In derivative or late epochs, men come to believe that art is at their service. . . . Yet at the same time, art becomes aware of its high status as a power and a force *in itself*, requiring from life only occasional and fleeting contacts, but then achieving supremacy by its own means. It is the awareness of this great mystery that removes the person of the great artist, in whom all is fulfilled, to such a vast height and distance from us. . . .'

The whole episode amused me; but saddened me far more, because it seemed to point to the impossibility of an intellectual

R

understanding developing between the Russians and our own people, as long as no one of their side dared to reject the rigid and deforming Stalinist tenets about art and literature. I saw it as a thoroughly bad omen for the future, that after three years of alliance the rigidity was totally unchanged. And the pressure was kept up to make it seem that if one did not accept the Soviet view about Soviet literature, one was being disloyal to the common cause. Only a few weeks before the end of the war in Europe, I was shocked to hear the incomparable Desmond MacCarthy, at a crowded memorial meeting for Alexei Tolstoi in the Curzon Cinema, maintain—on no evidence that could possibly have come to him from his own observation—that Alexei Tolstoi only began to achieve greatness as a writer when he decided to ' accept the Bolshevik regime '. Did he really believe this? The speech was woolly, even for Desmond at his most absent; it would be charitable to assume that he was speaking from notes prepared for him by someone else, and had not had time to go through them.

Desmond did not live long enough to hear of the event that exposed this horrible claptrap once and for all: the suicide of Alexander Fadayev, so long the cruel executor of the official Party line among his fellow-writers, when the Kruschev thaw began. Nor the hysterical persecution of that great writer Boris Pasternak (contributor, as it happened, like Tikhonov, to the first number of *New Writing*), when the freeze-up started again so soon after; an event that was to prove, in the most public and sensational way possible, how power without check allied to false dogma can warp and poison men's minds.

I I

AND then, gradually, the war began to change and enter its last phase. All the preparations that had been going on in secret while the surface of life in England remained so calm, all the campaigns on distant frontiers, were coming to harvest. Our hallucinatory fortress life of the three-year breathing space was over.

Even a mere publisher and poet, working outside the war bureaucracy, was sometimes permitted to catch a glimpse of that tremendous hidden work into which all the energies of the country had been absorbed; and the sense of pride and admiration these glimpses gave one was every now and then mixed with laughter.

I remember an occasion on which a visit had been arranged for me to an underground munitions factory in the Midlands, that had just been brought into production. Under cover of darkness, I was taken by car from the station in a direction I did not even attempt to locate. The sights revealed to my eyes were impressive indeed; but the real object of transporting me thither was, I fancy, to show me that a cultural life had been organized for the workers. In fact, in the buried concert hall of the factory, a performance was taking place that evening of *Twelfth Night*, with Wendy Hiller as the star. Great excitement prevailed, and the hall was full. It was a pleasant surprise for me to discover that Beatrix's old friend, Walter Hudd, was playing Malvolio; but a greater surprise was in store. The smallest speaking part in *Twelfth Night* is that of the priest: he only appears twice, with extreme brevity, and announces in his second appearance that he has, as he imagines, married Olivia to Cesario only two hours previously. I was astonished to see the tall bowed figure of a well-known young poet cross the stage with painful nervousness, clad in the priest's robes, and a few minutes later, with even greater nervousness, stumble through his half-dozen lines: David Gascoyne.

In his earliest war metamorphosis, David had become ship's cook on a naval vessel whose duty it was to intercept all shipping coming up towards one of the southern ports. Whether there was a mutiny among the crew, I have never been able to ascertain; at any rate David's naval career did not last long, and, with scarcely any of us knowing it, he had been released to join an ENSA touring company.

On another occasion, I was invited down to a ' WOSB ', one of the training centres that had been established in the larger country houses, where young officer cadets were put through a rigorous course and finally selected by a series of (to me) quite terrifying intelligence and field tests. The class-room tests,

devised with diabolical ingenuity according to the latest psychological theories, I knew I should have failed quite hopelessly.
After I had witnessed these wretched young men subjected,
during the whole of one afternoon, to every kind of trial of
physical endurance and agility of mind in the face of suddenly
presented situations, I joined the meeting of the selection board
next morning to hear the results and how they were arrived at.
There was one young man in particular, from one of the
minor public schools, of a pleasant unassuming aspect and with
an absorbed and dedicated look at the back of his eyes, who
had distinguished himself quite brilliantly in the bullying field
tests, and—so it appeared to me—reasonably well in the class-
room papers.   All the officers present seemed agreed on passing
him with flying colours at once; until the turn of the psychiatrist came.   To the astonishment of us all this person, almost
snarling with emotion, announced that he disagreed emphatically with our judgement.   Why? the senior officer asked with
some impatience.   ' I have never,' the psychiatrist replied,
' come across a worse case of a young man being in love with
his mother: all his answers reveal it.'   I had no voice, of
course, in these judgements, but I could hardly restrain myself
from exclaiming that this (if true) seemed the best qualifica-
tion possible for one called upon to defend his Motherland.

Now the raids on London began again: the ' tip-and-run '
raids and the fire-raids of the Winter of 1943–44, which could
not be compared with the earlier raids because they were made
by isolated aircraft, defying in high-speed sallies the massed
barrage of London's new ack-ack defences, for no worthwhile
reason that one could comprehend except to demoralize, to
maintain the idea of the imminence of the enemy—in which
no one seriously believed any longer.   Up on the roof of
Carrington House, in my tin helmet, I would watch fascinated
all the beams of the searchlights waving about like the antennae
of some threatened giant insect, finally to converge, in the clear
darkness of the sky which they pierced, on the little silver-
winged cabin streaking away, while the clanging, cracking and
reverberation of the guns increased and concentrated itself with
winking explosions in the raider's path.   These attacks were

disagreeable because of the suddenness of their violence, which broke up sleep; but considered from the dramatic–aesthetic point of view, they were rather beautiful, and the actual damage they did was comparatively small.

Meanwhile, Africa had been conquered at last, and the sunburnt victors began to trickle back to London, to infiltrate, with their bleached hair and dark-tanned knees, among the now almost entirely American soldier crowds in the pubs, to appear suddenly in their home villages, despising the tinned pilchards and Woolton pie that seemed to appear ever more frequently on our tables, but rejoicing almost with unbelief in the greenness of fields and gardens: at the back of their eyes, as they told their stories of desert camps and tank encounters in sandstorm and smoke and evening carousals along the boulevards of captured cities, there still seemed to linger a dream of Oriental horizons, a fading glimmer of something timeless, an adventure that did not quite belong to the iron schedules of industrial war, the tiered bunks in grimy tube-stations and the squalid rubble of the bombed insurance offices, mercantile banks and A.B.C. shops.

Among my own friends, John Lepper returned after long service with the fourth Indian Division all through the desert campaigns, as full of admiration for the Indian soldiers with whom he had fought as he was of contempt for the Arab inhabitants; Charles Dakers, youthful fan of *New Writing*, whose letters to me had been as much in poetry as in prose, describing hair-raising exploits with the Long Range Desert Patrol as if they had been the happy adventures of schoolboy explorers; Harold Acton from India, bringing refreshment with his sparkling affectionate courtesy and his chippendale flatteries, and describing for hours on end, with an inimitable flowery wit and Proustian eye for social comedy, goings-on in the bizarre, evanescent world that official India had become: compounded of the mixture of old-time colonial administrators with newly arrived Generals and Air-Marshals and Admirals, surrounded by their temporary staffs and an outer fringe of Hindu and Moslem politicians, prospering business contractors and frustrated intellectuals; Roy Fuller from East Africa,

happy indeed to be home with Kate and his young son John
but indefinably suggesting that some inspirational ghost of himself had been left behind; and many others, in their vizor-
peaked caps and worn battledress, veterans now who were once
the companions of drinking nights in the first winter black-out
of all; whose absence, though only two or three years in fact,
already seemed to have lasted half a lifetime.

At the same time, as a result of these triumphs in North
Africa, the intellectual silence between ourselves and the
French began at last to dissolve again. It had never been
complete: that excellent monthly *La France Libre*, directed by
André Labarthe with the aid of Moura Budberg, had kept some
devious contacts with Vichy France, some of Gide's *Figaro*
articles even found their way into *Horizon*, and Louis Aragon's
Crêve-Coeur poems had reached us and made a deep impression
by their powerful nostalgia, their lack of even concealed
marxist propaganda, and the beauty of the imagery that
evoked simultaneously the agony of still almost unbelievable
defeat and the splendours of the past:

> Drinking the wine of summer's haze
> In a rose-castle in Corrèze
> I changed this August into dream. . . .

> My love, within your arms I lay
> When someone hummed across the way
> An ancient song of France; my illness
> At last came clear to me for good—

> That phrase of song like a naked foot
> Rippled the green water of stillness.

The victorious armies discovered an intellectual life in Algeria
which had maintained itself with some dignity in spite of Vichy
prohibitions, and which immediately expanded under the sun
of liberation and developed an immense thirst for news of what
had been going on in England. This opening of windows
was good for us too; it must be admitted that the air in London was by now getting a little stale, and the malice that is
normal among denizens of the literary world when they talk
about one another would suddenly erupt in absurdly distorted

fantasies of envy and suspicion. Max-Pol Fouchet, the young editor of a notable new literary review, *Fontaine*, was brought over to London by the British Council, and with his chubby countenance, his enthusiasm, his Miranda-like air of continually exclaiming to himself ' O brave new world! ', charmed all of us, who were indeed happily excited to make contact at last with a Frenchman in the same line of business. Many parties were given for him, many long discussions took place on what had been happening to the arts in England, what attitude the outstanding French writers had taken towards the Germans and towards Vichy, and what could be done to bring our two worlds closer together again. Max-Pol planned a bumper special number of *Fontaine* on England and its intellectual life during the war, and persuaded as many as possible of us to write for him: to me was assigned the job of summing up the work and writing a funeral oration of Virginia Woolf.

Very soon after, I must admit to my immense pleasure, Jiři Mucha came back from Algiers to announce that he had met André Gide there and found him reading a volume of *New Writing and Daylight*. The sage, cordial as ever and unruffled apparently in his dignified seclusion by the tides of war that had swirled around him, had cross-questioned Jiři with voracious curiosity about all that was going on in England, and had presented him with a volume of his wartime ' interviews ' *Attendu Que*, adding that if I wished to translate and publish them in London he would be delighted. Thereupon a long exchange of letters and cables ensued, of the most flowery sort, but as the Americans had got a jump ahead of us, and Gide's pre-war publishers, Secker and Warburg, were already in touch with them, in the end I regretfully abandoned the idea of taking Gide at his word, especially as the directors of Secker and Warburg were my friends; and in spite of the fact that Gide in one of his letters to me observed (I think untruthfully) that he had never heard of them. With a grand gesture of accepting the inevitable, he added:

Tout se fait aujourd'hui a l'insu des auteurs et en se passant de leur consentement. On affirme toutefois que les ' royalties ' seront préservés. Je crois que c'est tout ce que l'on peut espèrer.

étant donné les difficultés des communications. Je laisse donc
faire sans chercher à protester, bien décidé à ne me point laisser
tourmenter par ces questions, alors qu'il en est tant de plus
importantes; soucieux surtout de maintenir de bonnes et cordiales
relations, autant qu'il se peut et se pourra, avec les maisons
d'éditions de l'étranger qui auront fait preuve de bon vouloir
et d'honnêteté; et tout particulièrement avec *New Writing* et
The Hogarth Press. . . .

Fontaine was not the only new French literary monthly that
came to us now from liberated Algeria. With the aid of his
Algerian friend Jean Amrouche, Gide had started *L'Arche*, the
chief virtue of which, if one compared it with *Fontaine*, was
undoubtedly that Gide himself was a fairly regular contributor.
I made great efforts to arrange that The Hogarth Press should
be the English agent for *l'Arche*: Gide was all for it, a first con-
signment was actually signalled as on its way, but in the end
nothing came of this scheme either. The only practical
result, from the publishing point of view, that arose from my
newly established relations with Gide, was that Raymond
Mortimer translated the brief but admirable and characteristic
sketch, *Ma Mère*, which Jiři had also brought back for me. I
printed it in the fifth number of *New Writing and Daylight*. A
small enough mouse to come out of the heavings of the bureaucratic mountain; but what rejoiced me was to know that in
future I could count on the interest and sympathy of the man I
concurred with Cyril Connolly in thinking the greatest French
prose-writer living at that time.

When I next saw André Gide, a year or two later, he was
re-established in Paris, surrounded by his acolytes and worshippers: the rituals of awe which gather round an eminent
French man-of-letters had resumed; and the air hummed with
murmurs of ' *cher maître* '.

In the middle of the fire-raids, Demetrios's death took place,
an event from which it took me a long time to recover.

He had been ill for several years, without knowing exactly
what was the matter with him. Before he left Cambridge to
work with the Greek Department of Information in the
Autumn of 1941, he had been told by a local doctor, to whom

he complained of persistently feeling out of sorts, that it was
all nerves and imagination. He even managed to convince
himself for a while that this was in fact so; coming up to London and entering into a wider literary and political world acted
as a tonic, and it was some months before he began to feel his
illness gaining on him again. At the same time he went
through a violent personal crisis, which brought on a complete
collapse: when I went to see him in hospital, he kept on speaking to me of ' experiences that can't be described ' when he was
on the brink of death, of a state of mind he could not even
entirely remember, which had transformed his whole outlook
on life and death. ' I'm afraid,' he wrote in a letter, ' although
I don't like it, that I am becoming a mystic. It was wonderful
to prepare oneself never to wake up again. I longed so much
for a night of freedom and rest, in which there is no memory,
no right and wrong, no suffering. But I had to wake up again,
and I shall go on and try to make the best of it. But I doubt if
the foretaste of the night I experienced will ever leave me alone.
. . . My new contact with this night reminded me that one
must never be too categorical with the things of the world.
Everything is changing in it. We have the right not only to
fear the worst, but also to hope the best.'

When he came out of hospital, his courage returned, and
spurred on by the immense interest his first English poems and
articles soon began to arouse among his friends and acquaintances, and by my persistent urging and planning, he settled
down to what he intended to be a long period of literary work.
Again his spirit triumphed; but again the disease, which his
new London doctor had realized was a dangerous sickness of
the blood, broke the new élan down. By the Autumn he was
feeling very ill again, and was sent away for a rest and change in
Devon. ' Today ', he wrote to me on November 12th, 1942,
' I feel much better, and people tell me that I do not look ill
any more. In spite of that I must stay here a little longer;
I am not quite prepared yet to face London again. My days
here are pleasant and peaceful, but my nights are full of terrors:
full of the most exhausting nightmares. In the morning I get
up extremely tired and I need all the peace of the day to forget
the terrors of the night. I know that it is ridiculous to get so

much affected by " things which are not ", but I also know that
my fate will always be to succumb to these things. That is
what destroys or threatens with destruction everything positive
given me by life.'

It was against this background of continual spiritual and
physical struggle that Demetrios, in the brief space of three or
four years, conquered the English language as poet and critic.

It would, however, be wrong to think of him as a pre-
dominantly melancholy and dispirited character. Not only
did his conversation sparkle when his literary enthusiasms were
under discussion, but also, when he was well, he displayed the
liveliest sense of fun and of teasingly malicious observation in his
social life. After Devon, he made his last, and most extraordinary recovery. He was suddenly very much happier in his
personal life, and for a time, in spite of what I was now privately told about the almost incurable nature of his disease, I
believed he might be on the way to getting well. During the
meals we had together two or three times a week, and the afternoon walks we sometimes took across the park, past the statues
of Byron and Achilles, he would occasionally speak with horror
of the oppression and starvation in Greece, of which nauseating
accounts reached him direct; but often his mood was gay, and
he would talk brilliantly of his latest discoveries in English or
American literature, and make witty and penetrating comments on our mutual acquaintances. In 1943 he accepted an
offer from the Friends Ambulance Unit to live for a time at
Manor Farm, to prepare the young Quaker volunteers who
were in camp there for work in Greece. He was thus brought
into contact with entirely new people, new problems and new
ways of thought. He found it extremely stimulating, and was
a great success, both with the Cadbury family and with his
pupils. His first letter to me showed his new mood of optimism
and gaiety:

> I was extremely pleased to find Donald Swan here, the most
> charming and attractive of my Quaker pupils, who showed me
> round yesterday evening. The camp is in the most wonderful
> park you could imagine, with Greek temples, rock-gardens, lots of
> roses and a huge lake. It belongs to Dame Elizabeth Cadbury,
> famous, it seems, not only because of the chocolates. I was told

that she is more than eighty, but she is full of life and energy. I met her last night and she asked me to stay at her house in the middle of the park. I was given a very nice room and a still nicer bathroom, and when I told her I was writing an essay on English poetry, she also gave me a very quiet and comfortable study with a lovely view and told me that I could use her library, in which I found excellent editions of all the English poets. . . . I had a very pleasant evening yesterday. Dame Elizabeth—who prefers to be called Mrs. Cadbury because she is a Quaker—talked a lot; she is interested in everything; in spite of her age she is even an admirer of the Sitwells. She also played the organ, a lovely instrument in the middle of the drawing room. Today she had to go to London where she will stay until tomorrow evening; so I shall have plenty of time for work. A little while ago, a strange, haughty creature, who introduced herself as ' Madame's French maid ' came to see if I wanted anything, and when I told her that I was perfectly happy, she gave me a long, long lecture on beauty: that beauty is to be found everywhere, not only in France and Italy, but in England too, that beauty in France is quite different from beauty in England, etc., etc. It was almost Gertrude Steinish. . . .

The recovery did not survive his return to London. He began to have long fits of dizziness and increasing nightmares, and knew at last that his only chance was to be treated in hospital. He waited in vain, however, for a hospital bed: they were as difficult to come by in those days as a bunch of bananas. In the end, it was only by deliberately causing himself to collapse and be found unconscious on the floor of his room in Prince's Gate, that he brought the emergency service into action and so gained admittance to Westminster Hospital. He was given every kind of treatment, including an extremely painful operation, which consisted in drawing all his blood out and pumping new blood in; but the leukaemia slowly wasted him away. It gave him great pleasure that all his friends visited him there, not only his devoted Greek friends but also the circle of English literary friends he had gathered about him, including William Plomer, Joe Ackerley and Beryl de Zoete, but he could never talk to them except briefly. He kept on telling me how unhappy he was to have disappointed me, because he had not written the many poems, essays and stories we had planned together.   His essay *A View of English Poetry*, which had cost him such an enormous effort just before he was taken to hospital, he thought could only be considered as a series of aphorisms, as there was so much more he would have liked to say;   and, as I have related in my own study of his work, *A Greek Poet and his English Language*, he felt that his last poem *Lazarus* was far too unpolished to be published at all.   In general, I believe that the wishes of the dying should be respected, but as I was sure that he was wrong in his view of it, I thought that he would have forgiven me for printing it.   Nothing he wrote haunts me more;   and I think it should be read in connection with the letter, written after his first crisis, which I quoted above:

> . . . Love is slow,
> And when she comes she neither speaks nor hears:
>
> She only kisses and revives the dead
> Perhaps in vain.   Because what is the use
> Of miracles unheard of, since instead
> Of trying to remember the great News
>
> Revealed to me alone by Death and Love,
> I struggled to forget them and become
> Like everybody else. . . .

Of his last days, while the nightly fire-raids were taking place —they were far too much of this world to trouble him—of his funeral, of my hunt through his papers and the essays and fragments I found there, and all that I did not find, I have given an account in *A Greek Poet and his English Language*.   It would have been inappropriate there to speak of what I personally lost by his death;   but I do not suppose that even now I have ceased to feel the wound of it.   Without his belief in what I was trying to do, as an editor and publisher as well as a poet, I have often thought that in the stress of war, in the torment of uncertainty about where one was going and what it was worth, in the baffling periods when one seemed to be misinterpreted even by those one thought to be one's closest friends and colleagues, I would have been tempted to throw everything up.   Not heroic, certainly;   but I am not one of the cold men of iron will-power; and even after Demetrios's death my natural pertinacity would sometimes have failed if I had not been able to think of things he had said to me—to hear as if his living voice, making a whole of all the disordered fragments.

Not very long after Demetrios's death, I was rung up one day by the *Manchester Guardian*, and asked if I would like to say anything about Alun Lewis, as news had just come in that he had been killed on the frontiers of Burma.

I have written elsewhere, in my essay *A Human Standpoint*, of the shock this caused me, of my admiration for the way his poetry was developing and of my greater admiration for the stories he was beginning to write. I was immensely proud to be able to publish the mysterious and beautiful last, long poem *The Jungle* (which reached England after his death), but his two short stories, *The Orange Grove*, which appeared in *Horizon*, and *Ward o3 (B)* which I printed in *Penguin New Writing* No. 18, showed him maturing, I thought, as a writer of fiction more rapidly and remarkably than as a poet. In announcing the dispatch of the latter story, in the late Summer of 1943, he wrote on an airgraph to me: ' Life follows Hobbes's description: excessively strenuous and brutish. There are however friends, and sometimes a gramophone, and I find a solid basis for myself in the Welsh colliers of my regiment. In many ways I'm glad I'm not in England. I'm sure I can see straighter here. Human behaviour is as clear as the lucid climate, and as hard and immutable. Change seems less simple than it did at home. Everything was possible there.' These words were the first foreshadowing to me of the profound changes that were taking place in his mind, that emerge so significantly and so disturbingly in *The Jungle* and the two stories, as if he were suddenly moving out of a narrow room into the open air of an experience of the universe of which he could not discern the limits.

And now he was gone, with his passionate sense of instinctive truth and elemental love that withstood the questioning of everything else, the ' tangled wrack of motives drifting down an oceanic tide of wrong ', only just on the threshold of becoming that kind of imaginative creator the world so badly needed.

Sidney Keyes had vanished one day into the desert, with the whole of his dawn patrol. Drummond Allison had been killed in Italy just as his first and only collection of poems, *The Yellow Night*, was being brought out. Drummond, in a long letter asking me to tell him what I really felt about his poetry and how he could improve it and pleading with me to persuade The Hogarth Press to take it on, had said, ' I expect Sidney is dead, you know, although, as John Heath-Stubbs says, " he may be wandering in some remote part of the desert disguised as a holy man ".' (But his grave was found in 1945.) I was suddenly filled with dread that what had almost incredibly not yet happened was going to be our doom in the last stages of the war. There were no miracles; the poets were going to be killed as they had been in the earlier war; how foolish we had been to think we could escape without the massacre of all that was best in our generation.

Then the sickles of war flashed out, reaching murderously across from either side of the Channel. The long awaited news of the Normandy landings under General Eisenhower came over the radio one June morning. And waking early another morning, sleepy and bewildered Londoners heard a strange spluttering noise, that grew louder, and then stopped, to be followed by a distant explosion: the first of the doodle-bugs had fallen.

V
THIS THEME, THEIR HOPE

I THINK it was largely owing to Demetrios's encouragement and quite extraordinarily intense perceptive interest, that during the lull I began to write poetry again, after an interval of several years. It surprised me to find the springs flowing as in my pre-Vienna days, to be covering page after page in my exercise books with notes and arguments and images for poems; but there was suddenly so much I wanted to say, and only in poetry, for (as I have already mentioned in *The Whispering Gallery*) the ' mysterious agency in the inmost chamber of my imagination ' had begun to co-operate again. Then, the very fact that one's life was so narrowly ordered and distractions were so rare—above all no travelling abroad and no motoring about—made it, I found, possible to draw a poem out of its sheath of invisibility by slow stages, adding perhaps a stanza every other day, two or three in a week-end, while remodelling others. Nevertheless, without the extra impetus that Demetrios's continual eager demand for new poems gave me, I doubt if much would have got beyond the scribbling and fragmentary stage.

Some of this work was done in London, in late afternoon intervals of other work; but a great deal more in the country, at Fieldhead, or staying with Rosamond or Helen, both of whom had cottages in the south, or on brief holidays by the sea. So it happens that the poems are filled with the imagery of English gardens and river-valleys, bluebell woods and sheep-cropped downs, cliffs and chines and sandy beaches of the Channel; but not all. Several of the earlier poems, for instance, evoke the Alpine landscape of Austria, *The Last Ascent* and *The Summer Story* most vividly, for at that time I would often find myself day-dreaming about the country I had loved so much; a nostalgia I worked off partly in my broadcasts, and partly in these poems. I remember one winter evening, reading manuscripts alone in my flat, I tuned in by chance on my portable wireless to a German station, and let it run on for

an hour or so while I prepared my supper. The massive allied
raids had just begun, and they gave a long list of places that had
been bombed during the previous week: as I heard the name
of each Austrian town, the place itself and the country round
it became almost unbearably vivid to me, and my memory was
flooded with images of holiday expeditions and explorations, all
with friends who were now officially my enemies. These
memories haunted me during the rest of the evening, and when
I went to bed I fell into a dream before I was fully asleep. In
the dream I was on a secret mission and had been parachuted
down from an aeroplane somewhere in Austria and captured
by Nazi soldiers almost at once. As I was being interrogated by
my captors my eyes kept on straying to the sun-drenched
landscape of Alpine foothills I could see over their shoulders—
the interrogation seemed to be taking place at a table in the
open—the fields full of corn that was just ripe for harvesting,
the farmsteads with their huge overhanging roofs and the bright
red flowers in their boxes on the windows, the purple onion-
domes of little baroque churches under the peaks; and when
they rebuked me for not paying attention to their questions, I
replied that it was impossible to answer questions in paradise.
. . . Then I was fully awake again, dizzy, and listening to the
raw clanging of an ambulance racing down the street below.
The feeling that oppressed me during the whole of the war, of
the tragic absurdity of a situation that turned friends into
murdering enemies as quickly as a thunderstorm blows up on
a sultry day, began to crystallize into verse:

> O in this cloud of darkness that endures
> Better by far, the guns say, greeting ill
> To barricade us for eternity
> Where the green wave the island dream immures
> And the Armed Guardian of the Cliffs can be
> Our classic, unrelenting stance, and kill
> The wandering birds of love that brave the sea . . .

The Summer Story came out of the same nostalgia at an earlier
date, but transposed and blended with other elements to make
a whole that is still mysterious even to myself: I can only
testify to its inner coherence and truth, which cost me many

hours and days of slow work. Though it would appear to be about despair and death, it seems to me to cover much more spiritual experience than that: inevitable, as it was in a sense a concentration into forty short lines of an idea I had for a long story or play, and as it went through the process of condensation and transmutation it attracted to itself unexpected images and phrases (in the musical sense).

By the middle of the war Fieldhead had been turned into a Red Cross Home, with some of the wards in the downstairs rooms, but we still had the dining-room and the library as well as several bedrooms upstairs, and were in general fortunate because my Mother had had much to do with the local organization before the war and was held in considerable awe by the Commandant (who was devoted to her) and the other officers. In fact I often got the impression that it was my Mother who was running the whole show, having for so many years been accustomed to run every show in the neighbourhood and get her own way. In addition, with the touch of sly New England canniness she never entirely lost, she took full advantage of the fact that she was partly crippled since the accident in the library when she broke her thigh, and was thus at the same time Supreme Patient and Grey Eminence of the home. She saw the joke of this herself, I think, and didn't mind being teased about it by her children. She had in any case grown a very tough skin, years before, against our teasing, which she treated as a kind of harmless half-witted fooling—an attitude no doubt justified by the fact that even then, when we were all in our thirties or early forties, we were apt to converse in a childish private language that dated back to the first world war. The long rest in bed did her good, and she looked extraordinarily young and beautiful when her worries cleared: even ten years later, when the cross-hatchings of age were far more minutely etched on her face, she retained a freshness of colour in her cheeks, a sweetness of expression and a sparkle in her grey-blue eyes that someone much younger might have envied.

As the thigh mended (though it was never entirely right), she began to go about again, and even made expeditions to London, occasionally attending my parties (as I have described). I also remember how she insisted on my taking

her to the famous Olivier production of *Richard III*, in spite of
the fact that rockets had already begun to fall in the London
area: she was, I believe, under the impression (luckily) that
sirens would sound before they arrived.

I had myself moved into a big first-floor room, next to my
mother's, which looked out over the drive and the yew-hedged
rose-garden, and used to work at my poems and *Armoured
Writer* articles there during my week-end visits, after Home
Guard parade on Sunday mornings. When I got stuck, I
would go for a walk along the river, or wander round the
flower garden, through the ' Lovers' Walk ' and the backways
of the kitchen garden, muttering to myself until I got a phrase
or epithet to my satisfaction. I find an August entry in my
journal, typical of many others: ' Tonight, after dinner and
the thunderstorm that broke up the week-end of perfect Summer weather, I went down the garden to pick some plums to
take back to London. It smelt incredibly good: wet grass,
roses and honeysuckle and lavender, ripening fruit and
aromatic leaves. I am still going over the poem, one of the
most difficult I've been working on, which, after a feeling of
confusion and heaviness, has suddenly begun to come through
properly, filling me with elation—confidence—insight. . . .'
As the Summer of 1944 advanced, and the battle of Europe
developed in intensity, a strange and terrifying contrast
developed between earth and sky. Where I walked, thinking
out my poems and articles, all was peace and fruitfulness, the
great garden of Fieldhead in its imperturbable and changeless
seasonal rhythm bringing flowers to bloom and fruit to ripening
as it had when I had been a small boy before the first world war.
The mottled red and yellow colours of the apples deepened in
the branches, the windfalls dropped into the heavy-dewed
grass where the wasps attacked the bruises, and hedgehogs
crept among them, snouts to earth; in the borders asters and
dahlias and snapdragons flamed in many-coloured fires, yellow
leaves began to appear among the limes in the drive and the
crimson drippings of the virginia creeper over the library
walls; squirrels leapt and swung from aromatic branch to
branch among the walnut trees, and late butterflies could be

observed asleep in window corners. Then, as sunset darkened into twilight on cloudless nights, slowly great armadas of bombers rose over the horizon and the tops of the chestnut trees, and their clustering formations, heading for the Continent, filled the sky for hours on end with their steady whine and roar. . . . One began to wonder whether one would ever live under quiet skies again: it was an awe-inspiring spectacle, this gigantic concentration of death-dealing power moving off to the kill, but appalled though one might be at what this revealed that war had become, for us they were there to protect. I could not help contrasting them with the outnumbered battles of our fighters in the same skies four years before, and the cease-less humming of the enemy bombers towards Coventry that moonlit night when I mounted guard by the railway bridge.

Sometimes, too, I took the jottings of a poem with me on night guards. These were now very often posted at various points in the hills, and I found them refreshingly stimulating and enjoyable. They formed an agreeable contrast not only to cooped-up London nights, but also to the morning parades and field exercises in which I had made no progress at all as a soldier, allowing ' enemy ' patrols to steal up to within a few feet of me without noticing a single sign of them, and proving myself ignominiously unable to hit the target at all in long-range firing practice on Cockmarsh. One June night, I remember, we were posted in the stables of Disraeli's old house at Bradenham, the bosky garden looming in the starlight, the edge of the deep surrounding woods showing in clear dark outline against the faintly luminous sky. In the midnight hours a young market gardener was on guard with me, and began talking about the war—about his life—about the changes that were coming. He had brothers who had emigrated to Canada and South Africa, and were fighting among the armies from those countries. ' I dare say, afterwards we shall be sorry we didn't do more,' he said rather wistfully, ' in many ways I'd rather be in the thick of it than growing vegetables for the home front.' Like so many countrymen, he was aware of, and anxiously doubtful of the speed of transformation in social relations we were undergoing. He told me of his grandmother, a village artisan's wife, her dignity and poise and long-living health, and the mutual respect that had existed between her and the former, vanishing gentry. ' It's the old rhythm of life we seem to be losing,' he said, ' the old contentment and free courtesy.' Then our time to go out came; and as we made our rounds the first phrases of a new poem came to me:

> At one o'clock the first patrol came in.
> We yawned and grumbled. ' Nothing stirring? ' ' No.
> Only old Jenkins' cow up by Saxon Wood
> Gave us a proper turn.' We slung our rifles
> Felt for our ammo, grinned, and stumbled out,
> The market gardener and myself from town,
> One Sunday night in June.
>
> Not a sound came from the stables, where the men
> Slept by the disused mangers, boys and warty
> Old village salts and veterans. The stars
> Marked the black roofline of the empty house
> With faintest diamond fire. . . .

Most of the poems I was at work on at this time were, it seems to me now, variations on one fundamental theme: the opposition of despair and love, the experience of the void that produced the will to destroy and was at the same time the product of it, and the spiritual affirmations that could fill it:

> The centuries blaze up behind your wrath,
> You shrivel continents you cannot save;
> When will you wake into the legend's truth,
> When will you know the daybreak of your love?

In my *Poem for Two Voices* and *The Ballad of Jack at the World's End*, which were Demetrios's favourites but neither of which seems to me now to have found quite the right tone of voice, I treated the same theme but in relation to the crumbling away of the old liberal belief in progress and beneficent power, that shaky temple whose ruin the war seemed about to complete: on the one side, the dream of the ideal state—the promise of justice and goodness as the natural right of man—on the other the incontrovertible imperfection of man and the fact that loomed larger and larger as power in the modern world increased, that power could be used by evil as well as good.

Gradually the sense of a civilization that had lost its way, a world out of control began to dominate my thoughts. I think this was a not unusual experience among reflective people, as the ingenuity of modern technology revealed itself more and more diabolically in the last phase of the war. At the back of one's mind grew the still tiny, but ominous apprehension that the conquest of the Nazis might only mean a pause and a change of partners before the process of destruction began again: the sense of something accelerating that should never have been set in motion. This, surely, was the impulse behind the revival of interest in archaeology and the science of vanished civilizations that began to be so marked at this time: not merely the new, still scarcely believable idea that our own civilization might join the rubble of the past without leaving a trace, but also that somewhere in the speechless mounds and crumbling stones, faint landmarks in a time–space stretching out far beyond Rome and Greece, a secret might be found that would tell us where we went wrong, what belief or intuition we had lost. Perhaps it could be found in the patient, cunning unriddling of the buried fragments; perhaps in the legends that had come down to us through the civilizations we knew. These ideas crystallized first in my poem *Invocation*:

> . . . When the lone mounds and mazes on the downs
> And shards dug up from ruins of old fires
> That blazed where Kings of Logres built their towns,
>
> Seem on the point of utterance, with lips
> Unlocked at last from their unreckoned sleep. . . .

I went down during a brief holiday period to stay with my sister Helen near Salisbury. At that time her husband Mounty was still in the Middle East, both her daughters, Maureen and Nancy, were engaged in war-work and Simon was at Eton. She occupied her energies, as a member of F.A.N.Y., in driving for the American Army, but so far from being tired of sitting at the driving wheel during her days off, she was eager to jump at any excuse to get back there. It is no doubt merely a masculine prejudice that leads men to judge women at the wheel as unreliable, unpredictable and irresponsible; but

Helen at least is one of the few women I would unhesitatingly award a certificate of exception to. I had, therefore, little difficulty in persuading her to drive me to Stonehenge, which I studied with a new curiosity and excitement. American G.I.s were wandering in and out of the rings, or nonchalantly lying against the trilithons, chewing gum: a ripple of the world storm had frothed up just to touch the unfathomably ancient temple. I noticed for the first time the megalith burial mounds to the west, and the traces of the tracks on the downs where the stones had been dragged up from the river. All around were the gigantic horizons with their suggestion of measureless realm and air. The visit stirred me deeply, and I began to find the first phrases and images for the long poem, *The Age of the Dragon*, in which I tried to define the mood of this time of massed Anglo-American raids, the contrast between the violence of the present, the loss of what my market gardener friend had called ' the old rhythm of life ', and the symbols of permanency, the reapers in the fields and the megalithic burial chambers and temple stones above:

> . . . The marble hands imploring from the past,
> The cities and the symbols are dismissed,
> And history, our home, is changed too fast
> Till all our lives grown thin as Autumn mist;
>
> O give us words, as strong as the ringed stones
> That still outlast forgotten priest and name
> Counting the years by thousands on the downs
> To cage the Dragon and transmute our shame.

In this poem I felt I had most nearly captured the tranquillity of tone, combined with intensity of image, that I was always aiming at; with the exception of *The Sphere of Glass*, it was the poem in which my own fragile-winged Muse seemed most completely to have inspired me to transform the disorder of living, feeling and thinking in a world cataclysm into the calm and order of art.

The Sphere of Glass came out of a Spring visit to Rosamond, who had taken a cottage at Aldworth in the Berkshire hills. As the bus from Reading wound up and down the country

roads, the fields looked so fresh and restful and softly green, the
bluebells a swimming ground-mist of azure-violet in the
copses, that my longing to have a cottage of my own in such a
landscape one day became a determination. Later, Rosamond
and I went for a walk in the woods. The light fell on the
young leaves of the trees, so that some of them looked like a
shower of pale green-gold coins pouring to earth. I told her
about the poems I was trying to write; and she excited me
very much by describing the new novel she was at work on, to
be called *The Ballad and The Source.* Then we began to talk
about the war, and the struggle that was going on at the time
between the Poles and the Russians, which seemed so ominous
for the future; and Archie Clark-Kerr, far away in Moscow,
struggling (as his letters revealed) to unravel the tangle in
lonely fury. As we talked, the air was filled with the distant,
ceaseless humming of aeroplanes; and I was aware of some
strange counterpoint between those aeroplanes with their
constant reminder of the war in which we were engaged, and
the Roman dyke, still visible as a lumpish heaving under the
soil, beside which we were walking. All this I tried to distil, to
bring into harmony in the poem I began when I returned to
London, starting from the key-line that came to me almost of
its own accord:

> So through the sun-laced woods they went. . . .

I was conscious during the walk, in a quite extraordinary
way, of the power of poetry, or rather of tragic art in a more
general sense, to resolve the discords of hope and despair, of
agony and triumph recurring in an eternal pattern in life, so
that the imaginative artist who dared to look far enough into
the truth was given a new dimension of being, as strong as—and
for an agnostic world stronger than—the consolations of
religion:

> Within the wood, within that hour
> It seemed a sphere of glass had grown
> That glittered round their lives with power
> To link what grief the dyke had known
> With voices of their vaster war
> The sun-shot bombers' homing drone,

And make one tragic harmony
Where still this theme, their hope, returned,
And still the spring unchangeably
In fires of its own sap was burned
And poetry, from love and death,
The peace their human contest earned.

It might have been all history
Without the sphere of wonder lay
And just beyond their colloquy
Some truth more pure than they could say,
While through the bluebells and the ferns
Sister and brother made their way.

It was on the return from this visit that I began to think
furiously about a periodical for after the war, a place where we—
that is people who put art and literature first but nevertheless
did not want to consider them in isolation from the rest of
man's activities and interests—should be able, without party
political bias, to discuss history and foreign affairs and the
impact of modern technology on civilization, as well as books,
pictures, theatre and artistic-philosophical questions. I believed such a magazine could be created; I longed to be its
creator; but not all the cards one dreams of are dealt to one,
and it was Stephen Spender who eventually found the opportunity, and the backing, to bring this idea closest to realization.

Very few of my poems at this time had a London background; for the most part the memories were too raw, the
tensions too immediate for the secreting process to be successful.
One of the rare ones which had this background, and one of the
half-dozen that still most satisfy me among those I wrote during
the war, is *In a London Terminus*. In this short poem I returned
again to the paradoxes with which I had first grappled in
Vigils, combined with the theme I had stated more pessimistic-
ally in *The Ballad of Jack at the World's End*. In *The Ballad* I
had been writing of the despair which engulfed young people
thrust into the horror of war, when what they had been promised in youth was peace, justice and happiness. In the new
poem I took this a stage further, seeing that those who go
through this ordeal and yet do not fall victims to despair are
in some way noble, endowed with a spiritual strength more

valuable for our life on earth than those who have not been tested ever could find. This complex of thought had been with me for a long time, as I wandered about London observing those soldiers who had returned from service overseas, whose aspect and bearing appeared to me to be so often marked so conspicuously with pride, courage and compassion. Particularly, of course, I had seen them in the major London railway stations, as I waited for my train to Letchworth, Bourne End or further afield; and these great ruined structures, through the shattered glass of whose vaults the sky could now on cloudless days be glimpsed in all its purity and infinity, seemed to me, as I started work on the poem, to be the essential, symbolic setting for my argument. The film of *Desert Victory* was in my mind:

> . . . Is the path through gulf and flame
> Love's one inexorable claim?

> Soldier, the riddles I would read
> In the mastery of your head
> Do not spell the peace you dreamed
> Once, while the scything bullets screamed,
> And will but sear the hopes of youth
> With their danger-volted truth;

> Here, in my trapped perplexity
> Turning to Heaven, I only see
> The broken girders, empty sky,
> Inscrutable to question why
> Love's grace must rot by Egypt's sea
> That we may grow as we would be.

As the tempo of the war quickened, and Europe became the main battlefield, the tempo of publishing activity quickened also. More countries were being liberated, more opportunities appearing for entering the foreign field again: not only sending one's own publications abroad, but getting hold of the most interesting books and authors from abroad to introduce to an English audience. Gradually my work for The Hogarth Press and for *New Writing* began to increase, and my other, more official work grew more complex; gradually the hours I could spend with my poetry exercise-book grew fewer, and I sadly recognized that the old division of my life was making itself insistently felt once more.

VI

THE LAST PHASE

I

LIFE in London during the V-weapons offensive was not
particularly pleasant; and yet it went on very much as
before. The trouble about the doodle-bugs was that they
came over at all hours of the day and night, and were continually interrupting work, meetings, parties and sleep with their
disagreeable splutter, like an aerial motor bicycle in bad
running order. If one was not in the open, and could not see
which way the beastly flame-tailed thing was heading—having
escaped all the obstacles erected in its path between London
and the coast—one had only the noise to go by. Gratefully
one heard the splutter fade away into the distance; painfully
one heard it grow louder, until it seemed directly overhead;
tensely one waited for the cut-out. If the splutter stopped at
the moment of maximum noise, one dived—if one had anything to dive into or under, shelter entrance, archway or table.
After all the years of war, Londoners were tired, and the
doodle-bugs frayed their nerves abominably. To me, they
seemed far less frightening than the all-night raids of the
Spring of 1941, with their massed bombs, land-mines and
incendiaries, because the area of fear was so much more precisely charted; but I know that many people felt them to be
the worst trial yet, and there were moments when it seemed
that human existence was not much better than beetle or ant
life. Even so, the alarm and despondency they caused was
never anything like as great as Hitler's propagandists gloatingly
reported.

Life went on: though the approach of a doodle-bug had a
markedly freezing effect on conversation at the luncheon or
dinner-table. I remember a luncheon that had been arranged
at the Savoy, in a private room, to discuss whether funds could
be raised to create a permanent memorial for Demetrios, in the
form of a poetry prize or some similar award. Sir Kenneth
Clark was there, the Greek Minister Monsieur Romanos,

George Seferiades,* poet-diplomat and friend of Demetrios, over from Cairo, and one or two other interested friends. It was the first time I had met Seferiades, whose poetry I had begun to publish in *New Writing and Daylight*, and I was deeply impressed by his charm, by his immense knowledge of everything that was going on in poetry all over the world, and by the look of brooding, philosophical reflection in the large dark-brown eyes under the domed brow: a true egg-head, if ever there was one. I was deep in conversation with Kenneth Clark about the war-artists: he seemed surprised at my interest in and admiration for all he had done to help them individually and to make it possible for an imaginative vision, and not merely a factual record, of the events of the war to be preserved for posterity, and he promised to show me some of the latest stuff that had just come in from Normandy. At that moment the familiar splutter began to be audible in the distance; as it grew louder, we all became a little more thoughtful; conversation faltered, dried up here and there for some seconds though the thread was never entirely lost; gestures were inhibited, not a fork was lifted to a mouth for the brief span of time that seemed an eternity. When the machine had evidently veered away again, it was satisfactory to observe that no member of the party had actually disappeared under the table.

There was another, famous occasion at the Churchill Club, in the Autumn. I do not imagine that anyone who was present will ever forget it. The three Sitwells were reading from their poetry. This attraction had drawn the whole of the smarter artistic and literary world, from Emerald Cunard and Sybil Colefax to those dapper young Americans in uniform whose war aim seemed to be to compete for the social place of ' The Sergeant ' (now absent in Normandy). Apart from the last-named, there seemed very little room indeed in the hall for the ordinary members of the allied forces for whom the Club was supposed to be run. As Edith got up to read, and began with her poem about the air-raids in 1940, *Still Falls the Rain*, the warning whistle was sounded in the Club. She had, I believe, never experienced a doodle-bug raid before; but she seemed quite unperturbed. As she reached the passage:

* As poet, George Seferiades has always taken the name of Seferis.

Still falls the Rain—
Still falls the blood from the Starved Man's wounded Side:
He bears in His Heart all wounds—

the rattle grew to ominous proportions, and it was impossible
not to think that the monstrous engine of destruction was
poised directly overhead. . . . Edith merely lifted her eyes
to the ceiling for a moment, and, giving her voice a little more
volume to counter the racket in the sky, read on. It was a
magnificent performance, worthy of a British Admiral coolly
dictating orders from the bridge in the middle of a fierce naval
engagement. She held the whole audience in the grip of her
discipline, the morale of her unspoken asseveration that poetry
was more important than all the terrors that Hitler could
launch against us. Not a soul moved, and at the end, when the
doodle-bug had exploded far away, the applause was deafening.

One grew hard about other people's misfortunes: one had to.
One did not try to picture the scene when a doodle-bug had
fallen, if it was sufficiently far away, out of sight and out of hearing. One registered a moment's relief at not having been
present, shut it out of one's mind, and carried on. One Sunday morning, looking out of my sitting-room window in Carrington House, I saw one fall in the middle distance, at a point
that seemed to be somewhere between the Palace and Big Ben.
A small column of black smoke arose: it was extraordinary how
little it affected the general view. It was only the next day I
heard that I had witnessed one of the most horrible disasters
of the doodle-bug offensive: that particular bomb had hit the
Guards Chapel just when it was full for morning service.

Life went on, in a way that would have seemed incredible if
one had imagined the situation before the war. The theatres
and cinemas remained open: most people bought tickets and
went, whether there was an alert on or not. The performances
of the Sadler's Wells Ballet always drew full houses. I remember one evening that Autumn going to see *Giselle* with Alice
Harding (who had been born an Astor and became an Obo-
lensky, a Hoffmansthal, and later a Pleydell-Bouverie, as well
as a Harding), always a devotee of the ballet and a profound
admirer of Fred Ashton's work with the Sadler's Wells.
Margot Fonteyn and my friend Alexis Rassine were dancing

T

the principal roles, and as they completed the famous love-dance in Act I, Alice murmured: ' They dance like a dream, they dance like a dream. . . .' Indeed the spell of a great ballet like *Giselle*, with music and movement and colour and physical charm all acting together upon one's mind and senses, did draw one into a dream-like trance where even all memory of the doodle-bugs was lost until the curtain came down.

The rockets—the V2s—which began a few months later, were, to my mind, much worse than the doodle-bugs. There were not many of them, and by the time one heard the after-roar it was too late to worry. But there was something singularly disturbing about their unpredictable imminence; it was uncomfortable to feel that one might at any moment, perhaps without even a second's warning, be hurled in frag-ments into eternity. Sometimes on a dark night, after one or two had fallen in the distance, perhaps at intervals of only a few hours, I must confess I found it difficult to concentrate on my work. There was one particular, grim Winter night, which remains in my memory. Beatrix had been appearing in *Uncle Harry* with Michael Redgrave, giving one of the most electri-fying performances in her career: so powerful was the effect she had upon the audience when she appeared in her prison clothes in the last act, that I was ready to believe that for the first time it had become exactly true and not a figure of speech, that one could have heard a pin drop. Suddenly one night, on leaving the theatre, she was taken seriously ill, and a very dangerous operation had to be performed. My mother came up to be at hand, and stayed with me in Carrington House. The drear, iron-chill Winter afternoon darkened into night, and the operation began. We waited, and waited for news: the time when it was supposed to be over passed, and still there was no news; in the distance the roar of a V2 falling could be heard, and still the hours passed; and another V2 fell, seem-ingly nearer; and still we waited. It was a tough endurance test for all of us, most of all for my mother, who first heard a V2 fall that night, when distraught with anxiety for her youngest daughter hovering between life and death under a surgeon's knife.

Another Winter evening which remains engraved on my

memory had a more comic side. Owing to the *Crève-Coeur*
poems, which had made such a deep impression on English
intellectuals, Louis Aragon had become a major symbol of
suffering France for us. When, therefore, it was announced
that he was intending to visit London, great excitement prevailed and every effort was made to receive him with festive
honours. Cyril Connolly arranged an evening party for him
at his flat in Bedford Square, and the most distinguished authors
then in London were among the guests, with Tom Eliot at their
head. Aragon quickly showed us that he had lost none of his
skill in charming people when he talked to them individually,
but perhaps the position he found himself in after the Liberation, as chief rhetoric-monger of the left-wing Resistance, had
somewhat blunted his sensitive responses on more public
occasions. After we had talked over drinks for some time the
word was whispered round that he wanted to give a recitation of
his poetry. Several of us took the cue and pressed him to let
us hear him recite some of the poems which had so profoundly
moved us while France was occupied. Flattered and happy,
Aragon settled himself by the fireside: the rest of us found
chairs or cushions on the floor and grouped ourselves round him
with an eager reverence that English intellectuals, so far less
insular than the intellectuals of most other nations when it
comes to the arts, rarely fail to show on such occasions. The
recitation began with some of the favourites from *Crève-Coeur*,
delivered by their author without a single hesitation and without a glance at the book. There were murmurs of appreciation
and pleasure from round the room. Then Aragon announced
that he would like to read us some more recent compositions
that we were less likely to be acquainted with. As if by magic,
he produced a sheaf of slim volumes from outer and inner
pockets. Do you know this volume? he asked, holding one up.
Or this?—holding another up. Murmurs of regret from the
cushions, noises expressing eagerness to hear them recited.
Without waiting a moment, Aragon, casting aside the texts,
lifted up his voice and began. . . . Time passed, the declama-
tion went on . . . and on. . . . In the distance the dread,
familiar roar of a rocket falling could be heard by English ears
attuned to these reminders of mortality. A frozen look began

to come over the faces of the audience, unable to banish problems of home-going from their minds as the quarter-hours
ticked away. It is doubtful if Aragon, intent on his rhetoric,
was aware at all of what was happening; but he certainly
heard what happened next. An intrepid young author,
arriving late, endeavoured to steal in through the kitchen,
could not find the light switch, and crashed into a row of empty
bottles on the floor. He then joined us, looking somewhat
ruffled, and conducted a running commentary on the recitation, in what was not exactly an undertone. Sweat broke out
on our host's brow. Faces reddened: even Tom Eliot's look
of kindly, enquiring attention seemed to freeze into something
more like a smile of embarrassment. I do not know how
Aragon interpreted this disturbance: but the flood of poetry
rolled on.

By then, the French Embassy had begun to function again.
One evening I was bidden by Sybil Colefax to a party at her
house, to meet the new French Ambassador and his wife: René
and Odette Massigli. Since then, Odette herself has told me
how, directly after the Liberation, she hitch-hiked from Switzer-
land to rejoin René in Paris, found the improvised Ministry
where he was working, and dashed up to his room to be met
by the dramatic news that he had been offered the London
Embassy and proposed to accept it if she said yes too. It was
an inspired choice, and the beginning of a great mission: one
that not only kept French prestige high through the most difficult years of political strain and confusion in re-born France,
but also transformed London's post-war social life. That
story, however, belongs elsewhere. At Sybil's party, I was
struck at once by Odette's exquisite elegance, the easy distinction with which she carried herself, the vitality that radiated
from her sparkling dark eyes—indeed from her whole being—
her charm and her wit. She promised to put me in touch
again with the French writers I had known before the war,
including Sartre, Malraux and Chamson, and then produced
Cyril Connolly's *The Unquiet Grave* from her handbag. Did I
think well of it? I told her that I thought the passages on plants
and animals among the most beautiful and original that I knew.
Did I think it would translate well into French? I replied that I

felt the task would not be too difficult, as a striking proportion of it already consisted of quotations from French authors.

That Winter had the peculiar terror of a recrudescence of struggle and uncertainty, just when the worst had seemed to be over. In the late Summer the great events had followed one another with mounting excitement—Paris liberated—Marseilles liberated—Rumania suing for peace from Russia—and success feeding upon itself, every day's news confounded the prognosis of the day before. Nothing appeared to stand in our way: allied troops would soon be deep into Germany, and all the sites of the rocket-weapons cleared. At Fieldhead we witnessed the astonishing armadas of aeroplanes with gliders in tow setting forth for the invasion of Holland. ' Dare one begin to say " Till we meet "? ' Christopher wrote at the end of a letter in September. . . . Then the checks began to occur. As the shortest days of the year approached—a time for me of strange perturbation for I have always for some unknown reason felt that the dying year was dying *in* me—the savage Greek crisis between the Communist-dominated E.A.M. and the West-sympathizing partisans broke out. I was glad then that Demetrios had not lived to know of it: during the last months of his life, after Canellopoulos's disaster, he had been very gloomy about the role that political factions were beginning to play in Europe on the eve of liberation, and especially in his own country, where he felt that embittered political division was a curse that had been laid upon it from earliest times. And at the same time the Germans launched their counter-offensive in the Ardennes, the last gesture of a nation at bay, to remind the world of the greatest military tradition of Europe. At Christmas at Fieldhead, my mother, Beatrix and I sat huddled over a fire blazing as high as the fallen bough of one of the poplar trees could make it (the boiler for the central heating had burst). A thick rime covered the grass and the trees, and through the french windows we watched a transformation scene of extraordinary beauty develop, as the mist cleared and the feathery white tree-tops were touched by the wan yellow rays of the sun, against a blue sky. There was even frost on the back of a solitary swan that came for food as Beatrix and I, wrapped to our noses, stood on the raft to watch the white sparkle of the willow trees all down the further bank. Behind us in the locked boathouse, the harvest of apples and potatoes lay snugly massed in the gloom under its straw and sacking, with the long unused racing craft resting on their racks above them. Here all was peace, and the unchanging Winter sleep of nature: but our thoughts were darkened by the news of the German break-through that had begun a few days before, the lengthening prospect of slaughter and ruin it seemed to foreshadow, and the suffering of many friends involved in the fighting. Some, including Jiří Mucha, Harold Acton and Lincoln Kirstein, I knew were out of harm's way in Paris, but the news they sent me was not reassuring: the French intellectuals were indulging in an orgy of accusation and counter-accusations, private vendettas were being worked off, and the Victor Hugos of the Resistance, in the intervals of soaking the public with their fountains of trumpery verse, were denouncing their distinguished but more reserved elders as all but collaborationists. Only Malraux, fighting under De Lattre de Tassigny in the Vosges, they told me, kept a dignified silence.

In the midst of this, it was cheering to have a letter from John Lepper with the B.L.A. in Belgium. '. . . After five days of residence in the best hotel in town we were ejected from our luxurious bedrooms to make room for some very senior officers, and had to seek fresh billets. However, I have benefited by the change, as I am now installed with a wine merchant, who has already treated me to a generous sample of his remaining stocks and presented me with a lovely early eighteenth-century drinking glass and two nice little glasses for Schnapps. My washing is taken care of, my bed warmed with a hot-water bottle, tea brought to me in bed, and I have been told to put my boots outside the door at night for cleaning. . . . Our prestige in Belgium has never been higher than at the moment; in fact many people have expressed a wish that they should be incorporated within the Empire on a federal basis. . . . Given one more month of good weather we could have settled the affair this year. Did you hear of the following couplet which appeared on the base of a statue of Bismarck, somewhere in Germany?—

Steig hernieder, lieber Reiter,
Der Gefreite kann nicht weiter.'

2

Two other visitors who caused some commotion arrived in our midst during the early months of the Spring, before the war with Germany was over. Both were from America: Edmund Wilson and Wystan Auden.

Edmund Wilson had long been one of the favourite American authors of the English intellectuals: an odd irony, as he was to prove himself singularly Anglophobe—at any rate in the English eye of disappointed love. I could remember what a stir *Axel's Castle*, which Wilson published in 1931, had made in Bloomsbury and Cambridge. Generally acknowledged now, I think, as one of the key books in modern literary criticism, this study of seven writers of our time, all in the symbolist tradition, profoundly impressed us at once not only by its intellectual energy, but also because of the confident attempt it made to see these writers in their deeper perspective, as part of a movement in the mind of man that had been going on for decades. *Axel's Castle* was followed in 1939 by *The Triple Thinkers*, in which Wilson brilliantly used his favourite X-ray apparatus, combining Marxist analysis with Freudian intuition, on Kipling, Henry James and other authors of the immediate past, with startling if not always entirely convincing results. The capacity of his mind, the restless movement of his thought, the vigour and bite of his writing were unexpectedly displayed in a totally different sphere when he wrote an elaborate—but immensely readable—study of the development of modern revolutionary socialist ideas, from an independent left-wing point of view, in *To the Finland Station*. Edmund Wilson explained the inter-war literary generation to itself more completely than any other philosophical critic: it was natural that there should be eager anticipation when we learned that he was to be one of the first from the other side of the Atlantic to break through our intellectual isolation. Again, as in the case of Aragon, the red carpet was laid down; again a certain dismay clouded the occasion, and seeds of bitterness were sown where the flowers of a happily renewed understanding should have sprung up. Hamish and Yvonne Hamilton laid on an evening party, to which everyone was invited; the literary ' top brass ' were on their best behaviour, but the little man in the drab clothes who was the guest of honour lurked rather silently in corners, was difficult to draw out, and gave a distinct impression of displeasure. ' He's just like a business executive,' sourly exclaimed a distinguished literary figure, who had hoped for a warmer and wittier response. A few days later, however, he came to luncheon with William Plomer and myself at my flat, and after a rather chill and wary start began to thaw, unable to keep up his reserve under the bubbling of William's grotesque stories and comic observations. For the first time I saw him laugh, and during an increasingly relaxed conversation he made a number of extraordinarily perceptive and incisive remarks about books and people, not all of them destructive, though the sharpness of a passing judgement on Willie Somerset Maugham (whose work enjoyed an unusually fervent highbrow vogue at the time), made me wonder whether part of the trouble at the evening party had not been that he was coming to the conclusion that the war had turned us all soft in the head. We parted on the friendliest terms. A few days later I saw him hurrying past the Poets' Fountain in Hamilton Place, coat flapping in the breeze, eyes on the ground, too absorbed in his own thoughts to recognize me or anyone else. Perhaps he was already composing in his head the *New Yorker* articles that caused such offence—in which the unkindest cut of all was his comparison of the atmosphere in post-war London to that of pre-war Moscow.

A week or two later Wystan Auden turned up. His arrival, of course, was of crucial interest to all of us who had been associated with him before the war. He had torn up his English roots and replanted himself in America without, it seemed, a lingering glance of regret: he had been reviled and indignantly defended in public on numerous occasions since 1939; but whatever doubts some of us may have entertained about the poetry he had written since leaving England, not only did we still think of him as *the* leading figure in our literary generation, but also we knew that he had established himself as an admired poetic master in America. Lincoln Kirstein had written to me that he thought the Prospero poem and the Oratorio ' the finest verse since the death of Yeats '. How much had he changed? How much was he aware that he had become a controversial figure in his native country? Edmund Wilson had discussed his transplantation with William and me, with shrewd understanding and sympathy; but, perhaps inevitably, could not give us much idea of what alteration to expect.

I very much doubt if there is such a thing as a completely detached point of view: one cannot change countries without changing one's outlook, even if only ever so slightly. Christopher Isherwood had written to me in the Autumn, about *Penguin New Writing*:

In Number 20, I thought the best things were the Stern story, your poem about the boy on the shore, the Gottlieb story (*What are we Waiting For?*) and Plomer on Forster. I like that poem particularly: better, almost, than any others you've written. And I must frankly say that the Gottlieb story seemed to me to stand head and shoulders above the British reportage—so bold and warm, after the half-tints and wavery lines. I do hope I'm not getting prejudiced in favour of my adopted idiom. I don't think so, though. Because I find the great mass of that kind of American writing boring and unsubtle; whereas the English nearly all have undertones and some sort of inner awareness. Of course the exhaustion of the war-mentality is apparent in all the English writing, as it should be. But a good writer can be exhausted and still maintain all his qualities. In fact, the best of the stuff in *New Writing*, and in Forster's letters, for example, has special qualities which perhaps only come with exhaustion; an extreme relaxation, a wider scale of values, a special kind of humour . . .

At a distance of fifteen years, this seems to me an intelligent piece of criticism; but at that time one was hyper-sensitive to any kind of implied slight or note of detached superiority. I had felt a tiny prick of dismay on reading Christopher's letter; when Wystan appeared, however, the dismay was more like a jab with a blunt hypodermic needle. He had been sent over by

the Strategic Bombing Survey to study the effects of bombing
on the civilian population in Germany. A slight shudder went
through me, as one who had also been bombed, at the coolly
clinical implication of this mission; but unjustly, because I
knew that in reality Wystan had longed for an excuse to get
back to the country which had meant so much to him before
the war. He arrived at my door one Sunday morning, complete with new American officer's uniform and new American
accent. A little overpowered by this, I was at a loss how to get
the conversation going; but it did not matter, for without
much beating about the bush, he launched into a long lecture,
quoting detailed statistics of pig-iron production and the
industrial man-power graph, on the world power position after
the war. Great Britain, her Dominions and Empire had
apparently been liquidated, while the two giants, the U.S.A.
and the U.S.S.R., towered over the world. Britain, in fact,
was lucky to have survived the war at all. There was no word
from Uncle Sam Auden about what we had endured, the
various skills, the faith, the unremitting industrial and military
effort without which the fortress of Western civilization could
never have been held; there was not even a personal word of
sympathy to a former friend about the discomforts of flying
bombs and flying glass and trying to work while a whole building shook and swayed about one under the impact of high
explosive. On the contrary, the second part of the lecture
consisted of an exposé of the superiority of American culture,
and a sharp calling to order of myself when, as a kind of desperate gesture of defence, I made some mild criticisms of recent
American fiction.

Of course I was wrong to be so furious. Wystan's prognosis
of the post-war situation was more than partly true; and I had
forgotten how impersonal he was by nature, and how habitual
it was with him to deal with a situation, when he felt uncertain
or shy, by immediate attack. Stephen Spender told me later
that he had had a violent row with him because of a similar
lecture, but had made it up almost at once and found Wystan
sympathetic and human as soon as the air was cleared: once
the idea that we were going to be morally superior with him
was out of the way. Indeed, I was disarmed myself when he

told me at parting, with a pleasure that found an immediate response in me, that the American Navy had ordered 1,100 copies of his collected poems.

3

THE long vigil of that Winter of torment and durance came to an end at last: the miracle month of April arrived, when one after the other the walls of Hitler's empire were breached, and the allied troops poured in to their victorious meeting among the ruins.

By a curious coincidence, I was at the Austrian Youth Centre in Westbourne Terrace, attending a memorial performance of Yura Soyfer's *Vineta*, on the very day when the Russians were overcoming the last resistance of the S.S. troops in Vienna. I had promised to make a speech; it was strange to be in the old ' Kleinkunstbühne ' atmosphere again, talking of my dead friend who had loved that world so much, just as the evil regime that had swept it away was in its turn disappearing into the past for ever; strange to be reminded in Yura's haunting poetic symbols of the Vienna I had known so well, where the despair was always mixed with dreams of better times, the tears with the wit, at a moment when my thoughts were daring at last to entertain the hope of seeing it again, even finding my lost friends still alive.

A few evenings later I attended a recital of Edith Sitwell's poems at the Polytechnic. Edith herself spoke very quietly and very movingly, with a face twisted with pain in the war poems; a singer then took over, in a group of poems set by William Walton; and the programme concluded with a choral work by Michael Tippett, the composer himself conducting. During the choral singing, I began strangely to feel that history itself had become like music: almost in a trance I perceived the freeing of the concentration camps that was taking place in Germany as against all expectation fitting and just and even sublime with the sublimity of great music; the revelation of degradation and bestiality not triumph of horror and darkness, but resolved at last, incredibly, in a final movement, an act of deliverance that repaid and justified all the struggle and suffering we had been through.

The trance-like feeling continued as the fantastic drama was being played to its close across the Channel, while the daffodils came out in the parks, where people walked freed at last from the fear of sudden death from the skies. The reality of the last days of Hitlerism seemed to eclipse the wildest imaginings of the fabulists and doom-warning dreamers among the poets and story-tellers. Only Shakespeare seemed to match the times: Birnam Wood was marching to Dunsinane while Hitler-Macbeth was dying in the flames of his bunker, and the theme that runs all through the last plays—of what seemed lost forever being found, of the rejected in the fulness of time restored and wickedness foiled by some mysteriously working power of justice and faith—was being daily illustrated. I tried to work these themes into a poem I began to write, using an image from one or other of the plays in the last line of each of the four stanzas, and picturing the swastika as the great axle of some primeval car that had tried to drag the world back to barbarism:

> Reunion and reprieve: the words like suns
> Blaze on the day these garland bells acclaim,
> And the great axle of doom that seemed to run
> Backwards forever to the unlucky dead
> Palpable over them as tank or gun,
> Dissolves in mist beneath those words instead—
> See: the veiled statue wakes, resumes her breathing name.
>
> The soldier drops his weapons at the door
> And from his forehead wipes the brand of Cain,
> The toasts are raised, the dancing shakes the floor,
> And that tall stranger with the eyes of ice—
> Look round, and laugh, for he is there no more
> To drain the tankard with the skull device—
> For the green springing host has come to Dunsinane.

The announcement of the victory over Nazi Germany had been anticipated for so many days before it actually took place that the celebrations seemed to go off at half-cock, and there was none of that sudden wild relief from unendurable tension that I remembered from my boyhood in 1918. It so happened that Stephen Spender was with me in my Carrington House flat when Churchill's voice came over the radio at three o'clock in the afternoon of Tuesday the eighth of May; and the coincidence struck me only when he left that he had also been with me, in my now charred and shattered Mecklenburgh Square flat, when the announcement was made of the German attack on Poland, six years before.

My chief recollection of V.E. day is of queueing for a bus to Paddington that never came, and finally having to walk right across Hyde Park with a heavy suitcase in one hand and a briefcase in the other, pouring with sweat. The crowds were more dazed than excited, and they seemed to gather and move in a slow groundswell, no wild battery of waves, good-tempered, a little bewildered and awkward about celebrating, like cripples taking their first steps after a miracle healing, not fully grasping yet the implication of the new life ahead of them. Now the noise of the last all-clear on the sirens seemed to prolong itself in the mind's ear until it was beyond the range of hearing forever: for surely far-away Japan could not in her most audacious dreams envisage sending a bomber fleet across all the continents and oceans we and our allies controlled at last and absolutely: Japan, who had still to be conquered, whose final annihilation no one could doubt but at what cost no one could reckon. This thought, I believe, was at the back of the minds of the crowds happily but not quite full-heartedly celebrating all over London—all over Britain—that Spring evening.

Like so many millions of other people, I had not been able to conceive any other fitting end to it all, than that the two great Anglo-Saxon leaders, who had conducted us to victory with such skill and staunchness, should write the peace that would inaugurate the new age their inspiration promised us. President Roosevelt's death came as the first shock. A news reel I saw of him, taken only shortly before, showed a face quite horribly drawn, pouched, exhausted, a man condemned to death by the gigantic burden of running a world war: the first victim, among many that were still to come, of political leadership in our distraught mid-century world. Then came our own General Election, lasting three weeks, from July 5th to July 26th, with the Potsdam Conference opening in the middle, so that no one knew whether Churchill and Eden, who went as our representatives to the opening, would still be there to speak for us at the end. In spite of a certain fantasy quality about the ' Caretaker Government ' after the Labour leaders left the war coalition, I must confess that I thought it might well be a near thing, but that even so Churchill would win. I had voted Labour before the war, but Churchill had swept the ' appeasers' away. Churchill had planned a series of measures for after the war, in harmony with the Labour members of his Government, that seemed the surest guarantee that social injustice would be abolished. Churchill's voice—which contained all his courage, his imperturbability, his capacity for inspiring others with his own sense of historic adventure, his wit and his generous compassion—had carried us through the darkest hours, turning panic as if by magic alchemy into hope and vision. Surely Churchill, hero of all the world, whom even the people of Berlin had clapped when he strode through their bomb-pitted streets, could not fail to be chosen by his own country? I should have been warned by such signs as the headlines that greeted the opening of the Potsdam Conference: ' The only news of Big Three is about their wines, melons, lawn-mowers . . .' What insolence towards the dead-beat hungry peoples of the world! Perhaps I should have caught such hints of a growing isolation in power of the leaders from the led, and taken more seriously the mistakes in electoral strategy that Churchill was making. Perhaps I should have understood more clearly from all the letters I had received from men in the forces, that to them the revolution to reverse the miseries of the 'thirties appeared postponed rather than already half-completed. Perhaps I should have remembered how, as if by a deep inherited instinct, the English ever since Cromwell's Protectorate have distrusted any man who seemed to them to have grown over-powerful. Perhaps, too, I should have known that the scurrilities and misrepresentations that had appeared in certain organs of the left, where the Russians were

still treated as political as well as military heroes, whose leader-
writers grovelled before Tito and reviled the luckless Mihailo-
vitch and had even been unable to grasp what was at stake in
the Greek civil war, were too clever not to have their influence
among those who still saw the pieces on the chess-board as
they had been twenty years before. Perhaps. . . . But I
remember a consternation growing, as a group of us sat round
the wireless in my Carrington House flat listening to the news
of the landslide that July afternoon, almost as great as the consternation on that November evening fourteen years before,
when the news of the other landslide came in. It was a
consternation that spread across the world, and which, I
believe, in America, to judge from my own experience of
bewildered questioning, has never abated.

Even though we knew we had entered the age of hideous,
death-dealing marvels, no one outside the innermost war-
waging conclaves, during those three months between May and
August, imagined that the end of the war would come so
suddenly and in the way it did. This is what I recorded in
my Journal at the time. . . .
' The explosion of the atom bomb over Japan has made me
feel physically sick for two or three days. I wonder how many
people reflect that it may cast doubt, not merely on the way the
world is going to be run now, but also on the whole course of
human *aspiration* for the last two hundred and fifty years.
That is the thought that won't leave me alone.
' The atom bomb announces beyond argument that the
supreme need of today, with priority above all other needs,
is that each living person should become aware of the reality
of every other living person in the world. Unless the imagination, the human imagination is at work, and can create a close
moral connection between the act and its result—in war, in
commerce, in government—modern Satanisms will surely
continue to flourish.
' On the first V.J. day, the Wednesday, I suddenly decided,
in my bath, that I would like to have some special memory of it.
So I raced through my shaving, and hurried in the light drizzle
across the Park to the Palace, where a sizeable crowd was

collected to see the State procession set off to open Parliament. The Guardsmen lining the route seemed to be in the same happy, informal mood as the crowd: then the sudden clap and rattle as arms were presented all down the Mall, the clatter of the black chargers of the Life Guards as they pranced out of the Palace courtyard heightened the tension. They were followed by the open barouche in which were seated the King, looking rather nervous and leaning forward in his Admiral's uniform, with the powder-blue Queen waving and smiling beside him— a cheer from the crowd—more Life Guards—more barouches filled with officials—no cheers, but " 'oo are these? " from my side—and it was all over (though long after they had passed a fussy explaining mother nearby kept on warning her schoolboy son that it might be difficult to see, he'd better keep a sharp look out, and so on, and so on). As I walked back, I passed a shabby little old woman stumbling along by herself, a beatific smile on her face, and muttering " lovely dresses . . . lovely dresses . . .".

' The evening was perfectly clear, warm and still: it was impossible to resist going out to see how London was celebrating, to join in somehow, somewhere. We went down from Carrington House by Whitehorse Street, and as we emerged into Piccadilly, we were confronted by an extraordinary sight: the brilliantly lit street—that was strange enough in itself—was packed with people as far as the eye could see, in both directions, with no wheeled traffic to be discovered anywhere, except one slowly moving car on to which people kept climbing and crowding. As we walked towards the Circus, the mass turned out not to be so impassable as it seemed, because everyone was quietly, happily, aimlessly on the move. One longed for bands and music everywhere; but it was, after all, a totally unrehearsed occasion, and people found their own haphazard way of giving vent to their feelings, as if scarcely able to believe that the long, long horror was over at last, bemused in their joy, with exhaustion suddenly coming over them. There were sailors giving girls endless, passionate kisses in the middle of the street; here and there people threw fire crackers; climbed lamp-posts; occasionally burst out singing; exclaimed to one another delightedly at the display of the searchlights; and most extraordinary of all, suddenly made dancing rings, performing strange, impromptu, atavistic steps, as they might have when the news of Waterloo, or of the Armada's defeat came through; then wandered on again.   We made our way past the Athenaeum, where torches were flaming over the portico and all around the Clubs were blazing with lights and hung with flags, down into the Mall, where we were confronted by the same perspective of massed crowds, thickening up to the Victoria Memorial: at the end the great illuminated façade of the Palace, with an enormous, raw half-moon hanging over it. As we came nearer, the noise of singing increased; the crowds were finally jammed beyond movement, and on the Memorial itself people were clustered as thickly as swarming bees.   Every few minutes the singing would pause, and the chant would go up: " *We* want the *King* . . . *We* want the *King* . . .". Until at last the french windows on the far, red-draped, fairytale balcony were opened, and the King and Queen, diminutive but glittering figures—the Queen's diamonds flashed into the night under the arc-lights—came out to wave and be greeted by cheer after cheer, waving of hands, and the singing of " For he's a jolly good fellow ".

' Then many dispersed—though many others, insatiable, waited for a later reappearance—and the squashed but happy crowd poured through the gates into Green Park, where the sudden soaring of fireworks lit up the innumerable couples on the grass and under the trees.'

I thought that night, on returning home, of the dark moments, the sinkings of heart that had inevitably occurred during the past six years, when vital fires were low and doubt was strong and no such happy ending as we were at last celebrating seemed possible. As our side, after 1942, had gradually gained the advantage, the intimations these moments brought were not so much of defeat and catastrophic humiliation—Britain after the gigantic proscription and the gas chambers reduced to the status of a helot colony of the world-dominating Third Reich—as of an endless stalemate, war continuing for all our lives with only the briefest respite leading to ever more feverish and exhausted efforts on both sides to

U

reach an absolute conclusion. Henry Moore's drawings of the sleepers in the underground stations were perhaps a prophetic vision of a condition that would become perpetual . . . while we sank into a darkness without hope or joy, only machines would grow more ingenious and more devilishly powerful. Perhaps the destiny of mankind was not to listen to the angels, but to go on perfecting machines, giving birth to machines in our own death, until machines were indistinguishable from life—in everything except mercy, pity, and love. . . .

It would be as well, I thought, even while the bells were ringing, not to forget that one had had these waking nightmares.

VII
TAKEN AT THE FLOOD

BEFORE V.J. day arrived, I had begun to plan a visit to Paris, whither Cyril Connolly, Raymond Mortimer, Eddie Sackville-West and other literary lights of the London war-time firmament had already managed to get themselves officially invited, not without slight twinges of envy on my part. At last, with the assistance of The Publishers' Association, The British Council and in particular Enid Macleod, who had put all her Scottish determination and intelligence into the task of re-establishing cultural links between France and Britain, and with the miracle-working approval from Duff Cooper and Diana, already established in the British Embassy, I managed to convince the authorities that my mission was urgent and found myself in possession of the necessary permits, orders and allowances. I left in the first week of September: a long, slow journey, the discomforts and delays of which, including hours of waiting for the right tide to float us into the still rather makeshift port facilities on the French side, were dissolved in a mounting excitement as the train jolted through the familiar landmarks which announced the approach of Paris. For a moment it seemed almost incredible that Paris had survived as mistress of itself and not as the subjugated second city of a triumphant Nazi empire, that one would see it almost untouched by bombs, and that one had actually survived oneself to be on this journey, after six years that were more like sixty.

Among many vivid memories of that first post-war visit, many wonderful occasions of reunion with friends, many moving sights, discussions and discoveries, one moment of deep emotion stands out. We arrived late in the evening, and tired, but before going to bed I went for a walk by myself down past the Madeleine to see the Place de la Concorde and the Champs Elysées again: I could not wait till the morning for that. There were still very few street lamps burning, but enough for me suddenly to notice that many of the chestnut-trees were already shedding their leaves, while new, Spring-green buds were appearing in their place. I had completely forgotten this peculiarity of the chestnut-trees of the Champs Elysées: and as when, after many years of separation, one meets a person one has loved very much and one catches one's breath on seeing again some intimate individual mark or trait, a dimple or a pucker of the eyes or a one-sided smile, that had slipped out of the picture one had tried to keep in one's mind, so I caught my breath on noticing this second burgeoning along the blackened branches, and tears started to my eyes with all the memories that came tumbling back.

At that time, Paris was still a city of austerity, suffering and want. The weather was mild, but the Parisians already knew that they would have little or no heating for the Winter, and that thousands of old and sick people, especially those who relied on savings and pensions in depreciated currency and were far too poor to buy on the flourishing black market, would die from cold and hunger and neglect. To bring to one's friends, or one's friends' friends, a pound of coffee, a bar of chocolate or a cake of soap, was acutely embarrassing, so overwhelming was the gratitude and relief. Very few restaurants or cafés were open, and those that were only provided the most meagre nourishment against the little ration-stamps with which one was provided. The allied occupation authorities had requisitioned a number of the best and most famous places, the British in particular having brought off quite a coup by collaring Maxim's and turning it into the British Empire Club. The bill of fare was not especially varied there but the cooking of course was first-class, and one felt slightly guilty, avoiding the eyes of passing Parisians as one slipped in for luncheon or dinner. Not that one came across any bitterness or envy; on the contrary I was deeply impressed by the warmth of the welcome one received from nearly all the French people one met, the fervour with which they spoke of our war-effort, our aid to the underground resistance in the cities and in the maquis, and the almost sacred veneration in which the B.B.C. was held. Duff Cooper and Diana were, I believe, the most popular figures in Paris at the time: applause greeted them whenever they left the Embassy. The French made it quite clear that they believed we were the only nation among the allies really to understand them: already a slight anti-American tone was discernible, which was unfair considering how much the Americans with their unlimited resources had done and were all the time doing for them; it arose perhaps inevitably from a thousand small occasions when some Americans unconsciously failed (in French eyes) to conceal the fact that they were not Europeans, that they considered themselves the new world-bosses, and that Paris had been created for the sole purpose of unlimited sexual gratification.

Getting about the city and making contact with all the old and new figures in the literary and publishing world was by no means easy; but I was lucky in having the constant help of the friendly officials of The British Council, and of Diana Cooper and her pretty young secretary, Penelope Lloyd-Thomas. A surprisingly large number of new literary magazines had appeared, and even more were being planned (most of which failed to appear): many of these magazines were eager to acquire the translation rights in various stories and essays which had been printed in *New Writing*, and I was kept busy negotiating with the editors and publishers who were also after the rights in Christopher Isherwood's, Bill Sansom's, Henry Green's and other Hogarth books. I found the literary situation in Paris even more confused than it had appeared the other side of the Channel: on the spot the opposing groups seemed more embittered, the accusations and counter-accusations more violent, and I was shocked by the power the extreme left wing appeared to wield in deciding whether an author should be allowed to publish (except in a hole-and-corner way) or not. It was sad also to see so much effort, money and space being lavished for largely political reasons on the floods of rhetorical ' Resistance ' poetry that filled the magazines. André Gide, however, François Mauriac and Paul Valéry held aloof from the more sordid public squabbles and still had their honour and their incense. The hour of the badly compromised Montherlant's return had not yet arrived, but Jean Cocteau, who had been in Paris during the Nazi occupation and friendly with the intellectuals among the German authorities (as Ernst Jünger's notebooks clearly demonstrate), had managed by another astonishing display of his natural conjuring powers to present himself as a poet of the Liberation. I even heard a story (no doubt apocryphal) that, as the last German lorries and armoured cars roared away and the population poured out on to the approaches from the west to greet the arrival of the liberating army, the first jeep that emerged out of the clouds of dust was found to contain the figure of—none other than Cocteau, in allied uniform, happily acknowledging the cheers of his fellow Parisians.

The scene, however, had changed radically in many ways. Among the now immensely influential Communists, Aragon, as I have already described, was bidding to be a kind of literary dictator, but Paul Eluard, former surrealist and a man of the most seductive charm and subtle artistic gifts, was already recognized as the Party's outstanding exhibit in poetry. Jean Paul Sartre, who before the war, at the time when I had published his short stories in *New Writing*, had been admired by only a comparatively small highbrow circle, had become the leader of the younger generation, high priest of the new cult of atheistic existentialism; his lectures and writings, one was immediately told, were driving hundreds of young people to despair and suicide, and his new novels and plays, *Les Mouches* and *Huis Clos*, were all the rage. Among those who were ranged with him as his disciples, one new name was, I found, repeated on all sides as a close competitor in influence: Albert Camus, a young writer-philosopher from North Africa, with two plays, *Le Malentendu* and *Caligula*—for which Harold Acton had already the year before whetted my appetite, describing them as ' of immense intensity and stark beauty '—and a first novel, *L'Etranger*, already published.

I made a special pilgrimage to see André Gide, whom I found writing in his huge library in the rue Vaneau. He greeted me with great warmth and enquired very keenly about our mutual friends in the literary world, about what people were reading in England, who the new authors were, and also about *New Writing*. As we were talking, the door-bell rang and a very small young man with a drawing block under his arm was ushered in. In a low, reverential voice, he reminded Gide that he had an appointment to make a drawing of him. The Master thereupon settled himself at a table by the window in a suitable pose, with a book in front of him, and the young man started feverishly to draw. While this was going on, Gide did not for a moment stop talking to me, discussing the Strachey family and asking about Virginia Woolf's death. Finally the drawing was done, and was presented to Gide for his approval. ' Pas mal! Pas mal du tout! ' he exclaimed, interrupting his conversation with me for a second. ' *Merci*, cher maître,' murmured the little fellow, almost prostrating himself to the ground; and then, as Gide turned back to me, bowed himself slowly out. Before I left, other young worshippers had already arrived.

André Chamson, the meeting with whom in the last days before the war broke out had remained so vividly in my mind, was not in Paris, but André Malraux had returned from the Eastern front at the end of the fighting to become General de Gaulle's ' chef de Cabinet '. I managed at last to arrange an interview, and went to see him at the Ministry of War the day before I left. I was shown into a large room with a thick pile carpet and a huge Empire desk: a young secretary who was busying himself with papers in a corner, offered me a chair and whispered: ' Le Colonel viendra tout de suite.' Ten minutes later Malraux came in, welcomed me with great cordiality, and dismissed the secretary. As soon as he had gone, Malraux hurried to the door in conspiratorial fashion, made certain that it was properly closed, and then turned eagerly to me and demanded at once to know what had happened to his English friends of the time of the Spanish Civil War. Had they changed their views about the Communists? I tried to describe the evolution of most of my contemporaries, who had been agitating anti-fascists a decade earlier, from direct political engagement to a more detached and reserved attitude, and an increasing preoccupation in their work with the deeper and more permanent problems of the human situation. Malraux kept on nodding vigorously as I spoke, and murmuring how he, too, with his closest friends were now completely disillusioned, at least with extreme left-wing ideology and agitation. He then suddenly asked me whether I thought there had been *progress* in Britain. Rather surprised, I replied, after a moment's hesitation, that in literature, art and music, certainly exciting new developments had taken place, but that, in a more general sense, perhaps the recovery of a sense of national community— the non-party planning of a Welfare State—could indeed be described as progress. He nodded again, and said: ' En France aussi on a fait beaucoup de progrès.' Anxiously, I enquired in what specific direction. ' Dans la reproduction en couleurs! ' he hissed triumphantly, and with his characteristic unsmiling nervous enthusiasm immediately launched into a long description of a plan for having the hundred greatest masterpieces in French painting reproduced in colours, life-size, and chucking everything out of the provincial museums of France to make way for them; so that, whether one went to Lille or Lyons, Toulouse or Bayonne, one would still see the same hundred masterpieces. . . . Malraux was out of office before this ambitious and disturbing scheme could be realized.

The previous Winter Philip Toynbee, returning from an official assignment in France, had written for *Horizon* an article about the literary situation there, giving the most illuminating information but at the same time sweepingly declaring that the literary production of France during the years of occupation had been ' incomparable and undeniably superior ' to that of Britain. I had joined issue with this attitude in a long letter to *Horizon*, saying that though I had not (any more than Philip) been able to read more than a fraction of the outstanding books published in France during those years, I thought that Britain's record, for which I gave chapter and verse, was sufficiently remarkable to make his proposition extremely doubtful— except perhaps in playwriting. My visit to Paris did not make me want to revise this view. France's intellectual vitality was as remarkable as ever, but it seemed to me to a large extent to be turning in a void. Whether it was the result of the shock of defeat and the humiliation of Nazi occupation, or of some deeper reason that went further back, the dominant spirit was, I thought, anti-humanistic, even nihilistic. It was the very reverse of what I had hoped to find, remembering Antoine de St. Exupéry's noble *Letter to a Hostage*, which I had published in *New Writing and Daylight*, with its cry: ' Human respect! Human respect! There's the touchstone! . . . If human respect is established in men's hearts, men will certainly end by establishing in return the social, political or economic system that will sanctify this respect.'

Human respect: was it not precisely this quality that emerged so strongly from what had been written in England during the war? Some weeks before the German surrender, I went down to Salcombe on the Devon coast for a few days' rest. I had been there for a holiday earlier in the war, but since my first visit the little harbour in the estuary had been turned into an American naval base, and in spite of the still continuing blackout in London, repairs on the ships went on all night under blazing arc-lamps. The little homely pubs were now filled with flushed and raucous young American sailors: to go in for a drink in the evening seemed at first like visiting the orgiastic celebrations of some strange barbaric tribe in Africa. To the limey eye they appeared exactly alike in their manner, their reactions, their thoughts; but as one got to know them one found that their ancestry was as varied as the map of Europe. The original suspicion melted quickly down into an immense friendliness, and on the third or fourth night an attempt was even made to persuade me to sample and praise a ' wunnerful ' drink they had concocted, which turned out to be spirits of turpentine and soda-water. In the midst of this weird transformation scene portending the future, I was jerked back into the past by meeting an old waiter in the hotel, who told me, his voice trembling with emotion, that as a young man he had been steward in a sports club of which my father had been a leading light, and produced ancient letters to corroborate his story. My thoughts churned up by these contrary encounters, I took a long walk in the Spring sunlight out along the cliffs, up the slopes of which armies of bluebells and primroses had marched, thinning out only where great broken ribs of grey quartz rock broke through the soil: seagulls perched and strutted on them, every few minutes planing off to dive and swoop and circle with piercing squawks over the blue-green clear-as-jewels ocean sparkling and foaming in a slow rhythm round the rocks far below. The sharp sea-breeze buffeted the meadow-brown butterflies in the nodding bluebell stems about my feet, and gathered as if to lift me from the cliff-top to an element of exultation and prophecy between past and future. I was suddenly filled with a kind of sublime joy in the knowledge that victory was approaching, that all our resolution and our tears had come to harvest, in the intuition that we ourselves had been changed in the process. Now at last in the new world that was taking shape behind the guns, we had, tested in a fire so different from, so much fiercer than anything we had envisaged, purged and strengthened ourselves to seize, if we would, a spiritual leadership out of the chaos. Surely now all the lack we had felt in our civilization before the war was being filled, the split in our culture healed; we had waged the war endeavouring not to loose our hold on the ideals of justice and humanity we had invoked against the Axis power; surely all the best that had been written in poetry and story, all that had been expressed in a thousand ways in articles and letters and speeches by those who were to inherit the peace, the spirit that more and more had come to inform all the pictorial and musical arts, pointed to a new awakening of the moral imagination, a new dedication in our islands to human respect. . . . Such was the inspiration that came to me on my cliff-top walk among the bluebells, promising so much in defiance of the chagrins of history; while the hammering and welding on the warships went on without pause in the estuary below.

In the last months of the war, I had thought a great deal about my future as a publisher and editor. I had gradually become aware that I had started something that looked like growing too big for me unless I did some drastic reorganizing.

Both *New Writing and Daylight* and *Penguin New Writing* were flourishing, the latter in particular bringing in an ever-expanding mail from writers and artists, from young people in the Forces who had been fired by it to enthusiasm for books and paintings and the theatre, or had begun to write and paint themselves. It kept up a circulation—it seemed incredible at the time—of 80,000, and sometimes, when Penguin Books could find the extra paper, of 100,000. The copies were gobbled up the moment they reached the bookshops, and so many addicts began to complain to us that they couldn't get copies, that with No. 21, in the Summer of 1944, we introduced a subscription scheme. At the same time, we made a second and this time effective promise to appear quarterly: since our first promise, with No. 13, we had not in fact produced more than three numbers a year, but by the middle of 1944 the labour position in the printing works had begun to improve. Allen Lane's enthusiasm remained keen, and at the end of the war we began to plan a bigger development: enlarging the format, improving the lay-out, introducing colour plates as well as photogravure reproductions, and a new three-colour pictorial cover design of enchanting beauty by John Minton. The first number (in fact No. 27) in this new series appeared in the Spring of 1946. By then we had also, in gradual stages, increased the number of pages again, using the additional space mainly for more critical articles—on all the arts—and more poetry. So many stories had been coming in that were fiction and yet had a background of war experience, that I decided to keep them separate from the first-person reportage: ' Report on Today ' was therefore abolished and the reportage sketches put at the end under the new name of ' The Living Moment '. I have always believed that the end of a magazine should be as strong, in a different way, as the beginning, and this change was in no sense intended as a down-grading of the reportage, or as a turning of the section into a nursery for unknown first-triers. In fact, on looking back at No. 26, I see that the three contributions to ' The Living Moment ' were by Keith Vaughan (*V. E. Day*), Winston Churchill's nephew, Giles Romilly (*Three Sketches from a Prison Camp*) and a young actor who had joined the R.N.V.R. in 1941—Alec Guinness (*Money for Jam*). The newly designed *Penguin New Writing* cost one shilling, but I doubt if such value for a bob had ever been offered before in a serious magazine of all the arts.

New Writing and Daylight also had its enthusiastic following, and sold out very quickly, sometimes going into a second impression: but of course on a much smaller scale. By 1945 our paper ration only allowed us to produce one volume a year. As at the beginning, there was considerable common ground between it and the *Penguin*, but I continued to use it for critical symposia of a more ' international ' or specialized sort than I would have thought suitable for the *Penguin*; for instance, in

the Autumn 1944 number, a section of appreciations of Demetrios after his death by Edith Sitwell, Canellopoulos, William
Plomer and myself, and another on the Polish, Chinese and
Nazi German theatre.   Often, however, if an article that had
seemed to me rather esoteric was very well received by non-
specialists I would reprint it later on in the *Penguin*.   The press
notices it received continued on the whole to be quite extraordinarily full of praise, which did not prevent me feeling
a sinking of the heart every time I opened the *Observer*, or the
Sunday Times, or the *New Statesman* just after it had come
out.

By this time the idea of miscellanies, or occasional magazines
in hard covers, had caught on in quite a big way.   *New
Writing* had started the movement before the war, but the reason for the multiplication of its imitators in the early 'forties
was as much that they provided a way round the regulations of
the Paper Control, which forbade the launching of new regular
periodicals, as that *New Writing and Daylight* had shown how
successful they could be.   There was *New Road*, in which Alex
Comfort had made himself the leading spirit;   more like a real
review and less like a miscellany than most of those that came
later, because it had a stronger intellectual flavour of its own,
standing, largely, for a kind of esoteric and anarchic individual-
ism, against realism and against what we would now call social
engagement.   There was also *Selected Writing*, run by Reginald
Moore, who in addition collaborated with Edward Lane in
The Windmill;   Henry Treece's *Transformation*;   and a late-
comer, *Orion*, the closest to *New Writing* in spirit, with a strong
editorial team of Cecil Day Lewis, Edwin Muir, Denys Kilham
Roberts and my sister Rosamond.   If only all of them had
succeeded in staying the course and turning themselves into
monthlies or quarterlies (as I am sure they intended) when the
Paper Control packed up, the literary scene in the early 'fifties
might not have looked so bleak.

I certainly did not want to give my editorial work up when it
appeared to be beginning to yield so promising a harvest; but
the combination of that work and running The Hogarth Press,
as all the opportunities of peace-time publishing began to open
up again, was, I could see, going to become a rather formidable

burden, leaving me very little time indeed for my own writing. If I were to go on as both editor and publisher—two aspects of the same purpose—I realized that it would be essential to run The Hogarth Press in a different way: to expand in order to carry a proper staff, to have the opportunity to train managers who could take as much as possible of the complex and time-wasting detail off my hands. I feared that Leonard Woolf might want to go back to what I considered the bad habits of the old days: that system of running things on a shoestring that had persisted because of the way the Hogarth had grown up from a hobby and a small personal venture. Never again, I vowed to myself, those damp and grimy basements of Blooms-bury houses, the homespun method of accounting and sales-manship, which had (I admit) charmed me so much in my early days when the business of publishing was illumined with almost as sacred a radiance in my eyes as the actual persons of Leonard and Virginia Woolf. The war had turned The Hogarth Press into a moderately valuable property, and it would, I thought, certainly be possible to find the capital for expansion. Before the war I had wanted to use it to complete the work of presenting the most interesting of the authors who came to *New Writing*, and to some extent I had succeeded. Quite obviously, with the large body of young authors *New Writing* had accumulated round it during the war years, the opportunities now were very much greater. In my more confident and energetic moments, it seemed to me not only folly from my own point of view to neglect these opportunities, but also a failure in responsibility towards the poets, story writers and critics I had brought forward. And I was already catching glimpses of new European and American authors who could be added to a list that aimed at discovering and gathering together the most significant talents, the most vigorous creative impulses of the time.

In addition, a more ambitious dream had begun to haunt me from time to time. I had become deeply interested in the other arts, in particular in painting, the theatre and the dance. I had come to know intimately many of the leading younger spirits in the revival of English ballet and the development of theatrical art. As I have already described, I began to see almost limitless possibilities in the new flowering of the romantic, visionary tradition of English painting: in their enforced isolation from the School of Paris, it seemed to me that the younger English painters were gaining in self-confidence and becoming more truly themselves. I would risk saying that nine out of ten English artists are lost if they attempt to transform themselves into the kind of visual explorers of daring intellectual concept and theory for which the School of Paris has rightly been celebrated in modern times: and the rare exceptions, who reject that ascendancy of the poetic which is so natural to us in all the arts, only prove the rule. I had reproduced, in *Penguin New Writing* photogravure supplements, the wartime work of nearly all of them, and several had become my personal friends, including Keith Vaughan, Len Rosoman, Leslie Hurry, Michael Ayrton, John Craxton and John Minton. The last-named had been brought along to my flat one evening by Keith Vaughan, where he sat on the floor with a drink in his hand, laughing a great deal and saying very little. I remember being struck at once by his gaiety and warmth, and the way these two characteristics gave a face that was not exactly good-looking, in fact had an element of the grotesque in its narrow axe-like boniness under the untidy mop of black hair—a face seen in an elongating fun-fair mirror—an aspect of compelling charm, almost of beauty. We discussed what had been happening to the arts in wartime that night, with hope and enthusiasm. The way we had tried to bring them together in *Penguin New Writing*, had already proved itself a success: could not a publishing house make itself a much more important centre?

So my thoughts had run, restlessly turning over the problems of the coming years. I was not absolutely certain I would decide to have a shot at expansion, still seeing the advantages of quietly exploiting what we already had, still hearing the plaintive call of all the poems and books I wanted to write; but turning more and more towards it. There was, however, another element in the problem. In the first year or two after Virginia's death, as I have already related, Leonard was content to leave most of the running of the Hogarth to me, and a greater harmony had been established between us than ever before. This halcyon period did not, unfortunately, last. I do not know why, but by 1944 our disagreements were beginning to grow more frequent and more difficult to resolve. In particular, Leonard appeared to me to be setting his face against allowing me to publish the new authors in whom I had invested so much capital of encouragement, appreciation and faith; and Virginia was no longer there to moderate between us. I had to remind myself all the time that I might have felt just the same suspicion and anxiety if I had been in Leonard's shoes; but it was frustrating at that particular moment when I felt convinced the tide was running so strongly with me.

Meanwhile I took one decisive step. I was tired of flat life, and rents were already beginning to shoot up. I remembered what Leonard had always said: to live in a house is really no more expensive than to live in a flat, and infinitely preferable. . . . I had accumulated an enormous mass of books and papers during the war, and had laid the foundation of an interesting collection of modern pictures. Most of my pre-war library was still down at Fieldhead. I wanted to have a place where all these possessions could be housed; and I wanted it to be large enough for me to entertain there on a fairly generous scale. I had grown more and more to believe that bringing authors together in social contact was an essential part of a good literary impresario's job; besides, it was fun. Vienna had grown too far away, under the long separation and the emotional pressures of the war, for me ever to make my home there again. In spite of the intimate nostalgic colouring my memories had acquired, I was quite clear about that; and equally clear that in London, not in Paris, Rome or New York, I had the best chance of combining, as I had always hoped I could, my spiritual and physical homes. I therefore discussed my plan of looking for a house with Ernst Freud, son of the great Doctor and father of Lucian. He was not only an extremely able architect, but a man full of ideas and enterprise. We were still in the early months of 1945, and I hesitated a little to commit myself while the chance of bombardment by various forms of V-weapons still existed. He brushed my doubts aside, with eager and persuasive arguments: the war

x

was as good as over, the risks were negligible, I must grab one of the many excellent properties still going cheap before everyone else joined the hunt. So off we went, whenever we could find an hour or two, exploring as many of the likely houses as possible; Ernst Freud sniffing for dry rot, pulling at peeling wallpaper, shifting piles of rubble-litter with his foot, calculating with lightning speed the cost of mending a roof damaged by incendiaries or a stairway shaken by explosions next door, remodelling interiors to my liking with a conjuror's dazzling patter—and dismissing the whole vision at once with a slightly diabolical laugh, when he saw me reluctant.

Eventually we decided on a house at the western end of Egerton Crescent, which was in a comparatively undamaged state, and with its fine interior proportions promised both room for all I wanted to bring there, and a welcoming, dignified setting for hospitality, in parties large and small. Besides, it had trees on all sides—an advantage that counted for much with me—including a tree of heaven, an acacia, and a pretty little laburnum leaning over the front door-steps. I was doubtful whether we could get a generous enough building licence to make it habitable in the way I wanted, but Ernst produced at once the most ingenious plans for making do with what was already there. The result was that the estimate was low, and was passed fairly soon; and work had already begun before I left for France. ' Where are the builders? ' was the despairing cry often raised in the press at the time; but Osbert Sitwell, passing by one Sunday morning at the end of August, announced that he knew the answer: ' at work on John's new house '.

In the late Summer, I finally decided that Leonard and I had reached a point of no return: if our partnership remained the same, with each of us able to veto any project the other proposed, not only would The Hogarth Press come to a standstill, but my own career would finally be frustrated. As I saw Leonard only at intervals, and communication even then was rather restricted, it was difficult for me to know what was in his mind: it was possible, I thought, that he might be glad to be relieved altogether of publishing preoccupations; was, in fact, inviting me to buy him out. I realized, however, that even if this was so, he might hesitate at the last moment, baulking at the thought that the handling of Virginia's books would be removed from his control. So I took the only course that was open to me. Our partnership agreement had a blindfold hazard in it: if either of us announced to the other that he wanted to terminate it in its present form, the other could within three weeks buy him out; if within those three weeks he made no move, the original challenger could make the same offer. I therefore tried to find some way of exploring Leonard's mind before taking the final step. I suggested a modification of our partnership agreement, allowing me to be associated with some other small publishing venture through which I could present my new authors, thus leaving our exiguous paper ration entirely for the reprinting of Virginia's works and other important Hogarth books. Perhaps it would not have worked; in any case it found no favour at all with Leonard.

I think I made up my mind that we should have to part very soon after I came back from Paris—a visit that had encouraged my belief that there was a more exciting job to be done in introducing new European authors than I had anticipated. Knowing the risks and difficulties involved, however, I let the decision simmer in my mind for a month or two, while I dealt with our return from Letchworth to London and various staff problems which had arisen. I did not actually write my letter telling Leonard that I was now convinced to my sorrow that our partnership would never work, and formally giving notice to terminate, until the end of January. I hoped that he would agree to a quiet tête-à-tête discussion, because I wanted to propose a scheme I had at the back of my mind, by which, if he allowed me to buy him out, I would arrange for him to keep absolute control over Virginia's books, including the posthumous works not yet published. Remembering how often he had spoken to me of literary work he wanted to complete, and political work he wanted to develop, I had some hope this would appeal to him. Leonard, however, immediately wrote a letter telling me he proposed to buy me out; and my subsequent attempt to put forward my scheme in writing, was in vain. If this result was a shock to me, if I felt more than a little chagrin

when I thought of all the work I had put into the Press, and
the authors I had brought to it; if I never ceased to regret not
having anything more to do with Virginia's books, I realized
that I had known that the course I had taken involved this
hazard. I have often, however, wondered since whether the
whole crisis may not have been due to a simple misunderstanding; the letter Leonard wrote to me later about the
problem that faced him (he had received an offer from Chatto
and Windus) gave colour to this idea.

Once more the confusing choice was before me. Temptation? . . . Or opportunity? I could at this moment have
decided to say goodbye to publishing, and explore at last what I
could make of all the other chances that offered themselves to
me. One precious child, however, I was extremely loth to
give up: *New Writing and Daylight*. Perhaps I could make an
arrangement to keep this going in some way, while I thought
over what was best to do in a more general sense. My friends
in any case were eager to see me carry on as editor and publisher, pointing out (perfectly accurately) how much was in my
grasp and how many young people were looking to me; and
my mother, my sister Rosamond and my brother-in-law
Mounty, with a loyalty and readiness that moved me, promised
support. But in order even to keep *New Writing and Daylight*
going, I needed paper. And paper was still very strictly controlled.

One is found out by one's illusions in the end. Because *New
Writing* had had such a success; because all the official and
semi-official authorities, the Ministry of Information, the British
Council, and the rest, had shown such interest in it; because
already I had received invitations from liberated France, Greece
and Czechoslovakia to go and lecture on the young writers—on
literature in wartime England—on my problems as a literary
editor; because I had always dealt, on the official level, with
people who knew exactly what I was doing, I fondly imagined
that I would have little or no difficulty in getting the tiny
allocation of paper I needed to keep *New Writing and Daylight*
alive. I had failed to realize that the Paper Control, that
Olympian body in Reading on whose decisions the fate of
publishers, great and ancient, little and striving, rested, was not

concerned with literature except in the smallest and most indirect way: cardboard cartons, wrapping paper, lavatory paper, official paperasserie and newspapers were the chief subjects of its weighty deliberations; and long after them the problems of the great publishing houses, the huge lists of technical and educational handbooks; after all those demands had been satisfied there remained a tiny area in which *New Writing and Daylight* was a pinpoint invisible to the naked eye of the Reading bureaucrats, whose previous lives had been spent, not reading books but manufacturing paper from esparto grass, wood pulp, rags and salvage.

Full of optimism, I made an appointment with a Paper Control official for a Monday in February, 1946, and went down to stay with Rosamond at Aldworth for the week-end. She drove me into Reading herself, and waited down below while I went upstairs for my interview. It was all over in five minutes. . . . *New Writing?* Never heard of it. Are you still a partner in, er, let me see . . . The Hogarth Press, Mr. Lehmann? No, but. . . . Ah, in that case, I'm afraid we can't do anything for you. . . . Sorry, but we have our regulations, and it would be most irregular to allow any such exception. . . . No, Mr. Lehmann, I can't suggest anything you could do about it. Good day to you, Sir.

It was then that my natural pride and obstinacy came into play. The choice was quickly made. I was not going to knuckle down under this refusal. As we motored back to Aldworth, I told Rosamond, who was full of indignant sympathy, that I was determined to carry on as a publisher. I hadn't the slightest notion how I was going to set about it.

Looking back on this moment now, at a distance of nearly fifteen years, I am inclined to think that it presented me with a much more decisive choice than ever before, in a career in which I seem to have come, with abnormal frequency, to a fork in the road, without any signposts I could clearly decipher to guide me. It has always, of course, been the same fork, however different the country has looked on each occasion; but this time I had far greater knowledge of my own capacities and

of the medium I worked in than when I first joined Leonard
and Virginia Woolf at The Hogarth Press in 1930, or when I
went back to them, to save *New Writing*, in 1938. I had
reached maturity perhaps rather late, but on the verge of forty,
in spite of the strain of the war, I felt full of energy, ambition
and confidence as never before. The beckoning mirage of the
poetry, the novels, the plays I could still write if I devoted myself
to them, was still as vivid, indeed more vivid than it had been
before the war: I still spent much of my leisure sketching out
plans for imaginative work I did not yet know I should never
accomplish. No one can truly tell what he might have done if
he had taken different decisions or been placed in different
circumstances; but that moment was surely the last when I
could have chosen otherwise than I did. Some things I have
always wanted I now realize only a miracle could put within
my grasp: as the years have gone by since the end of the war,
I have seen that, more irrevocably than ever,

> .... every day there bolted from the field
> Desires to which we could not yield.

And as I look back on that moment of choice, I am surprised
to observe how little I had to sustain me in the decision I made
except an obstinate refusal to admit defeat. I had no pre-
monition or crystal-gazing revelation that my difficulties about
paper would all soon be solved, that *New Writing* would continue and be transformed into *Orpheus*, that I should find everything I needed to build up a publishing house of my own and
fulfil the most audacious of my impresario's dreams—and lose
it again in a sudden catastrophe when its fame and its influence
seemed assured; nothing was clear, except the vision of all the
opportunities I was convinced lay before me if only the means
could be found to explore them.

INDEX